THE LANCASHIRE CARUSO

Other books by John Dennis Vose:

Lady of Connemara
Corner to Corner
Your Feet are Killing Me!
Tales of a Mountainny Man
Clerical Capers
Diary of a Tramp

Plays:

The Night Shelter – (One Act)

THE LANCASHIRE CARUSO

John D. Vose

JOHN D. VOSE
Blackpool

PUBLISHED BY JOHN D. VOSE
24 Norcliffe Road, Blackpool, Lancs.

ISBN 0 9501036 1 6

Printed in Great Britain by
United Writers Publications Ltd
Cornwall

[illegible] 2/10/82

To Dermot
Who would have had so much in common
with Tom Burke.

ACKNOWLEDGEMENTS

Without the generous help and co-operation of many individuals and organisations this book could not have been written. I thank everyone who corresponded with me, however small their help; and to those people who so kindly responded to my newspaper appeals. Particularly, I am indebted to the following individuals:

Joe Burke, Anthony Jackson, Alexander Hood, Harold Simpson, Joe Collier, Albert Houghton, Eileen Darwell, Paul Morby, Richard O'Hagan, Robert Stirk, Gerrard Warren, Mr Brassington, Mr Swarbrick, Frank Granville Barker, Walter Jones, Robert Gregory, Fred Unsworth and Alf Green.

Gracious thanks are also due to Tom Burke's contemporaries and fellow professionals: Joan Cross, MBE, Anne Broadhurst-Prescott, Dame Eva Turner, Isobel Baillie, Roy Henderson, CBE, and particularly to Robert Easton.

I am deeply indebted to Bert Jackson for his invaluable gift of musical magazines; to the following for permission to reproduce photographs and for the taking of photographs: The Stuart-Liff Collection for the Melba Photo; Harold Simpson, Harold Heaps, the Staff Photographer *Leigh Journal*, Thompson Newspapers, Jennifer Skempton, EMI for film stills. To Joe Burke for permission to publish his brother's photograph collection, London Palladium Management for programme copy.

To the Archivist at Covent Garden for her kindness in research and photocopying; Archivists of the following Institutions: Met. Opera House, New York; The Royal Albert Hall; San Carlo Theatre; New York Public Library; Manchester

Public Library and Microfilm Department; Liverpool William Brown Library, Leigh Public Library; BBC Archives of Recorded Sound; The *Daily Mail* Library; *The Times*; *New York Herald*; *Chicago Tribune*; Yale University Library; British and Albert Museum; British Museum Newspaper Library; British Newspaper Library for copyright permission.

To Donald Hanson for permission to quote from his newspaper article 'Leigh singer was Caruso's equal'. To Graham Nown for the article on Burke, and Granada TV for their kindness and hospitality; Fred Yates and Tom Lannigan. James Smith, Sydney Winstanley, John Hassell, and John Hamilton Jnr. for the Discography. Many thanks to Sydney Winstanley for permission to use his article in *'78' Mag.* as The Prologue, and for his critical comments on the records. To Messrs. Putnams for kind permission to reproduce sections of 'Two Centuries of Opera at Covent Garden' by Rosenthal; Likewise to Messrs. Nelson for kind permission to quote from Nellie Melba's Autobiography. To past and present Members of Heysham Amateur Operatic Company and to Morecambe Library; John Riley for permission to peruse his lecture notes on Burke. I must also acknowledge the kind comments of Lord Harewood.

Finally, I wish to acknowledge the help granted to me by Madame Marie Burke in correcting certain parts of the MS; to Patricia (Burke) Collingwood and to Jennifer (Burke) Skempton for their co-operation, advice and frankness. Great help has been given to me by Kay Saunders who deciphers my handwriting and sets it down in printed form. Also to my wife, Philomena, who has encouraged me despite the fact that she considers John McCormack to be the greatest tenor who ever lived!

J.D. Vose, Blackpool, October 1981.

PROLOGUE

Tom Burke never sang like an Englishman, and this was perhaps his greatest asset. His voice was a fine, high tenor, powerful, yet capable of a wide variety of expression, but these points alone do not make him unusual. He was quite uninhibited in his approach, and this unleashed his considerable physical resources. It is when this unleashing of pent-up fire takes place that something unusual starts to happen. No British singers allowed the traditional approach to singing to be so completely taken over and eradicated by the Italian style, as did Burke. Not Hislop, nor even Eva Turner became quite so completely Italian and free.

Even on records (I never saw him on the stage) he swaggered, and in England this is an unforgivable sin. But to sing Italian opera properly one *must* swagger. Even de Lucia, who was probably the most modest of opera singers, knew that the music goes flabby unless it is shaped and pushed along, by a strong (and musical) personality.

Just how much one can take from 'Personality' singers varies a lot. Chaliapine, Supervia, Callas, de Lucia, Battistini are names that quickly come to mind in this context, and they are all singers who are loved ardently or hated vehemently. Burke never reached their status (though there is no doubt in my mind that he would have done), but he stimulates the same reactions. Personally I can stand a lot of eccentricities if the singer can give a few moments which are really marvellous. Burke gave us marvellous moments, as well as fully satisfying performances and he remains for me the English singer who has consistently given me more pleasure than any other.

(Sydney Winstanley, Lecturer, Broadcaster and voice critic.)

OVERTURE

When the film *The Great Caruso* was making a fortune for its star, Mario Lanza, in the early nineteen fifties, another tenor, Tom Burke, was scraping to make ends meet, giving singing lessons in his home-town of Leigh, glad to be able to make enough to maintain a modest standard of living. Yet Lanza was a vocal pygmy compared to Burke whose renderings of the famous arias heard in the film had thrilled opera goers in America and the capitals of Europe. Caruso himself had forecast a great career for the Lancastrian of Irish parentage. Many singing enthusiasts today who heard the tenor in person claim that he was one of the world's 'greats'; a new breed of admirers has sprung up since the release of three long-playing records taken from the original 78's. Where has he been hiding, they ask. A good question. The fact is that Burke's recorded voice is seldom ever heard on radio programmes; he has been omitted from the vast majority of musical reference books; is seldom mentioned in operatic literature; was not included in the selection for H.M.V. *Great English Tenors* LP and failed to be represented in *Irish Tenors Through the Years* for which he could have qualified by parentage.

Undoubtedly many of the singers chosen for both these recordings fall well below the standard of vocalism attained by Tom Burke. It is as though there has been a concerted effort by broadcasters, recording companies and publishers to keep the name of Burke in obscurity.

Burke sang with the panache never achieved by an English man before or since. His voice possessed an urgent enthusiasm which was typically Italian. The warmth and passion of that wonderful country was captured therein. Most of all he was an exciting singer. What we would give for a man of Burke's vocal stature in England today. He would be a sensation. Tenor-wise we have always been dubbed second-raters in the world rankings, despite having produced many excellent singers. More than any other Burke has really shown that an English tenor can rank alongside the Italians in the top bracket of world opera. His is heart and soul singing by one who knows what he is doing and enjoys doing it. Lotte Lehmann had the same gift, a kind of vital fervency that communicated itself to the listener. By way of comparison, listen to Joseph Hislop, the highly-rated Scots tenor, who for all his beautiful tone sang slackly. Of other British tenors only Tudor Davies and Alfred Piccaver sang with the same enthusiasm as Burke. Davies, like the Lancashire man, was a favourite of Melba and to win her approval wasn't easy. Heddle Nash possessed a beautiful voice, but fervency wasn't his strong suit beyond a certain point. Walter Widdop, Yorkshire's great Wagnerian, was a heldentenor, a superb singer, who doesn't really enter into comparisons. Frank Mullings, certainly one of the best-loved tenors, had no real technique of singing other than his own which stood him in admirable stead. John Coates, that tenor par-excellence, lacked sheer voice.

But, perhaps because he was Italian-trained, Tom Burke possessed the warmth and range we normally associate with Italian tenors with all the uninhibitedness of singers from the sunny peninsular. Even third-rate Italian tenors are endowed with this 'heart and throat' style. The Italians alone seem to possess the secret of it. We tend to give too much consideration, nowadays, to singers who have more brains than voice and call them artistically intellectual singers. Burke was perhaps less 'intellectual' in his art, but far more thrilling to hear.

I think, too, we have to bear in mind that the singers with whom Burke sang – Melba, Pareto, Destinn, Tetrazzini, Dal Monte – are indicative of his own stature. Second-raters do not appear in such company, or if they do they very quickly sink into oblivion. That doyen of critics, Hermann Klein, found Burke a welcome change to Dino

Borgioli at Covent Garden when he was substituted for the Italian and he was a real judge of singing, none better. Tom Burke has been called 'the last of the great singers'. This opinion is open to argument. After all, singing is a matter of taste; singers are of infinite variety. Frank Granville Baker, a shrewd and expert judge of singing, wrote in his notes for *The Last of the Great* – Burke's first long-playing record: 'That Tom Burke belonged to the Great tradition of opera singing was proved by his magnificent vocal quality combined with a brilliance of vocal technique. Today's tenors seem able to acquire elegance of expression only by sacrificing any true masculinity of tone, but Tom Burke, like Caruso, achieved both thrilling virility of tone and the mastery of technique that alone allows the singer to express every shade of emotion.'

Immediately, the question will be asked, how does he compare with the leading operatic tenors of today? Again, one has to use one's own judgment when all is said and done. Take the beautiful aria *Donna Non Vidi Mai* from Puccini's *Manon Lescaut*. That fine Spanish tenor Placido Domingo sings this on record beautifully and is technically perfect, but after listening play Burke's version of the aria and say which is the most *stirring*. The English tenor's singing is passionately emotive, his phrasing and colouration has the power to clutch at the very soul of the listener, a power with which Caruso was so richly endowed. For all his beauty, Domingo – to my ear – tends to race the aria, denying the listener the true meaning of Puccini's words. And it was Puccini who said of Burke, 'Never has my music been so beautifully sung'.

Certainly Burke's career waned because of personal failings but that he was a *singer* is beyond question.

Tom Burke's story is one of the most remarkable in the annals of musical history. A notoriety surrounds his memory which far outstrips his fame. That he is partially to blame for this cannot be denied for Burke's public image was not always an endearing one. In the words of the aria which he often sang, he was a strange harmony of contrasts – often outrageous, rebellious, a blunt Lancastrian who was no respecter of persons, idolised by the gallery and loved by his pupils. Burke made enemies, but those friends he made grew to love him. Like his rich voice, he was colourful. A famous contemporary, who wishes to remain anonymous, wrote to me, 'Of all singers I sang with and have heard, Tom, more than any other, portrayed his character in his voice. He was a volcanic person yet with often amazingly soft facets to his nature which, like his superb voice, had great variation of colour.'

Another story confirming that Burke was a singer's singer is told by Laurie Higgins, theatrical tailor and ex-Rugby League International and personal friend of Burke. 'I was at a party where the guests included Richard Tauber and Hutch. Tauber was asked his opinion of Burke and whether he considered himself as good an operatic tenor. "No," replied Tauber, "Burke was one of the greatest of all operatic tenors. I was a lyric tenor. I just wish I had had Burke's training and, need I add, his voice!" '

On another occasion Mr Higgins was fitting the late Oscar Preus for a suit. Preus had been connected with the Columbia Record Company, responsible for engaging top-class artists for this prestige label. Says Mr Higgins, 'A friend who was with me asked him to compare Mario Lanza with Caruso. "If Lanza had managed to get into any opera in which Caruso was playing the lead it would have been as a member of the chorus" was his verdict. My friend tried again, this time with Gigli. Again Preus was not over enthusiastic. But, he added, there was one singer whom he did consider to be Caruso's equal and his name was Tom Burke.'

And so one could go on, for 'Lancashire's Caruso' was not only appreciated by the stalls and gallery but by the top professionals from whom it is difficult to win praise.

Burke's daughter by his first marriage, actress and film star Patricia Burke, had this to say when I told her of my idea for a book about her father: 'I wouldn't care to read a book about my father based on the 'plot No. 1' story which his public life appears to present – poor boy makes good, strikes hard times; poor boy dies unknown. To do him justice, any book about him should try to tell the truth behind the known facts.'

These sentiments echo my own feelings. Much that has been said and written about the tenor is simply not true. In writing this book I have exploded several myths. Yet it is in no sense an 'official' biography, even though I was aided enormously by Burke's own potted autobiography serialised in a Sunday newspaper in 1930 – *From Pit Boy to Grand Opera Star*.

Many years have passed since the events chronicled took place; bombing in the Second World War destroyed theatre archives in some of the countries in which Burke sang. However, due to the wonderful co-operation I have received in my research, I can state that, as his biographer, I have attempted to contruct an accurate account of the tenor's life. It must be stated, however, that some of the views expressed in this book are not necessarily shared by his family.

Clara Leiser wrote in the preface to her biography of Jean de Reske, 'A critical discussion of David Garrick as an actor which appeared in the *Theatrical Review* of 1763, ended thus: "upon a Review of the whole, we will venture to affirm, that impartial justice must pronounce Mr Garrick as the first of his profession: and that the amazing blaze of his excellencies greatly obscures, if not totally eclipses his defects".

'When one considers that in the case of Jean de Reske a like valuation is placed, most unanimously, not only upon his abilities as an operatic artist but also upon his qualities as a man, it is interesting to speculate on how a truthful book about him would have been received a few years ago, during the vogue for biographies which seemed less concerned about presenting 'the whole man' than about smashing idols. Almost any writer who had set out to debunk the great Polish tenor would, I feel sure, have given up the task in despair, for want of supporting materials.

'My own anxiety was of a somewhat different nature. The more I read about Jean, the more I discussed him with his friends, his fellow artists and his pupils, the more I realised that it might be very difficult to secure belief in the truly "amazing blaze of his excellencies". For any defects he may have had were certainly greatly obscured if not totally eclipsed. To illustrate: One of the first people I interviewed was Mrs Anton Seiol. She dwelt on Jean's lovable nature, on his simplicity and generosity, and then added that "Tony" and she considered him a perfect artist. I agreed that as an artist Jean must have been almost perfect: but I ventured to add that there must have been some natural frailties; that as a human being he could hardly have been perfect. Her answer was: "There *were* no faults! And if anyone tries to tell you otherwise, well it simply isn't true!" '

It seems improbable that any human being could have been such a model of virtue. Tom Burke certainly was not. We will never know whether Burke was as great a singer as the Polish baritone who became a tenor, but we do know that Burke revelled in his own reputation for being notorious and I am told by members of his family and those who knew him intimately that he would be the last one to wish to be 'whitewashed' in his biography. A 'warts and all' approach is the only way to reveal the true, rounded man. It is not my intention to smash idols. Rather it is my wish to bring to the public's attention that such a great talent as Burke's existed, and that, hopefully, this biography will reveal the singer and the man.

ACT I

From the steerage deck of the Liverpool-bound steamer, James Vincent Burke watched the Wicklow coastline receding into the distance, his thoughts a mixture of sadness and apprehension at what the future held for him in England. Like tens of thousands of Irishmen before him, he was seeking to better his fortunes in another land. He could not have known that he was a pawn in the great mysterious game of coincidence; certainly he had no conception that a baby boy back in his native Athlone was to become one of the world's greatest tenors. Even if he had been gifted with some mystic power to foretell that the young child, John McCormack, was to attain world fame, a premonition that his own first-born son was to rank beside the great Irishman as a world-class singer would have been more than miraculous.

He had neither job nor wife yet soon after finding work and accommodation in Leigh, Lancashire, he had found both. Leigh, a busy manufacturing town situated roughly between Manchester and Liverpool, was a depressing contrast to the lovely town of Athlone; yet despite its grime and sordid outlook to the eyes of a young man accustomed to pure air and the noises of animals on the family small-holding, the rattle of clogs on cobble-stones was an overture of hope. It represented work and that meant a living wage. There was stark poverty apparent in the mean streets of the working-class areas, a subsistence just above the breadline the contented lot of most folk. Vincent found employment labouring in a coal-mine and in 1889 married Mary Josephine Aspinall of St. Helens, of Irish extraction and by one branch of the family tree descended from the Lancashire Urmstons who kept the Catholic faith during the penal times, and whose name frequently figures in old parish records, having had to pay 'Ye double Taxe' as a penalty for being 'papists'.

Their cottage – one of a row all of the same soul-destroying architecture – 7 Mather Lane, was only a few strides from St. Joseph's Catholic Church, where the Burkes worshipped, and the school run by the Jesuit Fathers. The church – a large cathedral-like building – was designed by Hansom who gave his name to the cab.

Thomas Aspinall Burke was born on March 2nd, 1890, the first child of Vincent and Mary Josephine Burke. Hardly a year was to pass that didn't witness the birth of another Burke, until the family finally numbered nine, all of whom survived – no mean feat in those days. Thomas, or Tom as he soon came to be known, was Vincent's pride and joy and he would sit him on his knee after a day in the pit and sing Gaelic lullabies to him in front of the fire. Tom recalled later that his father had a very pleasing tenor voice. This was the first influence in the life of Tom Burke, an influence that was to swell and consume him with a compulsion to seek the joys of music wherever he could.

Thomas Aspinall was two years old when the disastrous pit strike of 1893 struck the town. Five and a half thousand people were fed daily from Charity Soup Kitchens, the Burkes amongst them. As winter approached Fletcher's Colliery at Atherton allowed coal-picking on their tips or slag-heaps as they were once commonly known. The Burkes joined the hordes of pickers in the expediency of collecting a bucketful of combustible waste; as most of the slag was comprised of 'bass' or rock, this could be an irksome task with speed and a sharp eye the chief factors of success.

As the years rolled by there was no surplus money to buy the musical instruments for which Tom pined. In a newspaper serialisation in 1930 he recalls those days:

'The existence of poverty still arouses that bitterness I felt as a boy when I saw poor old women, bent with years of toil, plodding through the snow to the mills. I know what it means. I have known hunger – have suffered the experience of never knowing what it was to be really satisfied for months on end. With bread and margarine as a staple diet and meat as an almost incredible luxury once a week – on a Sunday. For myself it did not matter so much. I was a fairly sturdy lad who could rough-it if needs be. But it was different with my mother, a gentle-faced woman who had always encouraged me in my dreams.'

The area around Mather Lane was a predominantly Catholic working-class community with Irish names very much in the majority; Jesuit priests, the midwife and the pawnbroker were the most important people. The degree of poverty in a town could always be judged by the number of pawnbrokers who did business beneath the sign of the Lombards – the three brass balls – and in Leigh at the turn of the century there were thirteen to a population of less than twenty-nine thousand.

It is interesting to hear about Burke's academic ability. Mrs Martha Kitts of Swanage, a sprightly ninety-year-old, was in the same class and recalls, 'Tom was a clever enough lad. Certainly well above the average, though he was something of a dreamer. Always singing to himself and I remember him telling me how one day he was going to be a singer and stand on a huge stage before a great orchestra. He was very determined too. But he was no softy; just the reverse and many a lad got a bloody nose at the hands of Tom Burke! I remember his mother, too. She had a terribly hard job to bring up the family, but she was a great manager. Always busy patching and sewing and working wonders with bits of scrag end and the cheapest cuts of meat. We were all very poor then, though I don't think we realised it at the time. Mather Lane area was no place for weaklings and we were rough-and-ready folks, but I'd say we were happy.'

'A young imp' was how another school chum described him to me. 'Don't think I am being derogatory about the Burke family, but we were all as poor as the lice on Job's turkey in those days. Tom's parents were respectable working folk and he was like the rest of us, a snotty-nosed kid up to all the devilment he could find; running around with holes in his breeches. We had a football team made up of lads from Mather Lane known as the Raggy-arsed Rangers.

We weren't always the best at football but when it came to a scrap there was no licking us. Tom's dad had a certain dignity about him – there was a pride in work in those days and a working-class dignity, a sort of 'walking tall' as they say today. I remember him once giving Tom a damned good belting. He was always being plagued by neighbours complaining about Tom. But it was all simple fun really, no malice in it whatever. Mind you, we were scared to death of the bobby in those days, not like today. He always seemed to be seven feet tall and built like a heavyweight boxer. Our favourite jape was to tie the large door knockers of two adjacent cottages together, then knock loudly on each. Neither occupant could open the door. We'd be hiding, watching the fun with relish! The highlight of the fun was when both householders came round the end of the terrace into the street to find out why their doors were sticking. Then we'd run like bloody hell! I know he was a great singer, but he was no sluggard at sprinting either!'

At the age of twelve Tom left school to work 'part-time' in Courtauld's Silk Mill, having had to pass a labour medical examination in order to do this. Children were used as the general 'dog's body', sweeping up and generally labouring on the operatives and spinners. Work began at 6 a.m. with breakfast a half-hour break between 8 a.m. and 8.30 a.m., then four hours until 12.30 a.m. For this he was paid five shillings a week. On his 13th birthday he attained full-time status, earning eight shillings a week towards the family exchequer. At this time silk was more important to Leigh than cotton, there being 4,438 looms in operation and the entire production being woven into dress material, unlike Macclesfield, the other leading Northern silk town, whose output supplied the ribbon trade.

Tom's ambition was to work in the pits, although he still nursed his burning desire to be a singer but he needed more money to face the realities of a world in which holding down a job in order to survive was the premier factor. But you can't stop a lad from dreaming. When he was accepted for the coal-mines at the age of fourteen he felt he was one step nearer to his goal; half-a-crown a day was his wage – twelve and six a week, a fortune. This meant being on the job at 6 a.m. and work finished at 4 p.m. Out of his wage he had to keep himself in clogs and overalls. Clog irons cost 4d a pair and thong laces a halfpenny; both rapidly expendable items when one considers that he walked four miles to the pithead every morning, followed by a three mile trudge underground along a pit road hardly high enough to allow upright walking. Some parts were so low he had to get down on his hands and knees to crawl. The reverse process was repeated at knocking-off time, a round trip of nearly eight miles. His official title was 'lasher-on', duties entailing hooking tubs of coal on to an endless steel rope as they were brought from the pitface workings – a boring, monotonous job if ever there was one. Tom hated work yet realised that he was fortunate compared to children of an earlier generation – boys and girls – who had had to drag boxes of coal along the pit road from the face. He relieved the tedium by singing. Soon the singing pit lad was dubbed the 'Minstrel Boy' by the colliers who loved to hear him sing the stirring Irish melody which somehow typified the struggle and determination of a young working lad out to conquer the world of Grand Opera: *'The minstrel boy to the war is gone. In the ranks of death you'll find him; his father's sword he has girded on – and his wild harp slung behind him.'* They found his singing was so enjoyable they sometimes took over his job so that he could concentrate on entertaining them. At this stage his voice was a rather fine contralto. Above ground, too, the name Tom Burke became known and talked about; his beautiful voice seemed to stand out like a beacon of hope to all who heard it. He still sang when he came home, no matter how tired he felt he always wanted to sing and, sitting in the zinc tub in front of the fire, he would entertain the family as he washed away the pit dirt.

Concurrent with his singing he was a keen member of Leigh Borough Brass Band and at fourteen was promoted to First Cornet, his hour of glory coming when the band competed at Crystal Palace. Tom won the silver medal for the best individual cornet soloist. By this time Burke senior, who had no musical ability, had formed his own band which he named the Irish Forresters Drum and Fyfe Band which rehearsed in the room over the 'Derby Arms' public house. They entertained at field days and, like McNamara's Band, performed at wakes and weddings and every grand affair – Vincent conspicuous in smart uniform as he marched proudly at the head of the band. Old folk in Leigh remember Burke senior as a man who always kept a smart appearance despite the hardships of the times; later on when Tom became famous he looked every inch the father of an international opera star – grey moustache, bowler hatted, yellow waistcoat, white gloves, silver-topped cane, accompanied by a tall aristocratic-looking borzoi dog. But this was all in the future.

In order to eke out enough to feed his large family, he turned his hand to all manner of money-making enterprises. One of these was keeping a few pigs in the back yard for tripe making. The pigs stomachs were boiled in a large tub to make tripe which was then dressed ready for sale by Tom who peddled it in a basket around the pubs and to anyone who cared to buy it. Such a Lancashire delicacy was easy to sell and there was no shortage of customers. Publicans vied for his patronage and gave him free beer to keep him in their pub singing to the customers. Some even offered to buy any tripe left over so that he was assured of selling all his stock. Pub singing became his hobby, the presence of a piano an irresistible magnet to the young singer, and it was in this environment, singing to colliers and mill workers in some of the town's roughest hostelries, that he served his vocal apprenticeship.

He is remembered also for the solo practice sessions which he held on waste ground or any quiet spot. It became quite common to hear him singing out loud and practicing scales, of which he had a very rudimentary knowledge at this time. This tended to create an anti-social reputation with his friends who wanted him to join them in 'chatting up' the girls and playing football and rugby on the colliery waste lands. Sometimes they would chase after him and call to him to join them but Tom would sing out 'I hear you calling me' then vanish down an alley or along the canal bank, singing the song at the top of his voice. But such dedication didn't turn him into a complete musical hermit. In every other way he was a perfectly normal lad. He enjoyed playing cards for pennies under the gas-lamps, a practice frowned on by the Jesuit priests, so in order to ease his conscience Tom had the bright idea of bringing a pot to the card parties into which went a donation made by the winner to be put on the collection plate at mass on Sunday morning. In this way he balanced his own conscience!

Mrs Kitts remembers the 'Monkey Run', a local name for Railway Road. 'It became a meeting place for boys and girls, usually on a Saturday afternoon or after mass on Sunday. It was perfectly respectable, a sort of promenading place for making friends with the opposite sex. You put on your best togs for you were on show. I don't know if it was peculiar to Leigh but I believe the same sort of thing was common in Spain at one time. Tom took the eye of many a girl for he was very good looking with a jaunty way of walking, a sort of swagger, and always stood out in a crowd, but there was never any big-headedness about him. Even then you could tell he was cut out to be something out of the ordinary. To him working in the pit was just a job of work.'

One of the highlights of these teenage years was when Father Fish heard Tom singing and asked him to join the choir. 'Would I?' recalls Burke. 'I would sing anywhere! I loved it so. And what is more, I had determined to be a singer and I would settle for nothing less. I remember once when I was about six years old, sitting curled up before the meagre fire dreaming away, my mother asked me what I was thinking about. "I want to be a great man" I told her and at that time I meant I wanted to be a singer, to give a message through the gift of song. I was determined that I would get on for I have always felt that the gift of God cannot be swamped by the environment of man. And if ever a man was helped by his parents that man was Tom Burke, and I pay tribute to the father and mother who gave me every encouragement and assistance in the fight against big odds.

' "He must be given a chance," said Father. "Let's get Tom

a piano." Things were none too rosy I can tell you, and it was still a bit of a luxury to get milk in one's tea as a regular thing. But somehow that piano materialised – materialised out of all the poverty by way of the higher purchase system. I remember father visiting the 'pop' shop or 'uncle', as we called the pawnbroker. Mother's sewing machine had to go too. Behold me the proud possessor of a piano! When I look back and compare that piano with some of those to which I have sung in the Capitals of the world I realise what a poor thing it was. But to me it was a golden harp, and never will there be a finer instrument in my memory than that piano purchased out of the self-denial of my parents and family. Neither must I forget my brothers and sisters who in their own way helped me too.'

Previous to buying the piano Tom had met two sisters at a local band concert. Discovering a mutual interest in singing, they invited him to their home on the next evening. He was delighted, not because he had taken a fancy to either of them, but because they had a piano. Such a commodity was unknown among his circle of acquaintances. Duly arriving at the appointed time, he was received with rather cold looks from the girls' parents, particularly their father, a colliery clerk, who didn't take too kindly to the idea of a pit lad from Mather Lane consorting with his daughters. The gulf between the aspiring middle-class and the working-class was very wide and never the twain must meet. The idea of one of them 'walking out' with a collier was abhorent. Snobbery – call it what you will – was more widespread amongst the lower strata of society than the upper; white collar workers were jealously proud of their status, a shabby genteel middle-class one though it was, due to the fact that their positions demanded a standard of living above their means to present before the public gaze. The old parody-jingle to the tune of the Red Flag could be sung in all honesty in turn of the Century Leigh:

The working-class can kiss my ass,
For I've got the foreman's job.

But Tom did get invited into the parlour where he almost committed the mortal sin of upsetting the aspidistra in its pot. Fortunately for him this emblem of middle-class respectability remained upright. But music not only soothes the savage breast it breaks down all barriers and soon the girls' parents were anxious to know when young Thomas (for Burke could be devious!) was coming round to sing to them again. Later on, when he was famous, they were very proud and would tell people how they had encouraged the tenor.

In Leigh some 'Burke' stories have become legends and are often grossly exaggerated in the telling. One of the favourites is of how the neighbours would stare through the parlour window at Tom as he played the new prized possession, his pit clogs resplendent on the polished top. Another is the locally famous tale of 'Burke's Donkey'. Joe Burke told me, 'Our Tom left the pit when he was nearly seventeen. My father bought a donkey and cart and set Tom up as a vegetable salesman. But he wasn't much of a business man. If I'd have had his voice – or vice versa – there would have been a millionaire in the Burke family. He couldn't resist the sound of a piano. He'd take the cart into the 'posher' districts calling at the houses, but if he heard the sound of music he'd be off in search of it. More than once he returned to find fruit lying on the floor and a cabbage or two missing. He lived for singing and everything else was only a means to an end.'

Another story that dies very hard is that Tom was too lazy to take the donkey to the end of the terrace and round the entry to the backyard, so instead he led it through the front door, much to the annoyance of his mother!

Certainly Tom became a local 'character', known for his eccentricities as well as his beautiful voice. At the age of eighteen he had the sudden desire to join the regular Army. He passed the medical A1 but after one week he was out again. After two days he was homesick, detesting the regimentation to which he was immediately subjected. Somehow the necessary ten pounds required to purchase his release was found by the family; a definite hardship was felt but they made no secret of the fact that they were delighted to have him back. In the light of Burke's subsequent reaction to authority and administration, one can plainly appreciate the traumatic effect such an institution as the

Army had on him. His rebelliousness had not yet manifested itself noticeably but it was latent in his character. Those who knew him in later life find the thought of someone yelling at him on a parade-ground quite amusing!

Home again, he turned his hand to various jobs. During the evenings he attended a general studies class at the local 'Tech.', one night particularly was his favourite – a voice production class at which he studied diligently. When Tom put his mind to it he could be a very determined young man and would certainly have made his mark in many another sphere besides music.

Choir rehearsal on a Wednesday night, then three Services on a Sunday, besides his intensive practice sessions at the piano, provided a full week of music. Gradually the true tenor voice began to develop and then came the need to earn more money if he was to have further singing tuition. This could be provided at Manchester College of Music if only he could be accepted and afford the fees as well as his rail fare each day. For a while he took on an Insurance 'round', at which he was quite successful, then debt-collecting for a pawnbroker, saving every penny he earned. As a sport he played rugby league for a local junior side as a second row forward. But he was more gifted as a boxer and, after joining a local gymnasium, toured the Lancashire Boxing Clubs taking on all the best boys in the county. Well over fourteen stone at the age of eighteen, he was no pushover and gave as good as he got. Next to singing, boxing was his favourite pastime, delighting in a really good scrap even when he came off worst. Rules of boxing were much more lax then and fights were allowed to continue even when it was obvious one of the contestants was getting by far the worst of it. A kink in his nose bore eloquent testimony to the fact he had gone through the rough and tumble of amateur pugilism.

In 1909, when he was nineteen, he walked the thirty miles to Blackpool to a concert which was to colour his life with impressions that never faded. His hero, Enrico Caruso, whose voice he had heard on cylinders and gramophone records, was to sing at the Winter Gardens, the famous concert venue for international artists, a theatre he was to sing at himself in years to come. The provincial music-world was agog with excitement, Caruso's first concert outside the Capital city had caused a stir seldom equalled in the concert world. It attracted people countrywide who packed all the leading hotels in the town. Tom was happy enough to purchase a seat in the 'gods' and for this he had to pay six times the normal charge. Seldom have such scenes been witnessed before or since in the flamboyant seaside town well-used to celebrities of all hues and shades. The great tenor arrived at Blackpool's North Station on the Friday in a private train with a special white compartment housing the great man's entourage. This white saloon, incidentally, had been specially built by the London and North Western Railway Company for the service of King Edward. Hundreds of people thronged the station concourse as the party were driven to the Metropole Hotel in a fleet of taxis; everywhere the tenor went he was followed by a crowd of sightseers eager to shake his hand or proffer an autograph book.

The concert was a tremendous musical success as well as a spectacular event for the socialites of the district. Tom took his place in the gallery queue several hours before the doors were opened in order to be sure of his seat. The *Blackpool Evening Gazette* reported:

> The moment had come – and now for the man. Every eye was fixed expectantly on the stage and there was not a sound. And although everybody was attentive, nobody seemed to see him come on the stage. Suddenly there he was standing before their surprised eyes, a firm figure, with pale and immobile features, strikingly suggestive of Napoleon Bonaparte, to which a somewhat Mephistophelian piquancy was imparted by the strong, arched, black eyebrows.
>
> It was he! And the audience, realising it, burst into a most cordial hand-greeting. Still preserving his statuesque pose, he cast his large eloquent brown eyes over the audience, and then his lips became less rigid and the faintest flicker of a smile was observed. That was his acknowledgment of the welcome accorded to him.
>
> The Caruso smile was a study in itself. It became more and more pronounced, as he mastered the emotions of those before

him: and whereas early in the programme he allowed a smile to escape from him, as it were, as he cast a glance at Mr Eugene Sandlow, the physical culture expert, who was in a box with a family group, and at Mr George Robey, the comedian, with whom he is on very friendly terms, it gradually beamed on all parts of the house. And when he made his last bow to the great assembly, his face was wreathed in one of the broadest and happiest of smiles.

MAGNIFICENCE OF PASSION

The silence was supreme when the pure and clear opening notes of the tenor's voice were heard in the recitative air, *Celeste Aida* from Verdi's opera, *Aida*. It was at once evident that besides being wonderfully gifted by Nature in voice, he is an artist of supreme power. His dramatic fervour in the repetition of the aria thrilled the audience. But that was as nothing compared with what was the master effort of the evening. First, he responded readily to the enthusiastic appreciation displayed with a Tosti song, *Ideals* in the native tongue. That trifle pleased. A second time he responded; and the piece was the heart-rendering motif in Leoncavallo's *I Pagliacci*, beginning "Ridi, Pagliaccio". Signor Caruso cast aside all music, closed his eyes to everything about him, and then, by a sort of self-hypnotism, he became the very embodiment of a great human passion, which seemed to be struggling to burst from the bonds of his quivering body. And then came the end. His arms thrown wide aside, his great bosom swelling to the full, his eyes firmly closed, there came from his throat a great and awful sob, as though the mighty heart of a giant had burst asunder in the direst depths of despair. It was magnificent! One fell under the spell so that, for the nonce, one could not applaud, but simply gaze on the singer who was now recovering from the tremendous strain of the passionate interpretation, just as though awakening from a trance. The audience coming to itself, too, burst into the wildest enthusiasm, many being brought to their feet in the ecstasy of the moment.

Now, more than ever, Tom longed to be a singer and resolved to practice harder than ever. He was so consumed with the tenor's superb performance that he couldn't contain himself once back in Leigh; everyone he met in the street had to be told about the concert. But one man, an ex-colliery mate, wasn't impressed.

"Thar's bin weer, Tom?" he asked.

"To the Winter Gardens to see Enrico Caruso."

"Aye? Who was he wrestling?" was the reply.

Tom's enthusiasm knew no bounds now after this exquisite taste of first-class singing and in the next few weeks he was back twice at Blackpool to hear John McCormack and Louisa Tetrazzini respectively. McCormack's rendition of *Il Mio Tesoro* left an indelible impression on Burke who always claimed that no tenor, not even Caruso, has ever sung this song so expressively as the Irish tenor.

Then out of the blue came one of the greatest events of his life, his first appearance on a stage as a paid performer. A choral society were presenting the Messiah in the town, but a few hours before the performance word came that the professional tenor was unwell. A frantic search was made around the Manchester area to no avail when someone remembered young Burke. He jumped at the chance and received great acclaim for his performance as well as a fee of thirty shillings, his first step on the ladder of a professional career. Around this time he did manage to afford a few lessons with Dr Mort an Atherton teacher of voice.

But pride goeth before a fall, we are told, and Tom was foolish enough to believe a friend who told him that J.W. Turner's Opera Company were sure to engage him when they came to Leigh theatre: "You've only got to open your mouth, Tom, and you're there," said the friend, a drummer in a local band. The conductor of the touring Opera Company reluctantly agreed to listen to Burke singing. Tom sang for all his life, but it was not enough to convince him. "Hmm," he grunted when he was through. "Not bad at all – but not good enough. Practice and more practice, knock off those rough edges then come again in a year or two."

It was a bitter blow to swallow at the time, but he realised after the initial impact of the disappointment had faded that the conductor was right. He was rough and must have expert tuition.

Fame is rarely attained without some form of help and

there is usually a dispute about who provided this initial opportunity for a foot to be placed on the first rung of the ladder of success. Tom Burke was no exception, several people have claimed the credit for his climb to the lofty dome of operatic greatness. The true account reads like a fairy story: A party of colliers were on their way home from a late shift singing at the top of their voices. Frederick Swarbrick was a baby in a cot being cajoled into slumber by his mother as the noisy colliers passed the house: 'What happened has become legend in our family. Naturally enough mother was annoyed when I started to cry. But then a solo voice rose above the rest and she stood almost transfixed listening to it. My crying was then the source of annoyance. She was an A.R.C.M. herself and possessed a lovely voice being a professional entertainer on the halls. She was so influenced by the singing that she told my father, a prominent local organist, about it. He arranged to be at home the next evening. Sure enough the rowdy lads passed again but this time they gave way for a solo by the singer of the previous day. The song he sang was *Lend Me Your Aid* from *Irene* by Verdi, a more appropriate aria it would have been impossible to imagine, for there was a lad as black as the ace of spades fresh from the bowels of the earth singing like an angel. My father was amazed and on enquiring the lads name learned it was Tom Burke from a miner's cottage in Mather Lane. Sunday night was music night in our house and it seems my parents invited young Tommy to come along. He turned up all scrubbed in his Sunday best and was put through his paces. Mother was playing the old Manchester Theatre Royal a short while later and arranged for the manager to hear Tommy sing. He was very impressed and arranged for him to go as a student to the Manchester College of Music.'

This was the fillip the young miner needed. Delighted to cast aside his clogs and overalls he became a full time student. His mining days were over. Casual evening work enabled him to scrape together the money needed for travelling and fees. At weekends he waited-on in *The Pied Bull* in Leigh and soon became known as 'Tom the Singing Waiter'. The landlord realised he was more profitable to him as a 'turn' than serving beer, and often did Tom's job himself so the waiter could entertain the customers with popular ballads of the day.

The aspiring singer never needed reminding that he had to study. He knew that if he didn't succeed it was back to the pit to do work he had grown to detest. After several months he was given an audition for the Halle Choir. Delighted, he sang for Michael Hallin, the Master of the famous choir. But again he was doomed to disappointment as Hallin shook his head and said "Nothing very extraordinary young man. Go back and knock that roughness off."

Unknown to Burke, Christian Neilsen, the conductor of the Halle Orchestra and Choir, had heard the audition. He was of a totally different opinion to Hallin and told Burke, "I know a man who is searching the world for voices like yours. His name is Hugo Gorelitz, a London impresario who is in Manchester now. Will you sing for him?" Burke was flabbergasted at this remark and duly obliged, though somewhat apprehensively. Gorelitz didn't go into ecstasies or tell him that he had Caruso skinned but did offer him a contract. He told him to go home and discuss it with his father and, if he agreed, to write to him in London. Tom couldn't get home fast enough. Burke Senior was delighted and saw this as a major break-through, but insisted on meeting Gorelitz himself to discuss the contract and his son's future. At the Midland Hotel in Manchester where the meeting was held, Neilsen, who had acted on a hunch, sat in on the discussions. At last it was agreed that Tom would sign the contract which stated that Gorelitz would eventually send the young tenor to Italy and take 50% of his earnings. First Burke would study in London and sing at Ballad Concerts along with Madame Amy Sherwin, an Australian soprano and the wife of Hugo Gorelitz. When it was considered he was ready, Tom would then go to Italy in search of the true Bel Canto sound. This was in 1913. His foot was firmly set on the second rung of the ladder.

Once more the question of finance raised its ugly head, but the Burkes were a very closely knit family and all very proud of Tom. Somehow they raised the cash to take him to the Capital City for his tilt at the dragon of fame and in his bag were several presents from well wishers, including four pairs of woollen stockings knitted for him by St. Joseph's Parishoners and a generous gift of money from a Mr Peter Ashton of Leigh, an old friend of the family.

Burke found 'digs' in a large house, sharing a room with several other young men, one of whom was a medical student. The arrangement was that you paid your weekly rent in advance which did not include meals. It was simply a roof over his head and a bed. The singer was an assiduous learner and studied the medical student's books whenever he got the chance, being particularly interested in the human diaphragm and voice production and would talk at great length with the student about anatomy and how the voice is produced.

Hugo Gorelitz obtained bookings for him all over London. Some days he sang at afternoon concerts before dashing across the city for an evening engagement. Victorian ballads were all the rage, songs which would be laughed at by many singers today were 'pop' hits of the day – such old stand-bys as *Come into the Garden Maud*, *Tom Bowling*, *Till the Sands of the Desert Grow Cold*, *Thora*, and duets with bass or baritone such as *Excelsior* and *Tenor and Baritone*. In concert-hall or drawing-room they were regularly called for. From Madame Amy Sherwin he learned the duettist's art and, together, they became great favourites. It may seem ridiculous that in these brash days of howling dervish-singers, screeching amplifiers and, that scourge of the ear-drum, the electric guitar, that ballad singing was a most popular form of entertainment right up to nineteen-twenty when the importation of jazz, swing, and the 'American influence' submerged it. They were halcyon days for the lovers of good honest ballads – songs of the 'road', adventure, love, and often sickly sentiment – the 'bread and butter' for a whole army of singers and often the launching pad for those with higher ambitions – Grand Opera and the Celebrity Concert Platform.

The most notable ballad concerts were those promoted by the National Sunday League, and Arthur Boosey whose celebrated 'Boosey Ballad Concerts' became the butt for the jokes of many a comedian. The Queen's Hall, Langham Place, was the venue for many of them. Gorelitz himself promoted ballad concerts at which his own contracted artists appeared and it was at these that the young Burke was most prominently featured. One critic at the time chanced to hear Tom singing at a house-party for guests of a prominent politician. He wrote in his paper on the next day that he had heard 'the voice of the Generation'.

'I thought I was made,' Burke wrote. 'But I was due for another think, for it was a hard and thorny path I had to traverse before I achieved anything like the fame I hungered for. Further study was necessary. Those engagements under the banner of Hugo Gorelitz had provided me with the necessary sinews of war and I went to the Royal Academy where I studied privately under Edgardo Levi, one of the greatest Masters in the country. The sinews of war soon diminished and in order to keep at it I had to sing at all sorts of concerts for all sorts of fees, and every day I would walk from the Academy in the Marylebone Road to a little restaurant in Windmill Street where I could get a lunch for fivepence. For months on end I lived on these fivepenny lunches and in between on cups of tea and snacks given to me at concerts and house engagements. I did not dare spend a penny more each day, and now and again when a concert did not happen along to eke out I had to forego my lessons for a time until I could scrape sufficient money together to carry on once more.'

Fortunately for Burke he didn't fall for the temptation of taking lessons from unqualified teachers. Pitfalls in the form of charlatan voice teachers lured countless promising vocalists to wreck their voices on the rocks of utter ignorance. Harold Williams, the eminent Australian baritone, in an article in *Music Masterpieces* stated that London was a paradise for 'quack' teachers. In a survey made during the 'twenties, many so-called teachers admitted to being fraudulent and capitalizing on pupils not able to afford college fees or the tuition of a qualified teacher. He also revealed that there were over five thousand teachers of singing in London. To sift out the genuine ones from the charlatans was a difficult task for an inexperienced beginner.

Walter Widdop, the great Yorkshire tenor, substantiated

this view: 'Several years ago I had a friend who was receiving instruction from one of these people – or rather it would be more correct to say he was paying fees for instruction – and I gathered from his remarks that his tutor was apparently a complete ignoramus. I advised him to tell the man in plain language that he was incompetent. He did so and the man then confessed that he knew nothing about singing, "but," he said, "I must get my living somehow". This is a shocking state of affairs, 'professors' with high-sounding names make all sorts of promises to young people anxious to be trained, and proceed to fleece them right and left. I was once told by an alleged expert that I had the most glorious voice in the world, and that after paying fees for a certain time I should be able to practically dictate my own terms to impresarios. But I soon found he was damaging my voice instead of improving it.'

In much more recent years a prominent Italian bass made the remark, "In Milan there are eight hundred music teachers, also eight hundred assassins." Obviously an exaggeration but would-be singers need to be extremely careful.

There were times when engagements were very scarce and Tom found himself unable to afford even a fivepenny lunch and still pay his lodging money. Finding himself close to Gorelitz's office he decided to approach him for an advance against future bookings. His luck was out, Gorelitz had gone away on business and only his secretary was in the office. Tom told her his plight. She was unable to help him herself so she took half a crown from the petty cash and made him a loan.

'And I'm not ashamed to say that I took it' wrote Burke in his memoirs 'Took it gladly, and had one of the most memorable feeds in the whole of my existence. She was a very beautiful girl with raven black hair and finely chiselled features. And – she was the girl who finally became my wife, Marie Burke, who has also acquitted herself well in the realm of song.'

Marie was a pupil of Amy Sherwin and they met again when booked to tour together. After the first tour there was no money immediately forthcoming and they found themselves on a London station with only a few coppers between them. Marie was met by her parents and she persuaded them to let the young tenor stay a night at their home in Balham. Romance blossomed and yet all was not happiness in Marie's home, for shortly afterwards her father was interned on account of his German nationality. Her mother, aware of the bitter feeling shown towards anyone bearing a German name, changed her name from Auefulditch back to her maiden name of Underwood by deed poll.

Hugo Gorelitz was also interned which left Tom without a manager; but before the internment Gorelitz had made sure that his protégé was not left unaided. He knew that his tailor, Mark Richardson Moore of Bond Street, was a lover of singing and had approached him to buy Burke's contract. Gorelitz however owed Moore for a suit and so after some haggling between them Tom, who had been described as possessing the voice of the generation, was sold for the price of a three piece suit.

So life went on singing under the flag of the Bond Street tailor and attending college to study voice. It was then he was given a remarkable opportunity to prove himself before one of the finest judges in the world. Tom felt sure that he was ready to sing operatic arias. Maestro Levi did not agree and steadfastly refused to budge every time Tom made the request. Matters came to a head when pupil and teacher had a row in the studio, the cause being yet another request by Tom to be allowed to practice opera. Levi laughed and told him that it was out of the question.

"What operas do you know, Burke?"

"If you want to find out then shall we start with 'Tosca'?" answered the tenor.

"I think, Mr Burke, you are becoming too big for your boots."

"You may be right, Maestro," retorted Tom hotly, "But I'm sure I can't learn any more from you." And with that he left the infuriated Levi to his own thoughts.

Knowing he had put his position at the College in jeopardy he waited for his letter of expulsion. It just wasn't done to approach one's tutor in such a way and his fellow students all forecast that by the end of the week he would be leaving them. Later in the week Levi sent him a note instructing him to report to his office. Expecting the inevitable expulsion, he was amazed to be greeted quite civilly by the Maestro. 'I stood there like a naughty boy,' wrote Tom. 'Then he said to me, "Burke, I want you to sing your best today. Signor Caruso is visiting College and I want him to hear you sing." I nearly jumped out of my skin. Many was the time I had stood outside the gallery entrance of Covent Garden for hours, having gone without a meal so that I could hear this greatest singer the world has known or ever will know. And now I was to sing before *him*. I had been at gatherings where he had been the lion of the evening and I had gazed on him from afar. It was a great day for me. The great man came in. I shall never forget him. His kindly, smiling encouraging eyes; and yet I felt as though my throat would burst. This would not do I told myself. I must pull myself together. I had to sing and one cannot sing when the muscles of one's throat are beating a tattoo. By a supreme effort I controlled myself and sang. Caruso listened, but I had forgotten him. I always forget everything when I am singing, and thank goodness, I forgot Caruso that day, otherwise I wouldn't have sung so well.

'At the end he applauded mildly. Then he spoke to Mr Levi, and Mr Levi came across to me with Caruso. The latter stretched out his hand and spoke to me in Italian. "In the days to come," he said, "one day you will wear my mantle. But you must go to Italy. There you will find your voice."

ACT II

Marie and Tom were married at a registry office and only weeks later did the news of the marriage reach Leigh. His mother was particularly heartbroken that he should marry outside the Catholic church. A registry office ceremony was not a marriage in the eyes of the Catholic religion and one can well imagine the stigma felt by his parents, both steadfast in the duties of their faith. However, in the fulness of time, fortified by their faith in prayer that their erring son would be reconciled to his religion, they strived to accept the situation. They were both very taken with his beautiful young wife and accepted her into the family.

Soprano Dame Eva Turner was a fellow pupil with Burke and she recalls him inviting her to Marie's parents home at Balham for tea where the newly weds lived prior to their leaving for Italy, where Tom was to study under the kind patronage of Mark Richardson Moore, who, inspired by Caruso's assessment of Burke's potential, had decided to pay his fare and give him an allowance.

Tom Burke was always sure that he was going to be a success, never doubting for a second that he would become an international opera star. Before leaving for London he had told his mother that he would sing at Covent Garden before he was twenty-five. McCormack had attained this pinnacle of opera achievement at the age of twenty-three in 1907 as Turiddu in *Cavalleria Rusticana*: and Tom had boasted that he would become a brighter star in the operatic firmament than John. But Burke was twenty-nine when he made his debut at the 'Garden'. In later days many of his most stringent critics called him arrogant; if he was then it was the arrogance of a man who sets out to scale mountains. With Burke's background it was imperative that he must believe in himself implicitly for there was no easy road and no influence.

On arrival in Italy, Burke's first task was to find somewhere to live. He and his wife found a tiny pension just about adequate for two people. Tom and Marie immediately fell in love with Italy but detested the cold winters. They found that the allowance was too meagre to provide such luxuries as coal or even wood. An antiquated stove was the only means of heating and for a while they collected sticks and anything that would burn. Then Tom heard about a shop that sold sacks of sawdust very cheaply. He discovered that it he packed the stove tightly with the sawdust, continually pressing it down, then poked a couple of ventilation holes into it with a stick, it provided quite a good fire. In time he became so expert at it that soon it was burning as well as solid wood. For food it was spaghetti and more spaghetti – and without butter at that.

The teacher to whom Burke had been recommended didn't impress him as the man to train his voice in the true Italian idiom. The subsequent search to find a teacher was both frustrating and amusing for the newly weds. There were many teachers but as in London the charlatans outnumbered the really competent ones. They encountered many bizarre characters who didn't inspire confidence. One was a woman who had played Desdemona and she greeted them clad in a long white dress and a golden wig. Tom and Marie could hardly keep their faces straight as she extolled her own virtues as a teacher of voice, and in the end had to run away like a couple of naughty children. A tenor called Chorchi was then tried but when he sang for Tom it was at once obvious that the pupil could sing better than the teacher who had an extremely nasally production.

While he searched Tom visited a man who had sung tenor professionally who helped him with the Italian pronunciation and coached him in the appreciation of Italian operas. It was an accepted rule that only Italian was to be spoken between Marie and Tom who insisted that if he was to sing in Italian he must master the Italian tongue. Here lies the reason why the Lancastrian's singing later on led Italians to believe he was one of their own countrymen.

The offer of better accommodation was made to them by the wife of a marine officer who let them rent part of her house while her husband was at sea. From her Marie learned to cook native dishes. In 1916 Marie gave birth to a daughter, Patricia. Tom had at last found the teacher he wanted. It was a case of was the pupil good enough? For maestro Colli was a noted teacher of many fine singers. He agreed that the young Englishman should audition for him. Colli was obviously impressed without actually shouting out for joy, but he did tell Tom that he had a very fine tenor voice. . . *but* there were many rough edges to be knocked off and re-polished. Lessons began immediately. With the family now numbering three a larger apartment was needed and they were very fortunate to find one directly opposite to the residence of maestro Colli. The allowance provided by Mark Richardson Moore was just sufficient to keep them in a very modest life-style with spaghetti, pasta and the cheap red wine of the district the routine diet; it also paid for the lessons but the new living quarters had burst the budget. Marie wired home to Balham for extra money which was provided by her mother.

Occasionally Tom, during his spare time, watched the racing at San Siro Racecourse, getting to know the bookmakers and generally soaking up the atmosphere of the turf. He became quite friendly with several of the punters, some of whom were professional gamblers. They needed a bet placer. Simply a polite name for a betting man's errand boy. Tom took the job. If the horse won he got commission, it not, nothing.

The training was rigorous in the extreme. Intensive practice of the scales, learning new techniques and unlearning so many things he had been taught. But he loved it. Singing study was never a fag, music was his life; true consummation of his intense passion for opera, its expression in song and its lore, lived in his heart which longed for that day when he would debut on the operatic stage. Colli, to Burke's way of thinking, kept him at scales for an interminable length of time. He studied operas when he wasn't singing arias until he could boast that he knew thirty by heart. French he studied seriously and still found the time to help Marie with her own studentship which she indulged when funds would allow the luxury of lessons.

Burke could never number patience among his virtues, he was always eager to move on to fresh facets of the vocal art, but still Colli was adamant. His pupil must not sing for money at concerts. Under no circumstances would he relent; if Signor Burke wished to be a singer then he must wait – 'Time, practice and the Italian climate'. More seemingly endless months of repetitive practice passed until it seemed that he could never satisfy Colli.

Away from studying Tom and Marie loved nothing better than entertaining their musical friends. Marie recalls one of them who made a great impression on her 'He was called Rubino and owned a most wonderful baritone voice. He was a Neapolitan and quite small but what a voice. After we had had our spaghetti and red wine – most of us sitting on the floor because we only had two chairs – Rubino and Tom would sing duets. Their voices blended beautifully, you will realise how good they were when I tell you that crowds would gather below the apartment window shouting "Bravo." and calling for encores. Poor Rubino must have got caught up in the war because he would surely have made a great career in opera, his voice was so marvellous. Another visitor was an American singer known as Smithey. Once he asked me to play *Mother Machree*. He wasn't very good really and after he had sung it he announced "you know when I used to sing that people would cry" to which little Rubino whispered in my ear "I am not surprised. I can imagine Smithey made everyone cry!" They were delightful evenings.'

Other visitors were 'Charley' Hackett the American tenor and 'Eddie' Johnson – Edward Johnson who achieved tenor fame when he changed his name to Eduardo Di Giovanni, finally becoming manager of the Metropolitan Opera House. Marie Burke not only recalls Johnson as a fine singer but as a really good comedian. It is often claimed that Burke studied with the great tenor de Lucia but Marie Burke disclaims this assumption.

Promenading on Milan's famous Galileo was a pastime of those smitten with the musical bug, for on this stretch of road one could sometimes see the great Enrico Caruso himself walking with his satellites; or other celebrated stars of the operatic and orchestral firmament. But not all the singers were La Scala material, certainly not the little Spanish colonel who wore a faded green frock coat. Tom and Marie were out for a stroll one day when he approached them, pulling a very large card from the depths of his frock coat. On it was a list of the operas he was ready to sing at a moments notice. Bowing very delicately he placed it before them. This amused them very much and they often chatted with him. One day they decided to put him to the test and invited him along that evening to sing at the house of a friend who was Grace Powell, another student of voice: 'It was rather unkind really. We told him that if he came along Grace might be able to get him an engagement in America. I was the pianist and when he arrived he told me he would commence with a song entitled *Spirito Gentile*. Really it was a fantastic noise! He came to a point which should be sung all in one breath. He suddenly stopped singing and said "all in one breath I sing this now". I was in hysterics, so were we all, and I had to leave the room. Tom was convulsed with laughter. We felt awful about it afterwards, so embarrassed for the man, that we would hide round a corner if we saw him coming!'

All this life-colour so engulfed by the Italians' love of singing made Milan a city of infinite charm to the Burkes, but not only did every Italian man fancy himself as a heroic tenor or lusty baritone, he also had an eye for a pretty face and a well rounded bottom. Bottom pinching was a national pastime, the lady so 'honoured' was expected to be pleased for it was a gesture of regard – or that was the excuse. Tom was very annoyed when a bold young man strode up and openly pinched his wife's posterior, so mad that he pulled off a glove as if to hit him with it 'But thank heavens he didn't!' Marie remembers the incident with some amusement now, 'But Tom was rather touchy and we were not long married and I suppose he was proud of his new wife – anyhow I restrained him otherwise there would have been a fight.'

Colli was still adamant that his pupil was not ready for the operatic stage, a point of view that Tom didn't agree with; he felt he knew the Italian language fluently, knew he was singing better than he had ever sung before – and he was very eager to take the plunge. But still maestro said no. There is a bluntness inherent in the characters of the people of Leigh. Tom made up his mind to do some straight talking to his tutor. He made it perfectly clear that he could not afford to continue tuition. Furthermore, he claimed, his voice was now ready for the operatic stage. The maestro remonstrated passionately. Tom bided his time. He was used to these outbursts of Italian temperament. Then Colli calmed down and said quietly;

"So you think you are ready, Signor Burke – you are very sure of yourself, Signor!"

"I feel I am ready, maestro," replied Tom.

"So you feel you can sing in opera?"

"I am sure I can. I *know* I can."

The Italian now turned cynical. "Oh! So the young man knows he can stand on the stage of the La Scala – or is that not a good enough place for you to begin? Or would you have us build a grander auditorium for your debut?"

Burke lost his temper. It was 'muck or nettles' as they say in Lancashire. "I can sing as good as you or any other Wop!" he roared and the two of them faced each other like street dogs over a bone.

Several seconds passed and then Colli said simply, "So! We will argue no more. You will hear from me in a day or two - Signor Burke."

Colli contacted another teacher who agreed to pass his opinion on the English tenor. Tom was summoned to Colli's house where he sang an aria from *Tosca*. "He is ready," was the simple verdict of the referee and preparations were made immediately for Tom to audition for a part at the Lyric Theatre, Milan. He passed with flying colours and was chosen to sing the leading tenor role in *Rigoletto*. So, at last, the great day. Many years before Caruso had made his debut at this same theatre. The opera was to be performed under the baton of a dictatorial conductor who made it plain right from the onset that he, and he alone, was completely in charge. Tom was content to do as he was told though the rehearsals were quite traumatic, with the conductor going into tantrums whenever he felt like venting his tempestuous nature on one of the musicians. It certainly wasn't going to be the easiest of debuts. But Tom, eager to please, conformed and gave the conductor no cause for complaint. That is until they were rehearsing *La Donna e Mobile*, without doubt the most popular aria in the opera, when the pedantic maestro began to lecture Burke on the singing of the aria. He insisted that not on any consideration must he sing the cadenza – the flourish at the close of the aria showing off the singer's flexibility, compass and expressive powers – it was not good musicianship! Burke agreed though very disappointed, especially as he had been practicing it for years. The aria is the culmination of the fourth act and by this time Burke knew he had impressed the audience. He could 'feel' the excitement, the chemical affinity between audience and performer. He sang the cadenza. The audience erupted, calling for encore after encore to which Burke responded with relish. At the conclusion the conductor was furious. It didn't matter to him if Burke had sung fifty encores it was bad musicianship and, furthermore, he had disobeyed him. In all his years he had not been so blatantly disobeyed by an artist. For a full half-hour Tom stood like a naughty school kid while the furious conductor marched up and down the dressing-room, gesticulating wildly and almost having a heart attack in the process. The tenor knew this was one occasion when he must keep his tongue in check.

Rigoletto was a triumph. It was also his first meeting with The Claque – an organisation of professional applauders. Marie had the business head of the family and realised that it would be foolish not to employ them – they could help to make her husband's big chance. She met the head claquer at an agreed rendezvous and over a glass of wine they decided that the two big tenor arias should be wildly applauded by his men. Marie handed over the fee and shook hands with the head claquer. A straight forward business deal honoured by The Claque in great style, who added their paid appreciation with great gusto to that of the rest of the audience who cheered out of sheer enjoyment.

After *Rigoletto* came an engagement to sing at San Carlos. Tom went alone. Several days later Marie received a sad letter telling her that he had been stopped from performing at San Carlos. He claimed it was because of his English nationality and in all probability it was on the orders of the Mafia. Several years later Amy Shuard suffered a similar fate in Italy. The disappointed tenor told Marie to sell the furniture and with the money pay her way to meet him in Naples. There was a strong possibility he would be engaged at Palermo. Marie did as she was asked and with her few belongings and baby Patricia, set off to join her husband.

This time all was well. Burke sang in *Cavelleria Rusticana* and *Rigoletto* with a young girl of nineteen, bearing the baptismal name of Antonietta Meneghel; trained to be a pianist she injured an arm so badly she was forced to give up her career. The girl was indeed a musical genius for it was soon discovered that she possessed a fine voice of remarkable quality, making her debut at La Scala, Milan at the tender age of seventeen under the name Toti Dal Monte.

She had been singled out by Mascagni to sing in his new opera *La Lodelleta* with another bright new vocal star – Beniamino Gigli.

Most of us can claim that life has its ups and downs. Burke's most certainly had. Luck was with him this time when Gigli received his calling-up papers. Mascagni was perplexed because rehearsals were already in progress. Burke was on hand and after hearing him sing the master knew he need look no further. He had two weeks to learn the new opera and he almost sweated blood over it: 'Tom was a very fine musician,' Marie told me 'I helped him all I could and he mastered it. We had a great laugh when Tom put on the costume. It had been made for Gigli who had put on a lot of weight. Tom was no sylph but my god it went round him three times! But the opera was a resounding triumph.'

'There was never a prouder man than I,' wrote Tom of that

time. 'But today I realise more than ever what a dream it all is – this success. What an empty thing is this glamour of the stage. It is not the success that matters, it is the fact that one is giving joy and pleasure through one's voice that matters, and I would rather have the applause of the men and women who have struggled to save their few shillings, and have waited long hours to get into the gallery, than all the trappings of so-called success. There is no greater success than that, especially to a man of the people such as I am. At that time, however, it meant so much to me and I am grateful.

'Palermo was a triumph. My greatest joy during this season was to go into Naples at night with some of the finest souls in Italy. I refer to the fishermen who would row me out in their little boats and there, way out at sea with the lights of Naples gleaming in the distance, they would sing to me their wonderful Neapolitan folk songs and ballads, as only such born singers could sing them. I used to join in, and many was the hour I spent with these fisher folk drinking in the loveliness of a summer evening.

'An extremely rich patron of the opera – a not unattractive woman with more money than sense – took a great liking to me though she had been very much against my engagement. After all, I was an unknown Englishman with an Irish name! The administrators suggested I alter it to Tomaso Buruski but I stolidly refused. I told them "Tom Burke I was christened and Tom Burke I'll stay" though, in retrospect, I know I would have done better than I have; however, I did melt a little and agreed to the Tomaso bit. After all, it's only Tom in Italian!

'This woman – dripping with satin and jewels – was so taken with my voice that she wanted to take me over lock, stock and barrel and, as a 'temptation', offered to turn over all her money to me if I would go to live with her. I have often found it quite amazing how money turns some people into incredible eccentrics – I refused and, as is usually the case, hell hath no fury. . . . The Italians can be very volatile when they are angry!'

Unknown to the performers, Nellie Melba was in the audience and she was completely overwhelmed by the sheer masculinity of Burke's acting and singing and found it hard to believe that he was an Englishman. She told her circle of friends that she had found another Caruso and in letters to England wrote about the striking resemblance, both physically and vocally, which Burke bore to the young Enrico. By this time Caruso's voice was in decline and she was thrilled to 'discover' a voice that was so like that of the Italian's when he was in his prime. However, she stated, as always when discussing or writing on the subject of tenors, no-one could ever equal her beloved Jean De Reske, the Polish tenor. Not even dear Enrico. Unfortunately there are no existing recordings for posterity to be the judge. The new British tenor soon found that the hot climate of Italy had invested in many of his musical acquaintances a fiery temper and explosive disposition; this was particularly the case with conductors and producers who could fly into tantrums at the slightest provocation. Toscanini was notorious in this respect. But Burke had the greatest respect for him and considered him to be the finest conductor in the world. Generally Burke was very critical of conductors, considering that in opera a singer was the more important of the two. Much later on he was to say, 'As to conductors, I'm afraid a lot of them are inclined to place more importance on their orchestras than on their singers, with the result that the voices are swamped. There's a certain amount of conceit in all of us, and in the case of the conductor it must be very tempting to show off by producing a glorious orchestral sound at the expense of the voices. Mind you, I'm not saying singers are not conceited too. The trouble is that there isn't often enough an ideal marriage between the two. If you get a really brilliant conductor, however, who really knows his scores and understands voices as well as orchestral instruments, then you can safely let him take charge. The conductor is, of course, responsible for ensemble, and it is up to him to ask a singer to produce a certain effect that he thinks will fit in well with the orchestra. But he can rarely tell the singer *how* to produce this effect – any more than the singer can tell *him* how to conduct the orchestra. There have been rare conductors, of course, who understand pretty well everything about opera – singing, playing and production. Toscanini was one, Serafin another. With conductors like these the opera is presented as a whole, with no question of the orchestra predominating when it shouldn't or the singer predominating the orchestra where he shouldn't.'

On the subject of producers Burke was often little short of scathing. 'What does he produce anyway?' In Italy he soon learned that producers considered their role over-rode both singer and conductor, a situation entirely unacceptable to both and guaranteed to cause a rumpus in such a highly dramatic and emotional art form as Grand Opera. The Italians *don't* bottle-up their emotions and Tom witnessed many a row at rehearsals and was not slow in speaking his own mind if he felt like it, yet this uninhibited volatile behaviour, which he saw exhibited so often, is inherent in the very genre of opera production and opera singing, and was evident in his own character to which his unfettered style of singing gave ample testimony.

After *Lodelleta* Dal Montes career really took off on its spectacular rise to those palmy heights habitated by only a select band of Divas. A concert tour followed which brought her to the notice of the Italian concert-going public who took her to their hearts.

No such adulation for Burke who was now similarly poised for a tilt in the lists of operatic fame. La Scala could not have barred its doors from the new English tenor for long. It was not to be. Immediately after *Lodelleta* he received a telegram from Mark Richardson Moore: *'Come back immediately. You have been called up for Army.'* There was no hesitation. The Burkes returned poste haste to London to see Moore, then on to Leigh where Tom was interviewed prior to having an Army Medical Examination. This was early in 1918. But Kitchener *didn't* want him. Dr Sturm, a local G.P., was a sensible man who had his priorities firmly fixed in their correct places. He realised that Tom, whom he knew from old, could do far more good singing for the war effort than he could if drafted to the Front as an Infantryman. So Burke, the ex-heavy weight boxer and rugby player, was classed as Grade 3. He was delighted, sent for Marie and Patricia who were visiting his mother-in-law in London, and put himself in the hands of an impresario currently arranging charity concerts.

The first concert of his tour was held appropriately at Leigh Hippodrome. Joe Burke remembers it as if it was yesterday. "The concert was for the Mayor's Prisoners of War Fund. Our Tom's return to Leigh soon got round and when the concert was advertised there was a rush for seats. Manchester's Jewish community supported all these charity concerts and took all the expensive seats. I've never seen the likes of it. At eight o'clock in the morning on the day of the concert queues were forming for the performance at eight at night. The prices were colossal for those days: five pounds for a box; one pound for stalls; fifteen shillings for pit stalls; twelve and six for the remainder of the bottom floor. The circle seats were twelve and six, seven and six and five shillings, and the 'gods' three bob. Many of Tom's old mates were in the 'gods' and he got a tremendous ovation when he came on the stage. Percy Kahn, associated with Tauber for many years, was his accompanist. Cecil Tate was violin soloist. Tom's wife, Marie, sang a song called *The Little Cuckoo*. It was a packed house – standing room only and outside hundreds of people milled around unable to get in. Tom sang twenty-two songs and raised £1,150 for the Mayor's Fund. It was a sensational concert and the whole of the Burke family were there in force.'

It was at this concert that Burke won his audience over immediately with a superb piece of theatrical timing and impromtu invention. As the applause died down after Tom's entrance on stage and the tenor stood poised to sing his first song, a voice from the gallery shouted, "How do Tom me old mate!" Burke looked at the sea of faces, waved, bent forward in a whispered consultation with the orchestra and broke into *I Hear You Calling Me*, a song he usually kept for an encore. The audience rose in their seats at the conclusion. A fantastic homecoming.

Several concerts followed at the Free Trade Hall, Manchester, and at one of these a young aspiring soprano shared the honours with Tom. That singer, Isobel Baillie, wrote to me from Florida. 'It is so long ago but I remember being struck with the exceptional quality of his voice. I later went to hear him in a musical play in London in which he was excellent, but after that he seemed to fade away. Perhaps he didn't

'Our dearest father' James Burke.

From the tenor's private photographic collection

'Our darling mother' Mary Josephine Burke.

From the tenor's private photographic collection

No. 7, Mather Lane, Leigh – where Tom was born.

NO CHARGE FOR THIS PROGRAMME

By Appointment
Jewellers to His Majesty The King.

PEARLS DIAMONDS
AND OTHER
PRECIOUS STONES.
PRESENTATION PLATE.

THE GOLDSMITHS & SILVERSMITHS COMPANY LTD.

112 Regent Street, London, W.1.

By Appointment
Jewellers to His Majesty The King.

The Opera Dinner & Supper
at the
WALDORF HOTEL
The Thé Dansant
Every Afternoon
6 to 6.30. Price 5/6
JAZZ BAND

Boots Chemists
TOILET SPECIALISTS AND PERFUMERS
Chief London Branches:
182, Regent Street, W.1
112-118 Edgware Road, W.2
52 New Bond Street, W.1
Boots Pure Drug Co., Ltd.

SCHWEPPE'S
TABLE WATERS
Ask for
"*Whisky & Schweppe*"

EVERY TITLE IN STOCK
Operatic Records
by all the most famous
ENGLISH & CONTINENTAL ARTISTES
can be obtained at
THE
GRAMOPHONE EXCHANGE
29 & 31 New Oxford Street

"*La Naturelle*"
is the natural-parting toupet which defies detection. Can be worn without parting if desired. Visit our Salons or send to Dept. 15 for an appro. selection, or Catalogue de Luxe.
Maison Georges
40 Buckingham Palace Road
London, S.W.1

SAVOY RESTAURANT FOR LUNCHEON

Royal Opera Covent Garden

Proprietors . The Grand Opera Syndicate, Ltd.

[1919]

THIS EVENING'S PERFORMANCE

OPENING NIGHT OF THE SEASON

Monday, May 12th, at 8.30

Puccini's Opera

LA BOHÈME

(In Italian)

Mimi	NELLIE MELBA
Musetta	KATHLEEN DESTOURNEL
Rodolfo	THOMAS BURKE
Marcello	ALFRED MAGUENAT
Colline	GUSTAVE HUBERDEAU
Schaunard	EDOUARD COTREUIL
Benoit, Alcindoro	POMPILIO MALATESTA
Parpignol	UMBERTO SCARAVELLI
Conductor	Sir THOMAS BEECHAM

Stage Manager . M. FERNAND ALMANZ

For future Announcements see inside

IMPERIAL RESTAURANT FOR DINNER

Telephone Mayfair 3368
Renée le Roy
CHAPEAUX
CHIC - ORIGINAL - BECOMING AND INEXPENSIVE
MODES FOR MATRONS & CHAPERONES
5. HANOVER ST. W.

THE WORLD'S GREATEST ARTISTES
including
MELBA, CARUSO
TETRAZZINI
MARTINELLI
DESTINNOVA, FARRAR
KIRKBY LUNN
McCORMACK, JOURNET
SCOTTI, BATTISTINI
CHALIAPIN
GALLI-CURCI
TITTA RUFFO
SAMMARCO
Will sing to you in YOUR home through the medium of
"His Master's Voice"
GRAMOPHONE RECORDS
Obtainable from Accredited Dealers throughout the Country
The Gramophone Co., Ltd.,
HAYES ——— Middlesex

GILL & REIGATE Ltd.
THE SOHO GALLERIES
THE LARGEST STOCK OF GENUINE ANTIQUES IN LONDON
Also Finest Reproductions from the Antique
Write for "R.O." Booklet, post free
73-85 Oxford Street, W

MELBA'S TRIUMPH.

Great Success of the New Lancashire Tenor.

The oldest habitué of Covent Garden cannot remember anything like last night; but a young subaltern, who must have been at Eton or Harrow when the curtain fell for the last time in July, 1914, assured a companion, equally positive, that it was just like old times.

Many things indeed were like old times, but the least imaginative could not help reflecting what changes there have been—and what they mean. More than once I heard men saying, "Last time I was here poor old —— was with me. I was with him when we went over the top."

Inside the theatre not much is altered. It looks fresher and newer, and it never looked more brilliant than last night.

Nearly every seat was full when Sir Thomas Beecham took his place in the orchestra, and after a few moments the familiar drum roll silenced the din of conversation as if by magic.

With the first bars of "God Save the King" the Queen was seen entering the

MR. TOM BURKE.

Royal box, and with her were Queen Alexandra, Princess Mary and Princess Maud. Then the audience caught sight of the King and the three young Princes, and a volume of cheers rose from all parts of the house, and grew and grew till the band was inaudible, and continued long after the National Anthem was finished. The Victory Opera Season had begun.

THE NEW TENOR.

When the curtain rose on the first act of "La Bohème" everyone was anxious for the first notes of Mr Tom Burke, the new Lancashire tenor, of whom the Syndicate expects so much. A few minutes sufficed to satisfy us that there was no mistake. It is a real tenor voice of pure Italian type, produced with rare ease and growing more brilliant as it goes up the scale. At first there was a little jerkiness in the singing, but the nature of the ordeal was enough to account for that.

As the moment for the entrance of Mimi drew near a sort of hush settled over the house, such as only comes on great occasions. When the first notes were heard from outside there was a sigh as of relieved tension. Some people tried to cheer, but the rest of the audience would have no interruption.

Mme. Melba looked if anything younger than when we saw her last. For a minute or two she was obviously nervous, but soon the voice came out limpid as ever, with that purity and evenness which have been the admiration of three decades of music lovers. There was even an added warmth of expression. Then Mr. Burke again became the centre of attraction. In the Poet's Song he firmly established his position. It is too much to say that his singing is perfect; the middle notes still leave something to be desired; the phrasing still lacks the ultimate polish and the temperament is not fully developed. But there is little doubt that it was the most successful effort made by any tenor at Covent Garden for a long time. As Mr. Burke is still under 30, there seems no reason why any position among the stars of the day should be beyond his reach. In the third act his singing had greater warmth and tenderness, and his success was confirmed.

Queues Wait All Day For Gallery Seats.

BRILLIANT SPECTACLE.

Melba And Thomas Burke In "La Boheme."

By "Mr. GOSSIP."

Long before the curtain rose at Covent Garden last night the grand old theatre was well-nigh full.

Queues had been waiting all day outside the unreserved portions of the house, and the opening of the doors was the sign for a stampede of musical enthusiasts, who flooded and crammed to overflowing the vast gallery in less than five minutes.

But eagerness and enthusiasm spread on this occasion to the stalls and boxes. Gone for the moment was the hallowed tradition that it is necessary to stroll in languidly between nine and ten o'clock, or be classed with those who eat peas with a knife.

Before even the footlights glowed on the great red curtain every stall and box seemed to be occupied, and there was a quarter of an hour or more of merry chatter.

1914—With A Difference.

Old friends were recognised and hailed, and there was a general atmosphere of "Here we are again!" about the whole affair.

Four and a half years of horror seemed to have passed in a flash, like some sudden nightmare that lasts but for a second.

The red draperies of the boxes, the grey carpet, the blue-green ceiling, even the faces of the attendants—surely it was just a week ago, and not July, 1914, that Covent Garden was last open!

It was only a close inspection of the audience that destroyed the illusion. Outwardly they are the same, dresses and jewels as wondrous as ever, and many, too, remain of the "old guard." But sometimes one looked in vain.

A Melba Night Again.

There is little that is new to be said about "La Bohème"; with Sir Thomas Beecham at the conductor's desk a brilliant performance was assured, and there was nothing to worry about. In fact, last night the interest, on both sides of the footlights, was mainly personal.

There was the personal touch in the return of Mme. Melba—Dame Melba now—to the theatre where she has triumphed for thirty years. Yes, it was a "Melba night" once again—the very phrase is redolent of the happy old times that have returned.

Mme. Melba—to call her "the Dame" has irreverent associations with lighter forms of entertainment than grand opera—was in splendid voice. The delicious bird-like purity of her tone is unblemished.

It has never been suggested that histrionically she is an ideal exponent of that consumptive little Parisian cocotte, Henri Murger's Mimi, but that has never detracted from the glory of her singing or the rapture of her welcome.

A Tenor From Lancashire.

Thomas Burke, the new English Rodolfo, with Lancashire as his home and Italy as his training-ground, came through the ordeal of following in the footsteps of Caruso, Zenatello, Bonci, McCormack, and the great tenors of former years, with remarkable success.

He was obviously nervous. But he is a true tenor, and not like so many English "tenors," a forced-up baritone. He has a pleasant appearance and personality, has some idea of acting, and has considerable power.

M. Magenot and Signor Malatesta, old Covent Garden favourites, seemed to be as glad to get back again as we were to see and hear them.

MR. BURKE'S TRIUMPH.

While our lot is to stare, through Act I., at an uninteresting attic while two evidently respectable young people are being rather unusually nice to one another, having never seen each other in the light. Such an ugly attic! Pierrot might well have a really fantastic attic, gleaming with broken Bourbon furniture and marvellous cobwebs the size of peacocks' tails.

Last night, however, one did not need [illegible] look and one could [illegible] it was worth [illegible]. A rich, flexible, [illegible]sionate young [illegible] that began [illegible] rather nervously but [illegible] as the act [illegible]; rang with [illegible] abrupt transi[illegible] lacked something in judgment, [illegible] was superb in [illegible] and beauty—[illegible] was the new [illegible], Mr. Thomas Burke. A hit, a [illegible] hit.

[illegible]

Mr. Burke must [illegible] done a further [illegible]—by no word or sign does he betray English origin. His assumption of the Italian manner is perfect. An Englishman who can pass for a pure-bred Italian tenor! The last act, with "Mimi se andata," showed of what an exquisite mezza-voce he is capable.

And Melba—Melba was Melba! What can the scribe at this time of day say of Melba, when all vocabularies were long since ransacked in her praise? Enough that when she lifted up her voice in "Mi chiamano Mimi" she prolonged the hour's illusion that the dark years had never been. The audience gave her ovations after each act, and the bravos' [illegible] rang out shrill. Sir Thomas Beecham, though a thought ruthless on the singers, obtained some brilliantly vivacious orchestral playing. The Musetta was not so pleasing as most of the generally excellent cast.

E. C.

ALL-DAY QUEUE FOR GALLERY.

As early as eight o'clock yesterday morning opera devotees began to take up their stand in Floral Street, and by four o'clock in the afternoon there were some hundreds standing and sitting about, some on portable chairs and others on boxes. There were many Dominion soldiers in the crowd.

The gallery was the only part of the theatre where seats could be obtained, all others having been sold long ago.

Many times also during the performance of "La Bohème" individual efforts were applauded, though, be it said, the applause on these occasions was quickly silenced. At the end of the arias, however, it burst forth with more [illegible] than Verdi employs in his "Requiem"! And the times Dame Melba and Mr. Thos. Burke (Rodolfo) were called and recalled! Who could number them? In very truth Time has dealt gently by Madame Melba, who first sang at Covent Garden in 1888. The voice is as glorious golden as before, the tone as full—recall the C as she and Rodolfo descend the stairs in Act I!—the style as easy as ever. Small wonder that folk applauded, and that many of Madame Melba's compatriots in various parts of the house cooed to her. In Mr. Burke the authorities have made a very valuable discovery for themselves. To a very fine and wholly sympathetic and powerful tenor voice Mr. Burke adds an excellent stage presence, and at once it was clear that he was thoroughly well received. For the moment I need say no more, for there will be many further opportunities for writing of him. He, as Rodolfo, was admirably supported by our old friends MM. Magenot, Hubendon, and [illegible] as Marcello, Colline, and Schaunard, whilst yet another old familiar friend was Mr. Malatesta in the dual rôles of Benoit and Alcindoro; and Miss Destournel, a newcomer, played and sang Musetta's rôle with a great deal of spirit.

A word of praise for the orchestra and for Sir Thomas Beecham, who did that they set out to do with magnificent spirit, and for all concerned on the stage. One and all worked with rarest skill to achieve a success, which most decidedly they achieved to a degree, all things considered, that is historical.

COVENT GARDEN REVEALS NEW ENGLISH TENOR SENSATION

Musical America

Thomas Burke, a Lancashireman, the Find of the Season—Karsavina Thrills with the Russian Ballet—New Works by Scott and Goossens—Albert Coates at Covent Garden—Moiseiwitsch and Lamond Win Popularity

London, June 2, 1919.—Brilliant is the only adjective that can be applied to the post-war musical season of London, still in full swing. More than a bird's-eye view it is impossible to give, but such a view will at once disclose certain high spots that are familiar to Americans. It is one of the paradoxes of the war that England, comparatively well fed and never despairing of victory, suffered at least a partial eclipse on its social side, while starving Germany, heading for certain defeat, was going full blast musically, theatrically and terpsichoreally, all through the war.

America, away off and untouched by the real terrors and well supplied with physical and mental nourishment, cannot be expected to know the emotions of the victory-glad Londoners awakening from a four years' nightmare of "Zeps" and submarines, any more than the feelings of hollow eyed, half starved Berliners listening to Beethoven symphonies.

LONDON "COMES BACK."

London "came back" musically with a whoop on May 12, when the Royal Opera, closed for four years, reopened its doors to give "La Bohème" for an immense and brilliant audience, including their majesties King George and Queen Alexandria. The audience was, according to the critics, "wonderful and wondering"—wondering if everything would be the same and whether we could really settle down to the old mixture of social and musical pleasure, as though nothing had happened." Something, to be sure, had happened to the audience itself—aside from that terrible something implied in the quoted phrase. It was not the same audience, in fact; for the galleries, the whole top of the house was filled with a new race of music lovers—the two shilling people whom Sir Thomas Beecham has been educating or indulging in the enjoyment of Wagner and Verdi. These people are now, that Sir Thomas has joined the Covent Garden syndicate, cheerfully paying their "five bob" to hear in a foreign language what they have been hearing in English at two. And they enjoy it in a manner that is new to London, so that the critics speak of the "hilarity" of the galleries.

THE GALLERIES CROWDED.

Every night since that first night they have been turning out in crowds, standing in line for hours to be admitted to the usual conventional cycle: "Traviata," "Butterfly," "Thais," "Rigoletto," "Manon," "Faust," "Tosca," "Bohème." Only two less hackneyed titles so far: "Thérèse," by Massenet, and "Louise," by Charpentier. It is the same old line stuff and, luckily, the same old line talent, for after all, people go to the opera to hear singers. The music is secondary.

No less a luminary than Melba shone on the opening night, and with her were such familiar figures as Huberdeau and Maguenat, but also a new "discovery"—Thomas Burke.

A NEW "DISCOVERY."

Burke is the sensation of the season. His origin is as plain as his name; a Lancashire lad who worked in the mines. He is one of the most talked of men in London, sharing the day's sensations with Hawker, one of the heroes of the air. His voice is a tenor of pure Italian flavor and for a debutant he displays an almost fabulous routine. Making one's debut as Rodolfo to Melba's Mimi, before their Britannic majesties on an opening night, is surely a large contract, but Tom Burke's nerves were not in the least affected by it. America will certainly hear more of him and in my imagination I can see his name in ten foot letters outside the Hippodrome!

June-26-1919

BURKE
at
Covent
Garden
Won fame in a single night!
At last—an English tenor with a voice equal to the greatest of the Italians
Britain is proud to be the possessor of a singer whose talent has startled and delighted the musical world. The great tenors of the world have met their equal in BURKE, the English tenor, whose marvellous renderings are reproduced with clarity, purity and fidelity to the original only on Columbia Records.
THESE ARE BURKE'S FIRST SIX RECORDS—
7201.—RIGOLETTO: La Donna e mobile
7202.—RIGOLETTO: Questa o Quella
7203.—MARTHA: M'Appari
7204.—MANON: Chiudo gli occhi
7199.—LA TOSCA: Recondita armonia
7200.—LA TOSCA: E lucevan le stelle
ASK TO HEAR THEM AT ANY MUSIC DEALERS
ONLY ON
Columbia
Columbia Records
MAGIC NOTES
TRADE MARK

Nellie Melba as Leda in 'Les Pecheurs de Perles'.

From the Stuart-Liff Collection

NO CHARGE FOR THIS PROGRAMME

Parfums de Luxe

MORNY

201 REGENT ST. W.1.

Bath Specialities

THE SMARTEST HATS IN TOWN SINCE 1914

MAISON LEWIS

152 REGENT STREET

PHONE 9420 GERRARD

LIBERTY SILKS AND DRESSES

PATTERNS & CATALOGUES FREE
LIBERTY & CO. REGENT ST LONDON

ROYAL FLORIST
By Appointment to H.M. THE KING

EDWARD . . GOODYEAR

Royal Arcade, Albemarle Street and OLD BOND STREET, W.

CHINA & GLASS
Originalité House

Soane & Smith Ltd.

462 OXFORD ST. LONDON, W.1.

Not to be excelled for TONE, TOUCH and DURABILITY

CHAPPELL PIANOS

50 New Bond St., London, W.1

SAVOY RESTAURANT FOR DINNER

Royal Opera Covent Garden

Proprietors . The Grand Opera Syndicate, Ltd.

[1919]

THIS EVENING'S PERFORMANCE

Tuesday, May 27th, at 8.30

PUCCINI'S OPERA

LA BOHÈME

(In Italian)

Mimi	MARGARET SHERIDAN
Musetta	OLGA LYNN
Rodolfo	THOMAS BURKE
Marcello	ALFRED MAGUENAT
Colline	GUSTAVE HUBERDEAU
Schaunard	EDOUARD COTREUIL
Benoit / Alcindoro	POMPILIO MALATESTA
Parpignol	UMBERTO SCARAVELLI
Conductor	PERCY PITT

IMPERIAL RESTAURANT FOR LUNCHEON

The Most Exclusive House in London for Tailor-Mades

Maison Arthur Ltd

20 DOVER ST. MAYFAIR

Exclusive Treatments

VALAZE SALONS

ensure the rejuvenation and preservation of complexion and contour

Mme. Helena Rubinstein

24 Grafton St., Bond St., London, W.1

Fan Maker
By Appointment

J. Duvelleroy

167 REGENT ST. W.

The RITZ RESTAURANT & GRILL ROOM

for LUNCHEONS and DINNERS

Telephone : Regent 60

BY APPOINTMENT TO H.M. THE QUEEN

ORIGINAL AND EXCLUSIVE MODELS IN DAY AND EVENING GOWNS.

Reville & Rossiter

OPERA CLOAKS
RACE GOWNS
AND
LIGHT WRAPS

Telephone: Mayfair 6380 (3 lines)

HANOVER SQUARE, W.

The CARLTON RESTAURANT & GRILL ROOM

for LUNCHEONS and DINNERS

Telephone : Gerrard 7820

NO CHARGE FOR THIS PROGRAMME

Royal Opera Covent Garden

Proprietors . The Grand Opera Syndicate, Ltd.
Lessees . The Sir Thomas Beecham Opera Co. Ltd.

1920

THIS EVENING'S PERFORMANCE

Tuesday, May 18th, at 8.30

BIZET'S OPERA

I PESCATORI DI PERLE

(In Italian)

Leila	GRAZIELLA PARETO
Nadir	THOMAS BURKE
Zurga	ERNESTO BADINI
Nurabad	EDMUND BURKE

Conductor . . Sir THOMAS BEECHAM

For future Announcements see inside

Tom and Marie on Rotten Row.

PROGRAMME

Sonata (Violin and Pianoforte)	"Andante"—"Allegro Vivace"	*Sjögren*

Mr. GODFREY LUDLOW and Mr. FRANK ST. LEGER

Aria ...	"Che Gelida Manina" (Bohême) ...	*Puccini*

Mr. TOM BURKE

Pianoforte Soli ...	(*a*) Nocturne (*b*) Etude (thirds) (*c*) Etude (posthumous) (*d*) Etude in A minor ...	*Chopin*

Miss GERTRUDE PEPPERCORN

Songs	(*a*) "Pourquoi me réveiller" ...	*Massenet*
	(*b*) "Un rêve" ...	*Grieg*

Mr. TOM BURKE

Violin Soli ...	(*a*) "Ave Maria"	*Schubert*
	(*b*) "Caprice Viennois"	*Kreisler*
	(*c*) "Gavotte de Renaud"	*Sacchini*

Mr. GODFREY LUDLOW

Old Irish Songs ...	(*a*) "The Next Market Day" (*b*) "An Island Spinning Song" (*c*) "Ballynure Ballad"	*Arr. by Herbert Hughes*

Mr. TOM BURKE

Pianoforte Soli ...	(*a*) "Marche," Op. 17	*Dohnanyi*
	(*b*) "Valse-Caprice" ...	*Strauss—Tausig*

Miss GERTRUDE PEPPERCORN

Violin Soli ...	(*a*) "Poême"	*D'Erlanger*
	(*b*) "Tambourin Chinois"	*Kreisler*

Mr. GODFREY LUDLOW

At the Piano - Mr. FRANK ST. LEGER

CHAPPELL CONCERT GRAND PIANOFORTE

Programme for 'Tom Burke Tour' 1920.

receive the right opportunities?'

As soon as the war ended the administrators of the Royal Opera House, Covent Garden, began to make plans for the first 'peace' season of opera. Dame Melba had instructed them that she would appear. Melba did not have to be asked, she commanded. Everyone was delighted – Melba was the queen of the 'Garden' and in the eyes of the opera goers could do no wrong. However, the opera hierarchy were astounded to receive word from her that she had chosen a tenor unknown to them, an Englishman with the unglamorous name of Tom Burke.

ACT III

With Burke's selection to sing Rodolpho to Melba's Mimi in *La Boheme* set for 12th May, 1919 safely under his belt, he was to receive a shock at his first meeting with the governors of the Royal Opera House. Here Burke's 'running war' with opera administration began. Here are his own words: 'If what I am about to say sounds bitter let me say right here that I do not speak any more for myself than I do for countless other British singers who have been driven abroad because they could get no engagement to sing at the Royal Opera House. I dare not take any concert dates at all and had to live on borrowed money because I knew it would spoil my chances of selection. Had I done so, the snobbery which exists over here would have killed my chances entirely. A 'concert artist'! The powers-that-be would have sniffed disdainfully, he *can't* be any good. That is the point of view against which Empire singers have to fight all the time. It matters not how fine a singer a man is, he must not sing to live, he must live to sing; and even if gifted with the voice of an angel if he is profane enough to break the opera code by taking concert engagements then he is doomed and damned to blush unseen as far as the operatic world is concerned.

'So we lived sparsely, with dignity, and at long last reaped my reward by obtaining that wonderful engagement to sing with Melba and that fine baritone Sammarco. I often laugh now when I wonder what the 'powers-that-be' would have thought had they seen me getting stuck into feeding pigs on my father's small-holding and mucking-out the sty while I waited to adorn their inviolate sanctum sanctorum!

'It was not far from the dawn of the day when I was to appear at Covent Garden, an ambition every singer strives to attain. At last I was called to London. I had been selected, purely on Melba's say so, for *La Boheme*. The fee I was to receive was twenty-five guineas. I emphasise this for the benefit of those budding Carusos whose appetites for operatic fame have been whetted by stories of fabulous fees paid to singers. Had I returned from Italy with an Italian name such as Tomasso Burkovitch, as one stupid person suggested, it might have been different. But how the hell could I have faced folks back in Leigh with a handle like that? I know what they would have said and it's not for publication! But proud Tom Burke, proud of his name, and his nationality, was offered the princely sum of 25 gns. When I demurred to the then General Manager of Covent Garden, Colonel Higgins – now dead – he told me with blunt and unemotional frankness that I ought to consider myself jolly lucky to get the engagement at all. "If you don't like it, Mr Burke, then you can leave it," he told me. "But remember this, if you don't sing here you'll never make your name in this country." And that is true. That is the whole iniquity of the thing. When I pointed out to him that foreign artists were getting more than I was he simply shrugged and repeated again that it was up to me. But I would have starved or sung for nothing rather than miss the chance. That does not make the position any the less unjust.

'I know that opera is a luxury entertainment and opera singers are a luxury, but, at the same time, if there is to be a government grant I would suggest that the major portion should go into the pockets of British artists rather than to subsidising foreign singers.'

This was written in 1930 but Burke began his campaign on behalf of British artists immediately after the *Boheme* triumph and was never afraid to air his views in public or through the press, for whom he was always good copy. Diplomacy was never part of Tom's character and his candidness was not always appreciated in influential circles.

Burke was very aware of the lukewarm reception the

announcement of his debut had received. It was the opportunity of a lifetime and he was determined to sing as he had never sung before. But anxiety is an affliction which can over-ride confidence in one's own ability and the prospect of the ordeal before him was traumatic in the extreme. And yet he enjoyed the weeks previous to the great opening-night; long hours rehearsing under the baton of 'Tommy' Beecham, enjoying the company of the other celebrated singers in the opera; living the part of Rodolpho, the Bohemian poet, in a conscientious effort to capture the very spirit of the character. Beecham's presence must have been a consolation; a fellow Lancastrian, born in St. Helens, the grandson of the Beecham who started the famous Pill Empire. Tom had often heard the tale from his mother of how the old man had stood on St. Helens' Market selling his pills with the notice 'Worth a Guinea a Box' displayed above his head; but Tom was sufficiently in awe of the great conductor not to mention that many folks in Lancashire associated his name with other forms of movements than musical ones!

Rosenthal, in his *Two Centuries of Opera at Covent Garden*, sets the scene which existed prior to the re-opening of Covent Garden Opera House after the war:

> 'During the 1914-18 war years Covent Garden was requisitioned by the Government, and used as a furniture repository. Opera in London was almost exclusively in the hands of the recently formed Beecham Company, first at Shaftesbury Theatre, then at the Aldwych, and finally at Drury Lane. Although the Beecham Company undertook provincial tours, London enjoyed several long and virtually unbroken seasons of opera from the beginning of October 1915 until the beginning of August 1916; from mid-October 1916 until mid-February 1917, and from May to July and September to November of the same year. In 1918 there were three months of opera in London, and then after the war ended, and prior to the re-opening of Covent Garden on 12th May, 1919, the Beecham Company was at Drury Lane from the end of February until 3rd May.
>
> The singing and ensemble of this company set a standard that had never before been experienced in English opera; and even today has seldom been surpassed. The repertory of the

company included works by Wagner, despite the hysterical outcry against German music in England at this time, as well as Mozart, the more popular French and Italian operas, and several of the Russian operas that had been heard during the 1913 and 1914 seasons at Drury Lane. The company included the finest British artists of the day – Jeanne Brola, Rosina Buckman, Mirian Licette, Mignon Nevada, Desiree Ellinger, Edna Thornton, Agnes Nicholls, Norman Allin, Frederic Austin, Maurice D'Oisly, Walter Hyde, Frank Mullings, Robert Radford and Frederick Ranalow among them. The conductors, besides Beecham, were Aylmer Buesst, Julius Harrison, Eugene Goossens, senior and junior, and Percy Pitt. With this strong artistic personnel it was felt that at last the foundations of a permanent British company had been laid. Beecham, in a curtain speech at Drury Lane on the last night of his 1919 spring season, just ten days before Covent Garden opened its doors for the first post-war 'International Opera Season', said that he felt that the cornerstone of English opera was laid. In July, they would re-open at Covent Garden (i.e. after the foreign singers had departed), 'a theatre more directly associated with opera', and there he intended to establish opera throughout the year. He was realising his ambition, he continued, 'to establish not only opera in English but English opera'. That this dream was not realised, and that disaster overtook not only the Beecham Company, but also its successor, the B.N.O.C., was due to a large extent to the Grand Opera Syndicate and its chairman Higgins. It was the story of the Richter-Pitt English *Ring* all over again; but its effects were even more crippling.

The first rumours that the Syndicate was planning a summer season in 1919 circulated in January that year. During February the preliminary prospectus was issued, which contained the expected news of the alliance between the Beecham Company and the Syndicate, and the promise of the English premiere of the Puccini *Trittico* (*Il Tabarro, Suor Angelica* and *Gianni Schicchi*) which had received its world premiere at the Metropolitan, New York two months previously. Verdi's *Simone Boccanegra*, Mascagni's *Iris* and De Lara's *Nail*, as well as productions of Gluck's *Alceste* and Borodin's *Prince Igor*, neither of which had previously been heard at the Royal Opera House, were also promised. By the time the season began in May, the Puccini,

> Verdi and Gluck works had disappeared from the repertory, and their places were taken by Massenet's *Therese* and Ravel's *L'Heure Espagnole*.
>
> The preliminary announcements also hinted at the engagement of Toscanini as chief conductor for the Italian works. That the negotiations with Toscanini fell through is something that London opera-goers have long regretted. The actual reason for Toscanini's non-arrival was a private quarrel between Puccini and Toscanini; and when the composer learnt that Covent Garden had invited Toscanini to conduct the first English performances of the *Trittico*, he asked his publishers to intervene: "I've heard about Covent Garden and I protested to Ricordi because I do not want that pig of a Toscanini. He has said all sorts of nasty things about my operas and has tried to inspire certain journalists to run them down"; so wrote the composer to an English friend in 1919. In the end neither Toscanini nor the *Trittico* appeared at Covent Garden that summer.'

Instead Puccini's *Boheme* was chosen as the opening Opera of the peace season, an excellent and popular choice, a tried and trusted favourite, the ideal work to link the past with the present, an opera with which 'Garden' devotees associated golden moments of sheer musical ecstasy before the war. And, most significant of all, was the engagement of 'darling Nellie' to play Mimi – what memories of those pre-war happy days were conjured up by the announcement which was reflected in the rush for tickets at the box office. Melba was adored in England and America, an adoration she did not enjoy in Europe, least of all in Italy.

Beecham had at his command an army of international vocal talent, singers who had sung for him before the war. Those selected were only too pleased to appear for they were well aware that the eyes of the musical world would be focused on the peace season at the Royal Opera House. But the singers not only brought their international reputations to London, they also brought their own temperaments with them and nobody could be more temperamental than Nellie Melba.

Beecham made no secret of the fact that he disliked the Australian Diva and the feeling was decidedly mutual.

The administrators were well aware of the volcanic situation they had created by bringing the two together. At their first meeting in the conductor's office prior to *La Boheme*, Beecham deliberately snubbed Melba, pretending he didn't recognise her, an action which infuriated her and caused a row before a word had been spoken about the forthcoming opera. Colonel Higgins and his cohorts had the task of reconciling the situation, not a new position for them to be in well accustomed as they were to shows of irascibility from performers who often behaved more like spoilt children than responsible adults. But such was the maelstrom of opera at the time. Both agreed to a smouldering peace which actually resolved itself into a happy and harmonious relationship. But Beecham, like Burke, was never one for disguising his feelings or opinions and he didn't care who knew that he did not consider Melba to be as great a soprano as most people imagined her to be. He admired her tonal beauty, technique and especially her superb professionalism, but claimed that she lacked a vitality which, had she possessed it, would have acquired for her the mantle of greatness. Burke, in later years, mirrored these views when he said that he preferred Louisa Tetrazzini to Melba but knowing Burke's preference for anything Italian in the musical sphere this is not altogether surprising. He also claimed that Melba, through her great influence, deliberately kept the Italian in the shade as far as Covent Garden was concerned. The two women hated each other. Melba described the Italian as 'looking like an Italian cook and sounding like one.' Perhaps as far as the appearance was concerned Melba was correct for Tetrazzini was in excess of fourteen stones in weight. The Italian, in turn, would claim to her friends that Melba faked her top notes and loved nothing more than to give impressions of her doing so. The truth was that they were both very great singers and there was so little room at the top. 'Darling Nellie' always received a larger fee than any other artist, even Caruso. This was an accepted fact. If, for arguments sake, her fee was a thousand pounds, Caruso would receive £995; to appease the tenor, and keep Melba happy at the same time, he would receive an amount for 'expenses'.

However, the fact indisputedly remains that she was a

magnetic attraction in England – the queen of song with legions of admirers who would have queued for days on end to hear her sing; and certainly there could not have been a more popular choice – the opening opera of the peace season *and* a Melba night! No wonder the operatic world was agog with excitement.

In the tenor division Beecham had three celebrated singers in his company – Giovanni Martinelli – considered to be Caruso's natural successor – Fernand Ansseau, the Belgian who, though possessed of a beautiful voice, did not appeal to Melba; and the 'thin man' of the operatic stage Spaniard Ulysses Lappas who looked as if a top 'C' would blow him over. To make up the quartet came Tom Burke, virtually unknown in his own country, yet chosen by Melba ahead of the others because, according to some critics, 'she was greatly taken by the sheer masculinity of his voice'. For a sum of twenty-five guineas Burke had a lot to prove.

The prima donna, as befitted the special occasion, was on her very best behaviour, not displaying any of the tantrums for which she was notorious; her reputation was known to Burke who had heard all the 'Melba legends' in Italy and was well aware that she was reputed to eat tenors for breakfast. Fiery Irishman John McCormack, who could throw a tantrum with the best of them, had never let Melba get the better of him. But she could never really forgive John for the sausage incident. Previous to a performance of *Aida* they had had an inevitable row. There was time to spare so the tenor dashed out to the butcher's shop where he bought a couple of fat sausages. Hiding them in his costume he bided his time until the heart-rendering aria *Che Gelida Manina*, in English, *Your Tiny Hand is Frozen*, when he thrust the two cold 'bangers' into his lover's fist!*

Certainly Burke was never overawed by any personality and felt no fear of Melba or her reputation. He loved to recount stories of this great occasion, often against himself. His favourite concerned two wealthy patronesses of the opera. *The Scene: Restaurant Frascati, Oxford Street. Two ladies are taking afternoon tea prior to attending the opera:*

First lady: (Looking at programme) Thomas Burke? I've

***The sausage incident has been attributed to Caruso but McCormack, in his writing, tells the story about himself.**

never heard of him. I'm told he was a miner of all things!

Second lady: Neither has anyone else heard of him, my dear.

First lady: Wouldn't you think the 'Garden' would engage one of the great foreign tenors. There's something magical in their names, never mind their voices. I mean, fancy engaging an English tenor. Let's face it, my dear, we don't produce tenors, do we?

Second lady: It's worse than you think, darling. I'm told he's positively Irish!

During that afternoon Burke mingled with the crowds lining the pavement hoping to procure seats for the gallery. The queue had first formed at 7.30 a.m. He overheard the words, "Tom Burke? Sounds more like a prize fighter than an opera singer." Although he was billed as 'Thomas' the newspapers had referred to him as 'Tom', one in particular causing something of a stir of curiosity in the man they described as a 'collier from Lancashire who practiced by singing to his workmates'. 'I thought it was only canaries that sang down the pit' was the final comment. Little wonder the lad from Lancashire was nervous; even though he had been described in one magazine as 'Probably the only coal-miner in Britain who can speak fluent Italian'.

It is doubtful if any other performer in the history of the stage has ever been as nervous as Tom Burke as he waited for the commencement of *La Boheme*. He was terrified. While he fidgeted and worried in the dressing-room his dresser periodically reported on the behaviour and the opulence of the tiara-clad assembly. . . . "The King and Queen have arrived, Mr Burke – you have never seen such an audience. . . Never!" The *Times* had this to say of the spectacle:

> 'The Royal Opera opened its doors last night for the first time after four years of silence, and admitted a wonderful and wondering audience. The audience was wonderful not only by the fact that the Royal Box was occupied by the King and

Queen, Queen Alexandra and many other members of the Royal Family, and that the stalls and boxes contained more than the usual number of distinguished patrons, it was wonderful in its heterogeneity and its homogeneity, the one shown in the contrasted decorousness of the boxes and the hilarity of the gallery, the other in the feeling of eager goodwill with which all assembled. It was a wondering audience because everything promised to be so familiar, so that one asked, will it be just the same, and can we really settle down to the old mixture of social and musical pleasure as though nothing had happened? The opera Syndicate had resolved to revive former glories as closely as possible to carry us back in memory a dozen years or more to the time when Puccini first became the ruling divinity of the Royal Opera House and when Mme Melba was – but there is no need to say what Mme Melba was, because last night she proved she is just the same today.

A "Melba Night" used to mean so many things besides Mme Melba. Last night was a "Melba Night" but only Mme Melba was quite what the phrase used to imply. Probably no season at Covent Garden has ever started with quite the thrill of enthusiasm which passed through the house as the audience rose to the first strains of the National Anthem, probably the cheers which greeted the Royal Party have never been quite so spontaneous and straight from the heart as they were on this re-opening. They expressed something of what we have felt during the opera's four silent years.

The presence of Sir Thomas Beecham at the conductor's desk, too, spoke of change. True, the opera was to be sung in Italian, but Covent Garden is no longer 'the Italian Opera'. The greeting which he got, chiefly from the upper part of the house, was a reminder that there is a wider and a more intelligent public for opera in London than there was in the old days, and that it is the hope of that public that Sir Thomas Beecham's alliance with the Grand Opera Syndicate is ultimately to mean the pursuit of a broader and more national policy at Covent Garden than that which used to prevail.'

"Five minutes before 'Curtain-up', Mr Burke," reported the dresser. Tom felt physically sick but he still managed to joke, "Anyone in from Leigh?" "How do I know that, Mr Burke?"

replied the dresser, seriously. "They'll be wearing flat caps and clogs, lad." It was a brave attempt to hide his real feelings, those of pure funk. But the behind-the-scenes staff were well aware that the new tenor was suffering badly from anxiety. For several hours he had been pacing up and down, gargling in his dressing-room, clearing his throat; and they noticed a decided wobble in his voice as he ran through the scales and it didn't help his confidence any when he overheard one of them remark, 'I reckon we'll have to push him on'.

The *Times* paints the scene in the auditorium during those few minutes before the start of the opera:

> 'With the opening bars of the National Anthem, the King and Queen came to the front of the Royal Box, with them being Queen Alexandra, Princess Mary and Princess Victoria. Their Majesties stood for some moments acknowledging the salutes of the vast audience, and were obviously moved by the warmth of their reception. After all it was a great occasion – a symbol of the return of peace.
>
> The Queen wore pale orchid velvet embroidered in silver and crystals, with a diamond tiara and a diamond and pearl necklace. Queen Alexandra wore black embroidered in steel and blue sequins and magnificent diamonds. Princess Mary was in white with silver leaves in her hair. Princess Victoria was in black and white. In another box were the Princess Royal with Princess Maud and the King's three sons, the Prince of Wales, Prince Albert and Prince George were also present. . . '

The article then gives a list of High Society that looks as if it came straight out of *Who's Who* – counts, earls, viscounts, lords and ladies, foreign dignitaries added sartorial lustre to the glittering assembly to whom this was a momentous social as well as a musical event.

> 'So it was with mingled memories and hopes that the audience took their seats and the curtain rose on the two Bohemians shivering in their garret. . . '

continued the *Times*. The reporter could surely not have been aware how truthfully he had captured the scene for one

Bohemian – Rodolpho the Poet – who was not only shivering but shaking.

For those who are not familiar with the opera, let me picture the scene: It is Paris and the year about 1830. The set is a garret on Christmas Eve, the living quarters of four Bohemians – Rodolpho, Marcel, Schaunard and Colline – the opera opens with Rodolpho the Poet and Marcello the Artist on the stage. Their hearts are a great deal larger than their purses, and share and share alike is the motto of the garret. On this wintry night the two are down on their luck. They haven't a franc between them; they are cold and hungry. Rodolpho is looking out of the window, gripping the window-sill – but so hard and tremulously did Burke's Rudolpho grip the scenery that the whole set began to shake, causing a stage-hand to call out, "For God's sake, Mr Burke, let go, you're shaking the whole set! Will you *please* let go!" Marcello asks Rodolpho what he is staring at. This was the cue for him to step forward to sing the opening phrases, to the great relief of the stage manager. Burke sang, *'Nei cieli Ligi guardo fumar dai Mille comignoli parigi – E penso a quel poltrone d'un vecchio cominetto ingann atore che vive in ozio come un gran signor'.* Translated into English: 'I am looking in the grey skies at the smoke of thousands of Parisian chimneys – and thinking of that old deceitful sluggard of a stove living in leisure like a grand Lord'. He sang the words tremorously but now that he was a participator in the drama the longer it continued the more confident his singing became until he was completely oblivious of the audience and everything else except the part he was playing. His beautiful natural voice of pure lyrical quality carried his audience along with it. Burke showed that he possessed all the elements of success – temperament, a good presence, finished methods and great musical intelligence. Yet, he claimed, when reminiscing about the occasion, that the crucial moment for him came when, upon Mimi's arrival in the garret, he accidentally touched Melba with a gesture. She gave him a look of instant defiance for she disliked any inefficiency in an actor, whereupon the tenor lost his temper. 'That was the spur I needed. I sang the knickers off the wench after that and stole her thunder. I sang like a man inspired. We opera singers are all a trifle jealous of each other and she didn't like it.'

After the first Act the two principals took several curtain calls. Already the cries were for the tenor. 'We want Burke! We want Burke!' The chant was taken up all round the house until it rang with it. Burke and Melba came out yet again and now the soprano was furious. Tom stepped forward to bow and as he did so felt Melba's elbow in his ribs as she hissed, "Move over, you Irish bastard!" Burke did as he was told, at the same time determined to top her remark later in the performance. He always had an answer ready for all eventualities, often caustic, which became known to his friends as 'Burkisms'. But Tom had to wait for his 'revenge' – the opera soared along to its magnificent conclusion – then, the finale. The scene is once more the garret: Mimi is dying with consumption. Rudolfo, distracted with grief, does his best to comfort her in her last moments in this life; Mimi touchingly assures her lover that he has been her only love and blessing him for his goodness to her she dies in Rudolfo's arms. Burke timed his riposte beautifully, "Now die, you Australian cow!" he whispered but loud enough for the orchestra to hear. A remark that amused 'Tommy' Beecham immensely and one that not even he could have bettered.

The two principals took umpteen curtain calls in answer to the audiences rapturous delight. At last when quiet was restored Burke spoke a few words of thanks before graciously (to the eyes of the audience) escorting Melba from the stage. But he hadn't finished with her and his pent-up nervousness and anger gave way to a torrent of fury which only halted when Melba shouted, "That will do, Mr Burke! It is quite enough! I am sorry."

After the heat of the occasion had cooled down she was gracious enough to congratulate Tom on his performance and awarded him the ultimate accolade – the treasured ambition of every singer – the offer to become a member of her touring company. Tom, in turn, was also gracious enough to admit to an American newspaperman that he owed a lot to Melba. "Madame Melba was kind to me during the performance. She was helping me all the time. Not every great opera singer would have done the same with a raw newcomer." But raw newcomer or not, Tom Burke had conquered London in one night in the most outstanding debut ever at the Royal Opera House. And it has known many in its exciting history. With one performance he had become the musical idol of the British capital.

Not surprisingly he found it difficult to sleep that night. Though he was aware of his success he still dreaded the views of the critics in the morning papers. He knew that it was one thing to please the audience but another to satisfy the critics. He was on the street early waiting for the first editions, but he left them on the breakfast table, unread, unable to turn the pages to read the reviews. When he did he was ecstatic with joy. Every paper praised him in glowing terms. His achievement shared the pages with the courageous efforts of Hawker to fly the Atlantic and demands of politicians to hang the ex-Kaiser.

Roy Henderson, C.B.E., celebrated baritone and teacher of Kathleen Ferrier, sums up the impact Burke made, 'The Press was full of the tremendous performance by Tom on his debut. At last a British singer had shown that he was equal to the foreigners. I only wish I could have sung on the same platform.'

Offers of engagements poured in by every post, mostly from abroad, and Colonel Higgins now looked on his new tenor in a different light, no doubt considering that he had got a bargain for his 25 guineas.

Many tales have come my way from Burke's pupils whom he taught in later life. Tom loved to entertain people with stories of his numerous disagreements with authoritarian bodies in the opera sphere.

Down the years elaboration may have altered the stories, but the Lancastrian was such a 'card' that one can quite well believe that he had plenty to say to Colonel Higgins on the subject of fees after his 1919 success. Higgins was a hard business man and when Burke asked for a rise he simply asked him how much he wanted. "Whatever Frank Mullings gets, double it and I'll settle for that." said Tom. "Oh will you?" replied Higgins, "Well, you can sing for your supper a few more times before you get that much my lad." For subsequent performances he did get larger fees but they were still very small compared to those the Royal Opera House were paying to Martinelli and Lappas to name but two of the international brigade, even though one critic hailed him as 'Next to Enrico the best in the world' and another dubbed him the 'Second Caruso' – a popular title with his host of admirers. To be called the second anything is the kiss of death. To Tom Burke it was more like a millstone around his neck than a compliment.

For several decades well into this century Pelmanism – the science of training the mind to achieve the success of which it is capable – was enormously popular as a correspondence course. The organisation which boasted thousands of successes in all walks of life were backed by a most efficient and enterprising promotional department who cashed in almost immediately on any feats accomplished by the 'ordinary mortal' not possessed by nature of a brilliant intellect or natural genius – whether they were already 'pelmanists' or not! National dailies carried large coverage of testimonial-type articles advertising the course. 'The three most talked about men in London today were once coal miners' stated one such article which went on to cite Jimmy Wilde the boxer, Bob Smillie a miner's leader, and Tom Burke as men who had overcome the odds by sheer strength of will and power of concentration 'Why do some men come out of a mine and others simply stop there?' the article wanted to know. 'Because those who come out develop their personalities and develop their will' is the answer given; Burke's great triumph was then given generous wordage 'His was a test of nerves as well as his powers as a vocalist. Read what Mr Chapel, the most severest critic in London today wrote: "A rich flexible voice – passionate and rousing – that began nervously, warmed as the Act went on; sang with too abrupt transitions; lacked something in judgement, but was superb in power and beauty – this was the new tenor Mr Thomas Burke. A hit, a direct hit! An Englishman who can pass for a full blooded Italian tenor!"

'Mr Kalisch of *The Daily News* wrote "It is too much to

say that his singing is perfect – but there is little doubt that it was the most successful debut made by any tenor for a long, long time. As Mr Burke is still under 30 there seems no reason why any position among the stars of the day should be beyond his reach." '

The article continues: 'No one who saw it can ever forget the ovation Mr Burke received. And nine years earlier he was working in a Lancashire coal-mine! What is the secret of Burke's success? He explained it to the directors of the Pelman Institute. "The fundamentals of success in Grand Opera are *memory* – parts are long and difficult" he said "*Constant study* which requires *patience*, *will*, and *concentration*. All my life I have been fighting, fighting, fighting – struggling to get out of a bad environment and striving to sing better, better, better; *I had a definite object in mind* and ceaselessly strove for it. All that, I understand, is a fundamental of Pelmanism.

' "To sing – to overcome temptations while training – you need a super will, an application which is almost superhuman. I suppose without knowing it I have been a Pelmanist all the time."

'Success is not further from your reach than it was to these three miners. Pelmanism is the bridge to which they would have been glad to have had the advantage.'

Seemingly all three did very well without! Burke, for one, could not have afforded the fees – but in all fairness to Pelmanism its principles have been praised by scores of successful business men who credit the course with their own success.

Burke, in later life, often advocated the system to his friends even though he believed that any person so motivated by the desire to succeed *can* succeed without help from anyone provided they are always ready to take advice when given by qualified experts in a particular field of learning. It was only as he got older and on the top of the ladder that he began to think he knew it all himself.

ACT IV

Burke's next performance of the season was as the Duke in *Rigoletto* on the 15th May. This was another outstanding success. Two days later he repeated *La Boheme* with Melba to a wildly appreciative audience. By this time Melba had made it known publicly that she considered that musical and social standards were lower than before the war, a state she deeply regretted. She was also very conscious that her audiences were recruited mainly from Hampstead and Chelsea rather than from Mayfair and Park Lane; aware, too, that Sir Thomas was the apostle of the younger generation who provided them with the latest thing in music, an apostle of change, a state Melba was loath to accept. The 'Garden', her beloved musical shrine, could never again be the same to her. And neither could London. In her autobiography she reiterates her feelings at the time:

> 'But London! It was not until I had been for several days in London that I realised the yawning gulf which separated this new, untidy, haphazard metropolis, so grey and so strange, from the London which I had known.
>
> "Don't you find London very dirty?" said the Queen to me, on the first occasion when I had the honour of seeing Her Majesty at Buckingham Palace after the War. And I was forced to admit that I did.
>
> It is an ironic comment on the frailty of human nature that the change should be most graphically brought home to me by a simple question of food. Adelina Duchess of Bedford rang me up a day or two after my arrival, and asked me to lunch at a restaurant. No sooner had we sat down to lunch than she produced

two little gold pots, and placed them with a gesture of triumph before her on the table.

"Whatever are those?" I said, because I am a curious individual, and want to know what is going on in the world.

"Ah!" said the Duchess. "That's something you won't often see in London."

"Really!" I exclaimed. "Do let me look."

Very gravely she took off the lids of the two pots and disclosed a small piece of butter and some sugar. I looked at her in astonishment. Had everybody gone mad? What I saw before me was obviously sugar and butter, and yet it was being produced as though it were some rare delicacy.

Then I remembered, and the memory made me almost cry. In Australia, and in America, we had had as much butter, as much sugar, as much everything as we wanted, and the delight on the faces of those around me at being greeted with such a simple commodity was infinitely pathetic. That lunch was full of surprises. We had paper table-napkins, and when eventually coffee was served, the *maitre d'hotel* discovered to his consternation that the restaurant had no sugar spoons. I think that was what hit his heart as hardly as anything else; but he rose to the emergency and gave us salt spoons instead.

I remember going back to my club at Dover Street after that lunch and asking myself: Is there anything I can do to help London to regain something of its old charm? Is there any way in which I can try to make people forget? And it was really this feeling that was uppermost in my mind when later on I accepted the honour of opening Covent Garden after the War.

That first night at Covent Garden will always stand out as one of the supreme memories of my life. To drive to the old stage door, to walk upstairs and down the long corridor to a dressing-room at the end of the passage, to sit down before the same mirror, to make up again; to put on once more the simple dress of Mimi – all as though nothing had happened, as though I had only been away for a holiday – and yet, to feel around me, in every shadow cast by the lights, in every bustling noise outside the door, in the very air that I breathed – ghosts. "It is not you," I said to myself, as I peered into the glass. "It cannot be Melba. It is somebody else. So many have gone, so many new faces have come – it can't be that you have remained."

I am standing outside the door of the attic in which the students of *Boheme* have been making revel. From inside I can hear Rudulpho sing his phrase *non sono in vena*, followed by the sudden change of key in the orchestra. And then I am mechanically finding myself singing, *Scusi!* And I open the door, to step once more on that stage which has been for me the scene of so much that is wonderful in life.

Rudolpho runs forward and gives me his arm, and I sink into the chair, the candle dropping from my hand, a few phrases coming from long habit to my lips. But it is more than the simulated exhaustion of Mimi, the little seamstress, which has gripped me now. For I find myself looking into the great space of the auditorium, and feeling once again that I am singing to an audience of ghosts. Lady de Grey had gone, Alfred de Rothschild had gone, and so many others, all gone, and yet I felt them there, I seemed in my imagination to see their faces again, looking out from the shadows in their boxes, and it was for them rather than for this great audience that I sang.

It was that night at Covent Garden that made me realise the full extent to which London had changed. There was little of the old brilliance. Can you imagine in the old days, men walking into Covent Garden on Melba Night, or on any other night, and sitting in the stalls in shabby tweed coats? Yet, that is what I saw on this night, and though I have no objection to brown tweed coats or to shabbiness, I could not help feeling a sensation almost of resentment that men who could afford to pay for stalls, could not afford to wear the proper clothes.'

Had she forgotten that England had undergone a terrible war?

Not once in the chapter in which she discusses the 1919 season does she mention Tom Burke; there is no doubt that his unqualified success, despite it being due to her own recommendation, had 'put her nose out of joint'. In fact, the book is a long recital of name-dropping, not fellow artists, but the Aristocracy, Royalty and the top echilon of High Society. Dame Nellie was, of course, an unashamed snob and her words reverberate down the years, applicable even to some present-day operagoers who look on it as entertainment for the rich, abhorring the habit of many devotees who treat it like the last night of the Proms – actually attending in sweaters and jeans, clapping and whistling instead of shouting 'bravo', and even having the effrontery to openly display signs of enjoying it.

Melba was very conscious of her own power as a lodestone on the music lovers of London. Burke, characteristically, though not deliberately aimed at Melba, takes the prima-donna down a peg or two in his statement which says, 'In the majority of cases opera going is only a pose with people and they do not go for the love of the thing, but simply because it is supposed to be the thing to do. It is a function, a social function, not a musical one, and, like Ascot Week, it is not the races which matter but the fashion display. Latest creations and jewels mean more than the opera itself.'

Bold words from a man who was earning his living from the box-office receipts whether from poseurs or genuine opera worshippers. At times Burke's outspokenness smacked of a jaundiced bitterness towards the higher bracket of society. For, like it or not, he was now one of them, a lion of London's swish society. Suddenly he was Britain's hottest singing property with an army of admirers and camp-followers, many of whom were the very ones who had sniggered at his engagement.

As the peace season progressed he sang with two other Mimis besides Melba, Margaret Burke-Sheridan and Jeanne Brola. The combination of Margaret Sheridan and Tom Burke in *La Boheme* on May 27th of the season had the papers making great copy of how the Irish soprano, who dropped the Burke out of her surname for her professional career, and Tom were the unlikeliest pair ever to grace the hallowed boards of the Royal Opera – ' "Street orphan and pit-boy" charm "Garden" devotees' was the way one paper described the affair. Miss Sheridan, it seems, had been put in the care of nuns in Ireland while a baby; the coincidence in the surnames came in for a lot of light-humoured comment but all agreed that Burke and Sheridan were equally as good as Burke and Melba. Another bright and shining star had appeared in the operatic firmament. But it was not in the British galaxy that her star was to shine. Lack of engagements, the constant fate of artists from these Islands at this time, drove her to Italy where she proved what a fine artist she was. Like Eva Turner, the distinguished soprano who became famous in Milan, she was a victim of the curious and wrong notion prevalent that British singers were not up to the standard of foreigners, particularly Italian and German artists. Tom Burke, probably more so than any other British singer, was able to refute this assumption. Altogether he sang in thirteen performances, always taking the principal role, during the season. No society hostess worth her salt omitted the Burkes from her guest list especially when she knew that she could rely on the tenor for a recital during the evening.

It has often been suggested that the young Burke was like a fish out of water in the London of that time. The opposite applied. The miner's son loved every minute of it. He took to it as if cocktails and dressing for dinner had been his birthright instead of the humble beginnings of a colliery cottage. Quite naturally and humanly he enjoyed the life style that his golden voice had won for him. He handled the ostentatious side of fame with ease. There was never any battle to bury the 'Lancashire Lad' in Burke's make up. He was natural, with inherent qualities of gentlemanly behaviour obvious. There are those who love to portray him as the coarse northerner who made noises drinking his soup and ate his peas with a knife. This is completely untrue. The ex-Lasher-on was as equally at home in the swish residences of Mayfair as he was in a working class kitchen. That he possessed remarkable qualities of adaptability there can be no doubt.

It was his blunt honesty which didn't appeal to people more accustomed to a subtle and often hypocritical approach. Consequently his 'out with it and be damned' style of south Lancashire speech was not always appreciated by the 'pretty pretty' brigade who were nice to your face and blisteringly abusive behind your back. His forthright style was sometimes construed as rudeness. He could never pander to the 'darling' set and could only be himself, keeping his own identity in the sort of world where poseurs are the rule rather than the exception.

Good looks, a magnificent voice, an excellent presence

both on and off the stage – the tenor was an immaculate dresser – a beautiful wife, a fashionable address in the city, a personal friend of the Prince of Wales – in modern day parlance Burke had arrived. He was fêted at soirées, took afternoon tea at high-society gatherings, horse riding in Rotten Row and adoration bestowed on him never known by a British operatic artist before and seldom since.

This almost incredible zoom to stardom was a reflection of the mood of jubilation in England. We had won the war, the flood gates of joy and happiness wide open and the huge success of a native singer another example of British supremacy. The public loved it all.

Yet through it all his true image was never submerged beneath a false façade. It is hardly surprising that he was considered an upstart by those who were jealous of his triumphant progress.

Like Beecham, he could be very blunt but whereas people could accept if from Beecham they found it harder to accept from Burke. He saw hypocrisy and tried to alter it with the delicacy of a bull in a china shop and pricked pomposity with a blunt knitting needle. He was not really ready for London or maybe it is nearer the truth to say that London was not ready for Tom Burke.

But Tom was not the only member of his family hitting the theatrical headlines for Marie had made her debut on the London stage as Isolde in *Afgar* in which she scored an immediate success. Later she became one of C.B. Cochrans leading ladies.

The 'Peace Season' lasted from May 12th until August 1st, during which time Burke sang in four different roles – Rudolfo, the Duke, Conte D'Almaviva in *Il Barbiere di Siviglia* and Pinkerton in *Madame Butterfly*. His greatest regret was missing the part of Cavaradossi in *Tosca* during July. This was his favourite opera but he never sang it at Covent Garden. Though physically strong, Burke was a martyr to nerves and on this occasion it had manifested itself into systemic illness. The fact that Giovanni Martinelli deputised is an indication that Burke had reached a status no other English tenor had previously obtained. At the end of the month the position was reversed when the Italian was taken ill before the gala performance in aid of the Housing Association for Officers' Families. Burke took his place and once more teamed with Melba to sing before Royalty, the choice being Act III of *La Boheme* as part of this great occasion. The critics could not make up their minds which tenor they preferred. Unanimously they reached the conclusion that 'both tenors are in magnificent voice this season'.

This was the occasion of the most famous 'Burke' story of all. It has been exaggerated grossly and even claimed as a reason for the tenor's subsequent decline. In fact, Burke committed two Royal indiscretions, not one, neither of which offended Royalty as is widely claimed. Opera is a strenuous business to any singer. To Burke it could be quite traumatic. He gave his all, he could only sing one way, afterwards he would be physically and mentally drained. After the performance he was relaxing in the dressing-room over a whisky when his dresser knocked on the door and called out, "Mr Burke, the King wishes to see you," to which Tom replied, "Tell the old bugger to wait!" It was simply the remark of a tired man and without malice for Burke was on very good terms with the Royal Family. The dresser, not the soul of discretion, stupidly blabbed out what Burke had said and obviously such a story made sensational copy for the press and scandalous gossip for the society vultures. It reflected badly on Covent Garden and the administrators were not amused when he kept the King waiting for twenty minutes.

Burke admired Beecham immensely although he preferred Toscanini as a conductor. Yet here again is an example of the tenor's preference for all things Italian; but working with Beecham was not without its ups and downs. He steadfastly defended British singers whenever possible, agreeing with Burke that they should be better represented at the Mecca of their calling – Covent Garden. Their relationship was not always a smooth one for in some ways they were similar. Both had the fault of being poor time-keepers, not bothering if they kept people waiting. On one occasion Burke was rehearsing with a visiting soprano, whose name he did not reveal in his newspaper serialisation except to say she was passionately fond of horse-riding, a fondness she shared with Tom who liked a 'flutter on the gee-gees' in the way of most colliers. It was Ascot week and as Beecham had not arrived for the rehearsal two hours after the appointed time, she suggested to Tom that they take a trip to the races. He readily agreed and both enjoyed themselves immensely, unaware that the conductor was calling them 'choice' names back at the Royal Opera House. The next morning they reported once more to be met by an irate Beecham who proceeded to tell them what he thought about them both in no uncertain terms. The conductor was a law unto himself and Tom and partner simply let him have his say knowing full well that all would be all right after his outburst. Sir Thomas not only kept his musicians and singers waiting, it was not unknown for him to start his concert performances well after the appointed time, knowing full well that his audience would always wait his presence patiently and be glad of it.

Like all who knew Beecham, Tom had his favourite story about the legendary maestro of the baton. He was rehearsing with the orchestra a particular work requiring the use of a saxophone. The clarinetist was striving to render his particular passages in the way the composer had written them but the instrument offended Beecham's ear to which a saxophone was abhorrent, considering such 'abominations' the property of jazz bands and café ensembles. After a few minutes listening to the sound, he abruptly stopped the orchestra and said to the saxophonist, "Would you kindly take that bloody thing out of here and throw it in the Thames, then come back and play your music on the clarinet!" Another, more well known, Beecham story is the one about him enquiring the name of a newcomer to the orchestra's ranks. With baton raised, he enquired, "Your name, sir?"

"Ball, Sir Thomas," was the reply.

"Beg your pardon?"

"Ball, sir."

"Oh, I see. How very singular."

The season finished for Burke with his performance,

yet again, in *Boheme* with Jeanne Brola, another singer whose name seems to have faded into obscurity.

Concert-goers now had the chance of hearing the new tenor both in London and in the provinces, although during the opera season he had been conspicuous singing at society soirées and charity engagements at which he was always willing to give his services.

Like Melba, Tom had for his agent and manager Lionel Powell who was a director of special concerts at The Royal Albert Hall. Amongst his sparkling array of international artists he could boast Maggie Teyte, Alma Gluck, John McCormack, Clara Butt, Signor Buson, and Vladimir de Pachmann. Powell arranged twenty concerts under the banner 'The Nellie Melba Tour'. A dynamic impression was felt in reverberations throughout the musical world when it was announced that her fellow artists were to be Tom Burke and Vladimir de Pachmann. Frank St. Leger, Burke's own accompanist, made up the quartet which appeared at the Royal Albert Hall and at leading concert halls throughout the provinces to the rapturous delight of starved concert goers.

Powell was so delighted with his new tenor that he made him the gift of a limousine and a chauffeur. Melba and Burke were so successful an attraction that he arranged further concerts to extend the 'Melba Tour'. It seems almost sinful that these two singers were not recorded on wax. The gramophone was still in its infancy, the realisation that personal appearances could make record sales bound astronomically had not dawned on the impresarios; truth was that some considered the new fangled gadget with the horn to be detrimental to the future of concerts.

When Nellie Melba moved on to further conquests Powell immediately sent Burke out under his own banner – 'The Tom Burke Tour'. He had declined the Australian Divas offer of joining her on an overseas concert tour preferring to await for offers to sing at Covent Garden in the 1920 season.

By this time he was able to command his own fees for recitals and with his star well and truly in the ascendancy attracted full houses wherever he performed, sharing platforms with many of the celebrated instrumental artists of the day, both British and foreign, including child prodigy Yehudi Menhuin. Holidaymakers heard Burke at Sunday Celebrity Concerts at most of the popular holiday resorts.

Dai Tanner, a retired choral singer from the Welsh valleys, recalls hearing Burke at Colwyn Bay one Sunday evening. 'I was on holiday with my parents. My father was very pro-Welsh where singing was concerned. Mother called his attention to a placard advertising a Tom Burke concert. "He's no Welshman" said my dad. We had a job to persuade him to book tickets despite the wording which proclaimed Burke as a star from Covent Garden. Very reluctantly he agreed to go. According to father only Welshmen could sing tenor. The transformation was quite amazing! I could feel his emotion as Burke sang. Mother whispered to me, "I think Dad likes him, you know." What an understatement! After the concert he said to us, "This evening you have heard the finest tenor ever. I have never heard Caruso except on record but if he is better than this man then he must be an angel." When we went home he made sure he bought all Burke's records and I have them to this day and wouldn't part with them for any money. He was a beautiful tenor.'

Robert Easton, celebrated bass and adjudicator, remembers a Burke concert in his native Sunderland. 'I first heard him in 1920 when on leave from hospital and I was quite amazed as he was the first international artist I had heard. It was quite beautiful singing, the like of which I didn't know existed. You ask me for an appraisal of Burke's voice – the most beautiful sound I have ever heard from a tenor. Of the Italian school and style. Lyric yet with drama and vitality. Never allowing expression to adversely affect immaculate technique. Interpretations showing a refinement and appreciation of the content of whatever was being sung. Performance comprehensive in the best sense of the word. In short – the finest ever! I have not heard him in person (the only real way) for so very many years, when perhaps my knowledge was less complete than it is now. But the impact was as if it were yesterday. And yet, surprisingly, my chief memory is of his casual approach.'

This last line of Easton's appraisal gives a definite clue to Burke's character. Though a dedicated performer who lived for singing, this casualness was the seed which grew into the 'slap happy' lifestyle which affected his career for it was carried over into his work, creating an impression of him that didn't inspire confidence. He was not a stable character and this instability was the root of his subsequent demise. A contemporary told me, 'You cheered Tom after you'd heard him, not before; he was never the essence of reliability and booking-agents soon grow tired of this sort of behaviour. Yet at the same time he could charm the birds off the bush, there was a winsome come-a-day go-a-day Irishness about him which I was very fond of. He could be extremely kind and helpful too, yet cross him and he could resort to basic crudeness. In the words of the aria he so often sang, he was a strange harmony of contrasts. The question is just how much of this sort of irrational behaviour can people take? I remember him hob-nobbing it with the London society – not crawling mind you – Tom was never that, just the opposite in fact. Perhaps if he hadn't been so open and blunt he would have done better. And yet I admired the man in many ways; but he found compromise between the two totally different worlds he knew to be so difficult although he didn't show it. But deep down it was there. Certainly he was an enigmatic character but not alone in that respect for the operatic world has always had its share.'

But Lancashire's Caruso was behaving himself at this early stage of his career and the tour went along smoothly, consummating in the provinces the fame he had won in London. In fact, it appears that Tom was a lamb rather than a lion at this time according to his press agent and promoter Lionel Powell: 'Although one of the most talked about men in England, Mr Burke is singularly shy and greatly dislikes talking about himself, so much so that he is the despair of interviewers. He cannot be coaxed to tell stories. In answer to questions he will admit that he likes the role in *Tosca* best of all and that his most treasured possession is an autographed scene of *La Lodaletta* given to him by Mascagni, but he gently refuses to be drawn and has the reputation of being the shyest singer in London. One story he has been known to tell, and though it is not about himself it appeals to his Irish sense of humour. It is about a certain performance of *Faust* which took place in Ireland. The singer who took the part of Mephiltopheles happened to be extremely portly and when he was descending he stuck in the trap door. Looking on at his violent efforts to get down to the lower regions one of the 'God's' called out, "Begorra the place is full up!" The sun and warmth of Italy invested him with some of the colour and passion of that country for his voice has the true Italian ring in it, particularly the high notes. He is very Italian in appearance and bears a striking resemblance to Caruso.'

So ran the 'blurb' notes on the broadsheet publicity for the tour.

Tom enjoyed touring, especially in the North of England where he delighted in singing to 'ordinary Joe Smith', the man in the street. 'He is my sort of man and he goes to a concert just to enjoy good music. He has probably saved and worked overtime to afford the tickets for his wife and family. These are the sort of folks I like to sing to.' He found concert work much more relaxing than opera, although the operatic stage was his true firmament. Whenever possible he visited his home-town of Leigh to lavish some of his new-found wealth on his parents and enjoy the company of his former workmates over a pint in the local pubs. Burke had great pride in his appearance but was always ready to discard sartorial elegance for overalls and a pair of clogs to help his father feed the pigs.

By this time Burke, Snr. had left the mines and around this period Tom put up the money for him to open a pork business, peddling his produce around the houses. He also bought the family a house. To the gratification of his parents, Tom attended Mass and sang in the choir whenever the opportunity presented itself, much to the delight of St. Joseph's Parishioners. Brother Joe remembers a straight-from-the-shoulder question from Tom, "Are you bothering with women yet?"

"No," answered Joe.

"Well don't until you find one that you think as much about as your own mother."

Tom had a great affection for his mother, whom he called Josephine, and was always glad to get back to Leigh for her home cooking, a welcome change to the more sophisticated hotel food. Homecomings meant more to him than even his own wife and family realised. Joe Burke has vivid memories of Tom's first visit to Leigh during the tour; 'Our Tom's car was a green Fiat saloon with a black top, the first saloon to come to the town. His chauffeur was called Mathews and had formerly been on the staff at Buckingham Palace. What a sight it was for the folks who knew him as a coal miner to see him sitting in a car driven by the King's ex-chauffeur! Tom had arranged for Mathews to collect him at our house in Mather Lane. When he arrived Tom was horrified. The chauffeur was in uniform. Tom told him to change back into a suit. He didn't believe in belittling any man.'

Wherever the tour took them Mathews looked after the money. If Tom wanted a pound he simply asked for it. It was perhaps a pity that the reliable chauffeur didn't become the tenor's personal aid in his later days because money and Burke were easily parted.

Another hugely successful concert took place in Bolton. Afterwards, admirers festooned the car with ribbons, tied a rope to the front bumper bar and pulled it all the way to Burden Park Football Ground where they gave Tom a rousing send-off on his way to the Midland Hotel in Manchester. Similar scenes were repeated in other Lancashire towns the bluff working folk saw in the great tenor the fulfilment of their dreams – a working lad who had 'got on' and they loved him for it. He was one of their own.

Fred Yates remembers those days as if they happened only last week: 'My father was one of the better-off in the district. He owned a nut and bolt works in Atherton. He loved to invite guests to Lynwood, the family house. To one party Tom and Marie Burke came. Dad was a typical Leigh-ite – straight from the shoulder. After the meal Tom said, "I suppose you want me to entertain your guests Mr Yates?" Dad really put him in his place, "I'll entertain my own guests lad – I'm quite capable." After a good while he asked Tom to sing and had to ask him to shut up in the end! You see we knew Tom when he was a waiter in the Pied Bull Hotel while he was attending college in Manchester – he was still plain Tom Burke to us. He was very good hearted though. I remember him and Marie, Kingsley Lark the baritone, and myself going to a victory ball. Tom and Kingsley were the singers of course. Well, the three of us got in but not Tom. Half an hour later I asked the door man had he seen Tom. He was a no-nonsense character and told me he'd sent him packing because he hadn't got a ticket. Tom had taken it OK but he was a bit upset when I met him in a pub having a quiet drink. His pride was rather hurt but he came at once when I told him that thirty lads in hospital blue where at the ball to hear him sing.'

It is not surprising that recording companies were falling over themselves to obtain the new tenor's name on their labels. After considering several offers, he decided on the prestigious Columbia Company for whom he contracted to record six single-sided operatic records, with a futher contract to follow for a second batch. Sales were excellent. These recordings are now extremely rare collector's items. Later on Columbia did marry some of the arias together to produce double-sided discs. These six records are listed on the Columbia advert illustrated.

In a review of these recordings, Sydney Winstanley comments:

> On 7199 *Recondita Armonia* – Burke was always happiest in Italian. His vowels are wide and generous, and the resultant tone is the real thing. His legato in the opening passages, and his excellent lower notes, make this one of my favourite versions of the aria.

> On 7202 *Questa O Quella* – Here we are shown that there are consonants as well as vowels in the Italian language, and that if they are used properly they can give vowels extra impetus to get the sounds clear of the mouth. This is a good but not outstanding performance; he is a little beefy for this gossamer-like air.

On 7201 – *La Donna e Mobile* – Burke is perfectly suited to this swaggering piece, and he gives it everything in the tenor's bag of tricks. He is shy and insinuating, he is full of indignation, and then gay, using different tone for each disguise. He brings off two nice Morendi and ends with a 'Scenic Railway' run and a dashing top note. I'm sure his performance would have the house on its feet anywhere in the world.

On 7203 *M'Appari* – Burke is in good voice here, but he misses the core of the thing somehow, and the result is a routine performance without fault, but also without heart.

Lacking heart is a surprising assessment of Burke's singing when one considers his great vitality, but appreciation of a song or aria largely depends upon interpretation. And in this department the great tenors often varied immensely.

The transition to wax was a successful one for Tom, though he once told a close friend that he had made a lot of good recordings but no great ones. Some singers have not made the transition so easily as did Burke, the early recording studios proved to be slaughterhouses for some singers who appear to have left their voices outside judging by some of the results. Literally, the singer sang into a box and with consequent traumatic results in many cases. Away from a concert platform and vast auditorium, some 'lost' their voices – there was no 'atmosphere' as the 'live' performer knew it. Frank Mullings, to my ear, is an example of a singer who never did his fine voice justice on records. Norman Allin is another, although in his case it only applies on certain recordings – again this is purely my own opinion, and may be considered ludicrous by Allin devotees. Conversely, there have been singers who have sounded better on records than ever they did in the flesh.

Strangely, during this period Burke selected a trite song, almost with no merit at all, *Dear Old Pal of Mine* – a typical sentimental tear jerker – a strange choice indeed following on the operatics. But here he brings to the song all the warmth and emotion embodied in his vocal organ – the 'heart and throat' style of delivery so typically Burke. Consequently it is raised to a state of sheer enjoyment and becomes a 'classic' of its type of sentimental ballad. A particular favourite of mine is *Lorraine* by Capel, recorded on a Columbia 10". Again, not a song of particular merit, but the tenor's enthusiasm and passionate longing for his sweetheart Lorraine is the very soul of vocal fervency and I can never listen to it without experiencing a thrill of excitement.

Though very favourably received by the critics on his nation-wide tour, he did not escape accusations of cheap effects to win the audiences' approval. By his own admission he would pick out certain passages and phrases to which he gave dramatic emphasis and, consequently, a thrilling effect to the piece; uninhibited singing endowed with the flamboyancy of his Italianate style was not the prevailing taste in England and considered to be the province of foreign artists from hot-blooded climates. Burke not only competed with the 'import' tenors, he sounded like them and his audiences loved him for it and he was undoubtedly an 'effects' singer.

Touring terminated with the advent of the 1920 Covent Garden season having been chosen to open with Russian soprano Marie Kousnezova on May 10th. She had changed her name from Kousnietzoff and her arrival at the 'Garden' is another romantic episode in its fascinating history. She had escaped from Russia aboard a Swedish ship because her artistic abilities were stunted in her own land by lack of opportunity. Before being allowed to sail, the ship was searched by Russian officials but the brave Marie had hidden in a trunk and remained there until well out at sea when she revealed herself to the Swedish captain, who was sympathetic to her plight. Eventually she landed in England where her singing attracted the attention of the Opera House 'scouts'.

Norah Burke, now living in America, told a subscriber to this biography, that she blamed her brother's fall from the palmy heights on his nervous trouble and certainly the beginning of the season was not a happy period for the tenor sensation of 1919. Though Burke never sang badly, his first few performances were not a credit to his reputation. Reverting to the operatic stage after a period of almost nine months on the concert circuit was a strain which impaired his performances. Once more the ogre 'nerves' took their toll. The opening opera was once again *La Boheme*. Of his Rudolfo the *Times* had this to say: 'Thomas Burke was not at his best and seemed only happy when he got safely landed on a high note with full open tone,' and, again, in another paper, 'He didn't seem to be part of the performance in the early stages, continually moving away from the action to seek the air and clear his throat.' While Rosenthal says of his Russian partner, 'She took liberties with the tempi and indulged in excessive portamenti.' Definitely not a performance to stand comparison with the *Bohemes* of the peace season.

As the season progressed Burke improved. Three performances as Nadir in *The Pearl Fishers* with Graziella Pareto were more like the Burke devotees knew. He appeared as Des Grieux in *Manon Lescaut* on three separate occasions, but undoubtedly his greatest success was in two one-act operas of Puccini's beloved *Trittico – Il Tabarro* and *Gianni Schicchi*. The tenor wrote: 'Puccini himself came over to see his beloved *Trittico* performed for the first time over here. I had been singing pretty well but did not dream that I would be selected to create these three single one-act operas. One of them was an all-woman opera and I did not sing in that, but out of all the tenors in the country I was selected at the express wish of Puccini himself to sing in *Tabarro* and *Gianni Schicchi* the other two.

'I remember that audition when he made known his decision. He was a very nervous man, highly excitable, and an autocrat of the first water. Nothing but the best would do, and whilst he would not hesitate to praise a good performance he also would not hesitate to condemn a performance if it did not come up to his high standard. So that when I knew he was to be there in the stalls when I tried out for him I was not feeling over confident. But I realised what it meant and I sang my best.

'In the dim shadows of the auditorium, with its ghostly sheets spread over the seats, I could just discern a shadowy figure pacing up and down the aisle. I had seen this before. Seen it when he was getting more and more agitated as he listened to a voice that did not come up to his expectations.

I wondered what it portended in my case – I was soon to know. I had sung one of the most difficult passages and suddenly found the old man on the stage beside me. He placed an arm around my shoulder and patted me affectionately on the back. "That will do, my boy," he said and there began a great friendship which lasted until his death.'

Marie Burke recalls this great event vividly. Prior to it she and Tom had had a break in their marriage when she was taken seriously ill with tonsillitis and forced to leave the cast of *Afgar*. After the operation she went to Italy for a rest to see maestro Colli and meet old friends:

'On my arrival back from Italy I was met at Victoria Station by a young man who was a complete stranger to me. He told me that my husband was unable to meet me but wished me to go to Covent Garden that very night to see him in *Manon Lescaut*. Puccini, said the young man, would be there and if Tom passed he would be chosen to sing the *Trittico*. I didn't want to go but the messenger was persuasive and so I agreed but I wanted to know who he was "Oh I'm a pianist, I've played at Tom's house. You don't know me." "But what is your name?" I insisted, "Noel Coward" was the reply. I attended the opera and sat in a box next to the great Puccini. He was obviously very moved by Tom's interpretation of his music. He turned to me and said "Never has my *Manon Lescaut* music been more beautifully sung." '

Auditions, rehearsals and performances were proving a tiring round and in between he still found time to entertain at society functions in the capital and home counties. One day he received a phone call from Colonel Higgins asking him to attend at the Opera House immediately. Ricardo Martin, the American tenor, had been taken ill and they wanted Burke to sing Pinkerton in *Butterfly* that very night. He was the only tenor available who could sing the role in Italian. Though familiar with the role, Burke refused much to the annoyance of Higgins. He would not perform without a rehearsal and didn't feel that he could do justice to the part at such short notice. He recommended that they contact his confrère Joseph Hislop, the Scottish tenor. Hislop only knew the role in Swedish so the rather bizarre situation presented itself where the tenor sang in Swedish, the soprano in German, the baritone in Italian, and the chorus half English and half Italian. "But I don't suppose the audience knew any differently," commented Burke rather scathingly "Most of them only go because it is the thing to do." His refusal was another blot on his Covent Garden record. He was to find out much later that the administrators had long memories.

On another occasion, he had the 'audacity' to stop the orchestra in the middle of rehearsal and complain that the trumpeter was playing in bad tone. Conductors did not take kindly to criticism from their singers, but if Tom felt like expressing a view he did just that. He was no respecter of persons. However, realising that he had upset the trumpeter – the conductor's feelings were of no concern – he invited him to lunch. The musician reluctantly agreed. The tenor then explained in detail where he considered the mistakes were being made. "Tell me, Mr Burke, what does a tenor know about trumpet playing?" asked the musician with a tolerant smile. Tom then told him how he had won the cornet solo prize at Crystal Palace at the age of thirteen. That altered it. The trumpet player went back to rehearsal and told the conductor that Mr Burke was quite right, he *was* playing the piece wrongly. Reluctantly the conductor had to agree also, but considered the tenor's intrusion a breach of his authority.

John Driver was a friend, having met Tom through Madame Amy Sherwin with whom Driver was a pupil baritone singer. The financial necessities of the time forced Driver to become an illusionist. His niece recalls his stories of concerts and music hall. 'One he loved recounting was about Tom Burke. Uncle John and he were on the bill at a theatre for a special Gala Show. The Prince of Wales was the principal guest. Burke was the main attraction and Uncle John asked him what he intended to sing. "Well for a kick-off" said Tom "I'm going to sing the *Minstrel Boy*," Well, Uncle nearly had a fit there and then! Anglo-Irish relations were very tricky and of course view points were extremely narrow in those days. The 'troubles' and the black and tans were causing a lot of bitterness on both sides. Uncle did his best to dissuade Tom to sing it but, seemingly, when he made his mind up there was no altering him. Uncle said it wasn't a gesture of anti-royalist feeling. Tom believed that songs were songs and refused to change it because of a situation. The house manager was very worried but Tom sang it and brought the house down. The Prince of Wales applauded and Uncle, peering from the wings, was glad to see a broad smile on his face!'

One certain fact is that Burke was not anti-royalist; he was proud of his Irish ancestry but had great respect for the monarchy of England. Unquestionably no singer of the time could sing the *National Anthem* with such patriotism and fervour as he. During my research several people have spoken and written of the intense fervour his singing of *God Save the King* evoked in them.

The 31st May, 1920 saw the closing of the second season with Tom again Rudolfo in the ever-popular *La Boheme*. This time his Mimi was British artist Miriam Licette. He was not to sing at the 'Garden' again until 1927.

ACT V

It is interesting to dwell on Burke the man as well as Burke the tenor as he quickly aquired an enviable musical reputation. In the light of much adverse comment which it has been this singer's lot to gather, his devotion and kindness to his parents must be emphasised in fairness to his memory.

Several people remember seeing Tom taking them out in the Fiat on shopping expeditions, the tenor attired in a Savile Row Suit. One old lady particularly remembers his shoes and the way he walked. 'They were Italian shoes, we'd never seen the like in Leigh. Grey suede, buttoned on the top and patent leather uppers. You could tell he was a theatrical by the way he walked – a sort of strut. His wife was very beautiful too. They made a striking couple together. Folks have said things about Tom but he was always very good to his parents.'

It was during this period that Tom presented his father with a bull-terrier. On its very first walk it broke loose from the lead and chased after a man on a bicycle. It was never seen again! During the 1920 'Garden' season Lord Ganley invited Tom to a dinner party in London but he turned it down for a further chance to visit his parents. Little did he or they realise that it would be his last trip home for a long time.

Brother Joe Burke remembers how Tom told them he had pretended to Lord Ganley he was giving a dinner party in Leigh to friends. 'It was simply an excuse. But he came home with a present just the same – a race-horse from His Lordship's stables. He wired me at Leigh – we'd left Mather Lane by this time and removed to a larger house – asking me to meet him at London Road Station in Manchester and to bring a pony and trap to meet the train. I wondered what this was for, but Tom being a rum customer I did as he asked and met him at the station. Porters were leading a fine-looking horse along the platform. In the street Tom asked me to take the pony out of the shafts. I obliged, wondering what was going to happen. He put the race-horse between the shafts, said 'cheerio' and left me to ride home on the pony.

'He could be a mad Alec at times and covered the thirteen miles to Leigh in exactly thirty-five minutes. He was going so fast up Leigh main street that a policeman stopped him and was going to book him for speeding in a horse and cart when another P.C. recognised the driver and said, "Hey, tha can't arrest this mon. It's Tom Burke t'opera singer from Mather Lane." '

But 't'opera singer from Mather Lane' had left Leigh far behind culturally although he never lost his love for the town and his affection for its people.

At the conclusion of the 1920 season it was mooted that 'Britain's Greatest Tenor', as Tom was widly acclaimed, should go to Paris to sing *Louise*. William Powell wasn't keen on the idea. He felt it high time Burke's income rose in keeping with his prominence as a celebrity. Marie offered to go with Tom to Paris to coach him in the French language which she could speak fluently. Powell was adamant; His tenor charge must follow the money. This meant accepting a fabulous offer from William Morris to undertake a concert tour of the U.S.A. Marie considered America to be too far away; France was so much nearer, offers had been made to her to perform in England. Very reluctantly she agreed to accompany Tom, mainly because Morris had 'sold' the tour on the happy-husband-and-wife theme with typical American expertise, and although the early bliss of those Italian days had faded from the marriage, she decided that her place was by his side. Baby Patricia was left in the keeping of her grandmother in Balham when the Burkes set sail from Liverpool in August 1920 aboard the *SS Carmania*.

It was a tearful parting. Josephine was very distressed that her son was going on such a long journey. She wanted him to stay in England where she was sure of seeing him from time to time. Vincent consoled her by reminding her that Tom had achieved the fame she had always wanted for him and he must go where it took him – besides he was only going to be away for six months. Josephine would have been more distressed had she known that she wouldn't see her son for another seven years. One consolation which must have pleased her for her son's sake was the agreement in the contract that he would earn the largest salary ever paid to a British performer in America. Both Vincent and Josephine found it hard to believe that their son would be earning even more money than the great Harry Lauder himself. The Scot was currently on tour in America under Morris's Banner. With a contract safely landed Burke was very secure financially; there was to be no operatic work and he looked forward to touring the U.S.A., establishing his reputation there, then returning to England to continue his operatic and concert career. And, hopefully, he would be invited to sing roles in his beloved Italy.

Many other European operatic doors were ready to be opened, such was the young tenor's standing.

On the quayside in New York Burke's party was met by a horde of reporters. Unknown to Tom, Morris's advance publicity had stimulated great interest in his arrival. The party was then driven to a press conference at one of the leading newspaper's headquarters and fêted like visiting royalty. The next day it carried the following article:

'Tom Burke, the Irish tenor, star of the Royal Opera Company, Covent Garden, for two seasons, arrived in New York on Wednesday aboard the Cunard Liner *Carmania* from Liverpool. With him are Mrs Burke and Harry Foster, London representative for William Morris, under whose direction Burke will make his first American concert tour, and Frank St. Leger his accompanist. Burke is an attractive young man who is only 30, with an engaging smile and a tinge of brogue which probably accounts for him having been called an 'Irish tenor' abroad, though he insists he was born in England.

"My first impression of America is so wonderful," he told me, "that we are immediately going to send for our baby." And Mrs Burke, also a singer, beamed at her husband with an expression of gratitude. "When we left England," continued the tenor, "my mother cried because we were going on such a long voyage – the longest I have ever been away from home, but she consoled herself with the reminder that we were coming to America. And speaking of Americans, I must add that the reputations of your singers abroad, such as Edward De Giovanni, Carlos Hackett, and Forest Lamont, who studied in Italy, are most enviable and quite justifies my belief that Italy, land of song and the home of music, is the most ideal place in the world to acquire what every aspirant to vocal fame strives for. During my five years in Italy and two in England, I have a repertoire of 35 operas none of which, however, is in German. Some time ago, Mrs Burke tried to teach me the language in case I should ever sing Wagnerian roles, but my accent was so unmistakably Gaelic that we gave it up.

"My program here will comprise what I consider every artist should arrange in his concert tour. I mean that he should sing those songs and arias which show his versatility and give the connoisseur his share of music as well as the great public which are classed as ballad lovers. I have arranged to sing a group of arias, a group of ballads and some old Irish songs."

Mr and Mrs Burke, accompanied by Mr and Mrs Morris, will start today for Albany to call on Gov. Smith and then will go to Saranac Lake, N.Y. where Mr Burke will make his first appearance in America at a concert in the Pontiac Church and Lady of the Lake Hospital. The tickets are 100 dollars each and every one of the 800 seats has been taken. He is to make his formal debut at New York Hippodrome on October before commencing a grand tour.'

Burke's arrival had been well and truly noticed, but not only by the press. New York's Irish population was incensed by the notices billing the Hippodrome concert. As the party travelled from the newspaper offices through the city, the Burkes were staggered to see poster after poster proclaiming 'Ireland's greatest living Tenor'. Across several were scrawled the words, 'Not while John is alive!'. Hand-out bills showed a picture of Tom, edged with Shamrocks – and Burke had never set foot on Irish soil!

The popular story – another of the Burke 'legends' – is that he insulted John McCormack by deliberately giving himself this ridiculous billing. This is utter nonsense. Burke was no man's fool. The fact is that he was horrified at Morris's stupidity and bluntly told him that he had ruined his opening concert and possibly the whole tour. Not at any time was there any animosity between McCormack and Burke and, at this time, the Lancashire man was probably an unknown quantity to the Irish tenor then domiciled in America. Although Burke was certainly egotistical enough to believe that he could surpass the Irishman in popularity, he had great respect for him and was an ardent admirer of his voice technique. Naturally enough, Tom always preferred those singers trained in Italy as was McCormack.

Which brings a question which cannot be dodged. More than any other native singer prominent during the 'twenties, Burke was considered to be McCormack's number one rival. Comparisons are indeed odious, but if they are to be made then I feel that Burke would come second best. For McCormack's range of expression made him outstanding, was a sweeter toned one than Burke's and allied to quite outstanding technique that enabled him to sing florid music such as *Il Mio Tesoro* faultlessly and he could spin out a note like a silver thread. Burke had the more exciting voice with a splendid top C and although he excelled in the heavier operatic roles he was also a polished exponent of the sentimental song. Both were singers who thrilled the audiences, each in his own inimitable way. There are few like them today. The Athlone tenor was the complete artist who attained world fame over a long period. Burke was a tremendous potential who, sadly, faded when he should have been one of the world's leading tenors. Voice-wise they were totally different, both completely distinctive in sound and style. Certainly McCormack, by his own admission, was a 'ham' actor, while Burke was above average. McCormack is often dismissed as a typical Irish tenor, not a derogatory title though hardly doing justice to a superb singer. Many people associate him purely with Irish ballads, such as *Mother Machree* and *Macushla*, usually basing their opinions on his last recording spate for H.M.V. when he had become nasally and was in vocal decline. The young McCormack sang Irish ballads in a style that has never been emulated, for his renderings of these songs sprang from the very soul of his bel canto training and dramatic expression gained in the operatic field. The late Dermot Troy, James Johnston of Covent Garden fame, and the current 'McCormack' Frank Patterson – all gifted with beautiful voices – never sounded quite as Irish as did John. It is this Irishness in the voice which endeared him to his own people, especially the emigrant population of America, yet I know many lovers of singing whilst appreciating the beauty are not enamoured of the Irish sound.

Probably Cavan O'Connor, the 'Strolling Vagabond', more than any other tenor since McCormack has identified himself with the Irish ballad. This veteran of the halls, still in remarkably good voice for his years, possessed in his younger days with a sweet, lyrical voice of distinct Irish quality – the personification of the 'typical Irish tenor'. He was sensible enough to realise that he did not possess the compass or power of voice for the more classical field. Even Father Sydney McEwan, a truly beautiful tenor, could not be classed alongside the legendary John. Even though of Scottish birth he has often been mistaken for Irish and compared to McCormack. He once told his recording company's publicity man, "I have often been compared with Count John McCormack. I simply smile. With the old John, maybe, but not with the young one."

Several fine singers have shared McCormack's fate of not always being taken seriously. Tauber, because of his penchant for operetta has been dismissed by many 'serious' critics as a sort of lightweight tenor, fitted only for the ephemeral world of Franz Lehar. Yet Tauber was an operatic *great* to which his early recordings bear testimony. The vast legacy left by this prolific recording artist leans far more heavily on the 'popular' side of his repertoire than it does on the classical side of his art.

Nelson Eddy, though not warranting the title 'great' had a fine voice full of confident virility, but was doomed to remain the idol of the celluloid screen, admired more for his good looks and romantic baritone, than ever he was for his operatic appearances and concert recitals at Carnegie Hall.

Richard Crooks, to my ears a superb vocalist, falls into

the same category. Likewise Grace Moore.

I am naive enough to believe that singers of the type discussed in these pages should sing to entertain the masses and not just one section – the so-called 'highbrows' – of musical audiences.

It was this 'popular' side of McCormack's vocal art that Tom Burke had to contend with on his tour. And he fully realised the great love and esteem in which he was held. The idol of the American-Irish, a folk-legend amongst the hibernian hordes of New York concertgoers. They went to his concerts not to hear German Lieder, Mozart, and operatic arias. These they sat through patiently waiting for that section of the tenor's programme in which he sang the old favourites one after the other – taking them with him back over the seas to their native land, and there is no more emotional race than the Irish in this respect – and always finishing up with *When Irish Eyes are Smiling*.

Follow that you might say. Burke knew in his heart that he couldn't follow it. He would never ever have tried to emulate John in this respect. But that ridiculous billing, not just making him into a 'second McCormack', but calling him an even greater singer meant that in the heart and soul of every Irish emigrant in the Hippodrome audience there would be a definite assumption that in front of them was an upstart who dared to imply that he was the greatest living Irish tenor. He was the unwitting red rag to the bull. No wonder Burke felt a sense of foreboding doom. But before this 'official' debut the Saranac Lake Charity Concert was an ideal pipe-opener for the tenor. He sang superbly before a packed audience which included Sir Harry Lauder. The comedians' vaudeville tour was proving an enormous success and naturally William Morris was hoping for similar results with Burke. No one, of course, could dispute the fact that Lauder was indeed 'Scotland's greatest living comedian'.

The few days spent at the Morris's residence were idyllic ones for Tom and Marie. 'We canoed around the lake clad only in bathing suits,' wrote Tom. 'This with the snow on the ground. Never have I beheld more beautiful country than that which surrounded his home on Lake Saranac. Can you imagine a vast tract of forest land with swaying firs rising from the carpet of snow with the sun shining as warmly as on a summer's day over here. They were four of the happiest days I remember, but they were the prelude to months of misery such as I pray no other may ever experience. During the time I was up there I met the sufferers from consumption who live amongst the pines to try to recover their health and I am delighted to say that as a result of my concert I was able to present the St. Bernard's Health Camp with a cheque for 11,000 dollars. Then it was back to New York and that fateful Hippodrome debut before an audience of pro-McCormack fans. My spirit quailed as I thought of the ordeal. With all the good intentions in the world, William Morris had practically killed my chances from the outset. John had already established himself firmly, and deservedly so, in the hearts of the American people. I felt there would be those who would resent this newcomer whom they had not heard so far and of whom *they* were to be the judge. They were not to know that I had not made the claim for myself. The Irish are a romantic race and here I was entering the stronghold of their hero, billed like a circus act not a concert artist.'

As Burke stepped onto the Hippodrome platform on the Sunday evening he could almost smell the hostility in the atmosphere. He felt doomed. The knowledge that he could sing to please any audience in the world was overwhelmed by the certainty that his art mattered for nothing because of that incredibly tactless billing. It was he, not impressario Morris, who was on trial and he felt condemned before he uttered a note. This was the great Irish tenor's second home – it was not unknown for him to give ten concerts during a 'Sunday' season. Tom could even joke about it afterwards – 'Slightly larger than Leigh Hipp and not half as friendly' he quipped in a letter home to Josephine.

At first polite applause was his reward, to be followed by booing and foot-stamping as the concert proceeded.

The tenor noticed that the culprits were seated in the rows immediately beneath the platform. As the attendants seemed to be ignoring them he decided to take the matter into his own hands. What followed is unprecedented in the sphere of celebrity concerts. Burke ran down the steps, lifted the ringleader out of his seat by the lapels of his jacket and told him in a loud voice that if he and his cronies didn't shut up he would give him a hiding there and then. The furious sixteen stone tenor then proceeded to shake an apology out of the man who hurriedly left the theatre with his friends. The Irish love a fighter and Burke's stock rose. But he knew in his heart that thc concert was already a disaster. 'My reception was good after this incident. But I was right and Morris was wrong. I knew I sang well. I would be the last one to deny it if it had been otherwise. What I had gone through at the performance was nothing to the vitriolic attacks made upon me by the critics the next day. They went all out after me in the press, and never have I read such bitter notices as were written about me. And they all mentioned the extravagant claims that had been made for me. My worst critic was a man who called himself P.V.K. I had been so anxious to please – so anxious to make good, and the knowledge that I had failed, not because I had sung badly but because I had been billed foolishly, was too much for me. I broke down beneath the weight of my sorrow and disappointment and for *eighteen months I never opened my lips in song.*

'My voice was gone and if any man suffered agony I did throughout those despairing months when I did not know whether it would ever return. For eighteen months this nervous breakdown had me in its grip and then I gradually began to improve.'

Marie nursed her husband at the home of a friend, Eleanor McCullen who was a voice teacher and had a home at Nyak. She says that Tom's statement about the breakdown is not completely correct. 'If I remember rightly he did sing at six concerts before he was forced to give up. He didn't lose his voice, it was his confidence he lost. Eleanor was a marvellous friend to us. Tom chopped wood in the wonderful fresh air, we went for walks in the woods and Eleanor gave

Tom lessons. Gradually she nursed him back until his confidence was restored. She was a great healer.'

When he started to show signs of improvement it was agreed that Marie should strive to further her own career. One of them had to be the breadwinner. At the New York Winter Garden Theatre she starred with Eddie Cantor of the organ-stop eyes and later, in 1922, took the part of Sophie Lavalle in the *Lady in Ermine* at the Ambassador. Upon the termination of her contract with the Schuberts she was affected by home sickness and a pining to be re-united with her daughter Patricia. Tom whole-heartedly agreed that she should go to England to visit her family then return to him in America where, hopefully, a fuller family life would restore their wilting marriage. Marie departed in a mood of optimism for the future. Her dreams were soon shattered. After she had been in Balham for a very short period a telegram arrived from the States. It read: *Have found supreme happiness. Desire my freedom. Tom.* It was an utter bombshell, completely shattered she sought legal advice to be told that there was nothing she could do in England with her husband in America. Taking the advice to ignore the telegram she was now faced with the urgent necessity of earning a living. No money was coming from Tom who was slowly finding his feet again after the illness. Marie found a partner and together they worked on and perfected an act. They were seen at Putney and engaged by the Williamsons Theatrical Agency to tour. Subsequently the act visited New Zealand, Australia and South Africa.

After his wife's departure Tom had begun to practice very hard, and after a short while it was apparent that his voice had not suffered through the illness. Once his confidence returned he sought engagements. Vaudeville and revue appearances were offered and he was forced to accept them. As he became more confident that his vocal powers were as good as ever he determined to fight his way back into Grand Opera. Burke, as he proved throughout his life, was a great survivor. Cautiously he took whatever engagements were offered. Revue, vaudeville 'spots' and then, far more to his liking, the odd concert appearance. For a short period he got a tour and the notices were very pleasing. Back to revue again, at the *Ritz* where his name was prominently displayed in brash Broadway fashion. He detested revue but when it was the only work available he took it, sharing bills with jugglers, black-faced comics, trick cyclists and once with Trini, a C.B. Cochran beauty described as 'the most beautiful girl in the world'. In between these shows he obtained the odd Sunday concert in New York. This time the critics sat up and took notice; in the course of time a concert tour took him to Chicago where his singing was heard by Harold McCormack, the millionaire patron of the Chicago Opera Company, who engaged Tom for the company. Burke's joy new no bounds. Ironic indeed that it should be a McCormack who proved to be the fairy godfather. Here he was back on his beloved operatic stage, part of a tenorial school that included Tito Schipa, Muratore, Ansseau, Cortis, Hackett and his old London confrère Joseph Hislop. All exceptionally fine tenors and during this period 1920-1925 all at the peak of their vocal powers.

'I was in better voice than ever, so that I was more than elated when I heard that the company was going to New York for a season at the Manhattan Theatre. I shall never forget that opening night. I knew what I was up against, but I knew from the first moment that I was in touch with my audience. The critics were there in full force, but I did not care this time. I knew in my heart that this time I should achieve my ambitions and confound my own worst enemies.

The opera was *Rigoletto* and I was playing the Duke. On the last occasion (the McCormack fiasco) my most vitriolic critic of all had been one whose initials were P.V.K. The morning after our opening night I had the pleasure of reading the following notice by P.V.K:

> 'Last night at the Manhattan Opera House we had the pleasure of hearing the Duke in *Rigoletto* sung as we have seldom heard it sung before. Burke's Mezza Voce was a thing of rare beauty, and I question if in my lifetime I shall ever hear it sung better.'

It is not hard to imagine the feelings of mingled bitterness and joy which this notice – a fair sample of them all – caused the tenor to feel. After the torture of the Hippodrome debacle and its traumatic wake, the minstrel boy from Leigh had shown them he wasn't the man to go down easily and without a fight. But there still remained a hard struggle to establish himself in the top echelon of opera in America.

On another occasion, again at the Manhattan, he sang the Duke, this time with Edith Mason an American girl new to this opera house who took the role of Gilda. This time it was as a guest artist deputising for the indisposed Tito Schipa, not an enviable task for the Italian had an excellent reputation in the role. Mary Garden was unable to obtain another famous Italian so she called upon Burke of whom she had had good reports. She was not disappointed. One critic wrote:

> 'Not as Tomaso Burkini or Tomovitch Burkousky – as he would have done a generation ago – but as plain Tom Burke did a new operatic tenor appear suddenly at the Manhattan last night. On this side of the Big Pond he is known mainly as a concert singer but he got along very nicely without a rehearsal. He has an agreeable voice, knows how to handle it, and Verdi made sure that whoever sings the part of the naughty Duke of Mantua gets plenty of applause.'

Another critic whilst praising Burke's singing of *La Donna e Mobile* regretted that Verdi had ever written the song considering that it did not belong in the tradition of Grand Opera. In actual fact, the composer was well aware that he had written a tune to be whistled by window-cleaners and warbled by butcher boys – a 'popular' song in the middle of an opera; so sure was he that it was destined to sweep the world with its captivating lilt he didn't allow the tenor chosen for the inaugural performance to see it until the very day of the opening knowing that, if sung, it would fly all over the town and he would be accused of having stolen a popular tune.

Popular tune or not, it was always received with howls of joy and of all the arias Burke sang this was his most requested encore and ideally suited his flamboyant personality.

Edith Mason, too, received excellent notices. 'In the *Caro*

A TENOR FROM BRUSSELS: M. ANSSEAU.

THE LANCASHIRE TENOR AND EX-MINER MR. THOMAS BURKE.

A GREAT GREEK TENOR: M. ULISSE LAPPAS.

SINGING AT COVENT GARDEN: MME. AYRES BORGHI-ZERNI, SOPRANO.

A SOPRANO NEW TO COVENT GARDEN MISS MARGARET SHERIDAN.

IMPRESARIO AND CONDUCTOR SIR THOMAS BEECHAM.

THE FAMOUS AUSTRALIAN SOPRANO: MME. MELBA.

A SOPRANO WELL KNOWN TO LONDON: MME. EDVINA.

"LA BOHÈME". SIGNOR MARTINELLI, A WELL-KNOWN TENOR

FORMERLY KNOWN AS MISS EMMY DESTINN: MME. DESTINNOVA.

A FIRST-RATE BARITONE: SIGNOR SAMMARCO.

London Illustrated News: Hall of Musical Fame, 1920.

THE ILLUSTRATED LONDON NEWS, JUNE 26, 1920.—1105

PUCCINI'S TRIPLE BILL AT COVENT GARDEN: "AN OPERATIC "TRIPTYCH."

DRAWN BY OUR SPECIAL ARTIST, STEVEN SPURRIER, R.O.I.

THE END OF A TENOR!

An artist's impression of the dramatic climax of 'Il Tabarro'. Michelle (Dihn Gilly) has just strangled Luigi his wife's lover (Tom Burke) and casts him at her feet. Ida Quiatti is in the role of Giorgetta, Michelle's wife.

'Bound for U.S.A.'

(c) Underwood & Underwood, New York.

Marie Burke

(c) Nicholas Muray, New York.

Note the Shamrocks!

TOM BURKE DISAPPOINTS

A big house waited in eager expectancy at the Hippodrome on Sunday evening last for the appearance of Tom Burke, who had been brought to this country by William Morris. Those present had been told in advertisements and press notices that Tom Burke was the greatest Irish singer that had ever come to this country.

When Mr. Burke appeared he was accorded a hearty reception. He proved to be a personable man with a pleasant smile, but his voice and his method disappointed. He has some fine clear notes in his voice but he lacks some of the fire and the poetic feeling one expects from a singer of this type. Particularly was the audience disappointed when he sang typical Irish songs and in which he did not mkae as strong an appeal as in some of his other numbers.

John McCormack need not worry. *N.Y. Star Oct 16.1920*

TOM BURKE AT THE HIPPODROME

It is very easy to conceive of Mr. Burke as regretting having permitted his press agent to advertise him so lavishly as "the greatest living Irish tenor," for even taking into consideration the discount to which all advertising is subject the audience at his first American recital was clearly disappointed, partly, no doubt, because of the inevitable comparisons. Bold, indeed, must the singer be who aspires to project his voice fittingly into the vast space of the Hippodrome, and when to Mr. Burke's inability in this respect is added a most unimpressive style, one might easily say lack of style, small wonder that his hearers were quite unable to wax enthusiastic. Of those accustomed to strut and posture on our concert and operatic stages we surely have more than a sufficiency, but Mr. Burke goes too far the other way; in his delivery life, fire, genuine feeling, as distinguished from mere emotionalism and sentimentality, were almost entirely lacking. We had been told of Mr. Burke's connection with Covent Garden, but in his operatic selections on Sunday evenir again and again came the conviction that here was one more of th

lyric tenors being forced beyond its limitations, especially in the "Quest: O Quella" from Rigoletto. Obviously it was in the group of Irish songs at the end of the program that Mr. Burke was to carry his hearers with him if ever, but strangely enough it was just there that his failure to do so was most apparent, though in one of them, Charles Stanford's "The Bold, Unbiddable Child," he came nearest to making a genuine impression on an audience in which the wearing of the green was everywhere, from green hats to green spats.

Town Topics Oct 7 1920 *The Treble Clef.*

N.Y. Times Oct 4 1920

Tom Burke, Irish Tenor.

An Irish tenor new to this country, said to have been successful as an operatic singer at Covent Garden in London, made his first appearance last evening at the Hippodrome, where a large audience heard him with some sympathy and considerable applause. It was hardly fair to Mr. Burke to announce him as "the greatest living Irish tenor;" or perhaps it was an oversight; for a much greater has recently been heard in New York. Mr. Burke has a voice agreeable when he allows it to be heard at its best, which is not when he forces it and delivers it continually from the chest, or when he fails to maintain the pitch; and there are matters in production and delivery in which he discloses technical deficiencies and a lack of style.

The voice is essentially one of lyric quality; but he is fond of urging it to dramatic or at least operatic effects; and his personality seems to be one that can make its best or its most plausible showing in the simulation of such effects. There were evidences of nervousness in Mr. Burke's singing, especially at the beginning; and it is likely that this nervousness prevented him from showing the best that he is capable of.

He sang the prayer from Verdi's "Otello," the aire "Pourquoi me reveiller" from Massenet's "Werther," the Duke's air "Questa o quella" from "Rigoletto"; Grieg's song "A Dream"; a group of Irish songs arranged and a bit sophisticated by Herbert Hughes, and an amusing Irish song by Stanford. He was curiously ineffective in the Irish songs, and hardly caught the rich native flavor that belongs to them.

Mr. Burke was introduced by Father Duffy of the 69th Regiment, who disclaimed a knowledge of music but gave full assurance of the singer's admirable qualities as a man. Assistance was given by Miss Helen Scholder, 'cellist; Francesco Longo, pianist, and Frank St. Leger, accompanist.

TOM BURKE FAILS TO SCORE

Tom Burke, the Irish tenor brought over by William Morris, the vaudeville manager, made his debut at the Hippodrome on Sunday night and failed to score the big success which his extravagant advertising led many to expect.

"The greatest Irish tenor in the world," his advertising matter read, but he is far from that, judging by the way he was received by the Hippodrome audience. Possessed of a rather pleasing voice and some knowledge of vocal art, his singing, however, left much to be desired. An explosive style of voice production, particularly in the upper register, robbed his voice of much of its natural pleasing quality and also led him, on several occasions, to sing out of tune. He was at his best in his operatic selections. The group of Irish folk songs at his program's end were, strange to say, far from effective. The lilting style which one expects from Irish singers was absent and his enunciation was far from good.

Burke was visibly nervous at the opening of his concert, which may have affected his singing. The audience however, was disappointed that he did not live up to his advance billing.

N.Y. Clipper Oct 6 1920

TOM BURKE'S DEBUT.

The "greatest living Irish tenor" is a phrase that had achieved some publicity before it was applied to Tom Burke, who came from Covent Garden to the Hippodrome last night to sing his way into American hearts. Although the newcomer has the trick of delivering his native folk songs, he devoted much of his opening programme to operatic and other elaborate music, and specialized in the loudness of his top tones.

In its gentler moments Mr. Burke's voice showed a very pretty quality. There was some good 'cello playing by Miss Helen Scholder, and Francesco Longo contributed piano solos.

N.Y. Mail Oct 4 1920

RUSSIAN MUSIC

SHORT'S 'RITZ REVUE' OF GORGEOUS BEAUTY

'A Triumph on the Visual Side, but Is Somewhat Lacking in Comedy.

HASSARD SHORT'S RITZ REVUE, in two acts, conceived and staged by Hassard Short. At the Ritz Theatre.
Principals: Charlotte Greenwood, Raymond Hitchcock, Tom Burke, Jay Brennan, Madeleine Fairbanks, Chester Hale, Adele [illegible] Hetton, Ja[illegible] Dorothy [illegible] Mrytle Schaaf, Stanley Rogers [illegible] Brown, Ladd, Albertina Vitak, [illegible] William Frances Lee, Floyd Jones, Hal[illegible] Brown, Conrad, Leila Ricard, Joel Forde, Eddie Moulton Montgomery, [illegible] Hurlbert, [illegible] Allis and [illegible]

The new revue at the Ritz Theatre has much to commend it. It was to have been expected that Hassard Short, with three Music Box entertainments behind him, would produce a beautiful and tasteful revue. Of beauty "The Ritz Revue" contains as much as any current musical production: the show is nearly always lovely to behold. Unfortunately Mr. Short's good taste has not extended to the spoken word. Not a few of the jokes manage to be downright offensive.

The program credits more authors and composers than have ever been assembled before on behalf of any single entertainment, but unquestionably the principal honors should be pinned on Mr. Short. He has done a gorgeous job. In particular, a series of tableaux depicting the scarlet woman of all time was beautifully presented. So was a golden number entitled "Sun-Girl"; so were divers chiffon-draped and delicately lighted episodes. Distinctly, a triumph for Mr. Short on the visual side.

As for the comedy, it should not be hastily inferred that the production is devoid of laughter. On the contrary, it has several delectable moments in a comedy way. Many of these occur in a sketch entitled "Her Morning Bath," written by Norma Mitchell and Ralph Bunker, thespians both. In addition to providing a handful of laughs, this sketch demonstrates that at least one person's opinion of Charlotte Greenwood has been wrong all these seasons. Miss Greenwood is an excellent actress when her material provides the opportunity, and last night the opportunity was provided.

Raymond Hitchcock was less fortunate when the comedy was allotted; not even his unctuous and persuasive personality was able to compensate for some of the drearier moments of his monologues. On the other side of the ledger, however, should be entered the splendid voice of Tom Burke, the undeniable cuteness of Madeleine Fairbanks and the dancing of Albertina Vitak.

The girls are generally beautiful; the costuming is all that even Mr. Short could desire. Only the team of Brennan and Rogers disturbed the good taste of the evening. And these two, it must be recorded, successfully managed to make one positively ashamed of the the-

SEP 18 1924

Musical Comedy Should Develop Sense of Satire

Tom Burke Predicts Great Future for This Type of Entertainment.

TOM BURKE, opera tenor featured in "The Dancing Girl," at the Winter Garden, believes that the American musical comedy not only has a great present but a greater future.

"America leads the world in this field of stage entertainment," said the singer. "In melody, in sense of comedy, in originality of humor, in smartness and taste of staging, in resourcefulness and vivacity of singers, dancers and comedians and in the general pulchritude of girls no nation can excel you. If you can boast a superiority you should by all means do so. This country is as yet far behind the European in serious drama and in grand opera and operetta composition, but they cannot begin to approach America in your lighter musical form of theatrical amusement."

Mr. Burke believes that the musical comedy of America will have a greater future when it develops a greater sense of satire and burlesque.

"Librettists here don't take enough advantage of the material that lies all around," he said. "They are too content to follow the conventions of yesterday just because those conventions made for substantial financial success. They should make their musical comedies reflect American life in all of its humorous aspects, political, social and intellectual. Americans must be ready to turn the spotlight upon themselves, to laugh at themselves spontaneously and understandingly. They must do in musical comedy what Gilbert and Sullivan did in light opera. Satirize national fads and fancies. In this way they will be accomplishing a splendid thing for America. They will be assisting in no little way in broadening national culture and outlook.

"There is no reason why a musical comedy cannot express American life quite as humorously, quite as wistfully and whimsically, as, say, a straight comedy such as 'The First Year.' I would have the music as representatively American as the comedy. Now this may sound like a tremendous order. As a matter of fact, it is easily within the capabilities of Americans once they set about it. If I can be of any aid in fostering such a movement I shall consider that my stage career has been well spent."

HERALD 7-29-20

FEB 18 1923

Singer Rides Bicycle Daily to Keep in Trim

Tom Burke, the singer, who is appearing in "The Dancing Girl" at the Winter Garden, has undertaken a rigorous athletic schedule for the spring and summer in order to keep the physical trim necessary to his role. He rises at 6 and goes to the Velodrome at 225th [illegible] rides a bicycle for two hours. At the conclusion of this exercise (he estimates that he travels twenty-five miles during the course of it) he has a vigorous rubdown for half an hour. He then goes home for breakfast, followed by a nap of forty minutes. His breakfast consists of one orange, one egg, two slices of bacon, one slice of toast and a cup of tea. This is followed by a nap of forty minutes, after which Mr. Burke attends to his correspondence and indulges in a little reading.

At 2 o'clock he goes for a two hour walk (on matinee days he takes the walk between performances) and then comes [illegible] practice. His dinner, his only other meal of the day, consists of ve[illegible] sup- ply [illegible] 6:45, after which he goes to the theater. The performance is over at 11:30, and Burke is in bed at midnight. During the last week he has reduced ten pounds.

APR 29 1923

'PINAFORE' LAVISHLY REVIVED AT CENTURY

Fay Templeton Little Buttercup of Splendid Cast in a Gala Production on High Ship.

7-29-00

H. M. S. PINAFORE or THE LASS THAT LOVED A SAILOR, a comic opera in two acts. Text by W. S. Gilbert, music by Arthur Sullivan. Costumes by Ernest Schraffe; settings by Rollo Wayne; staged by Milton Aborn; revived by the Shuberts. At the Century Theatre.

Sir Joseph Porter, K. C. B.	John E. Hazzard
Captain Corcoran	Marion Green
Ralph Rackstraw	Tom Burke
Dick Deadeye	William Danforth
Bill Bobstay	Charles E. Gallagher
Bob Becket	Chester Bright
Tom Tucker	Master Durkin
Sergeant of Marines	Emmet Douglas
Josephine	Marguerite Namara
Hebe	Nydia d'Arnell
Little Buttercup	Fay Templeton

That not uncelebrated "nautical comic opera" entitled "Pinafore" was produced again at the Century Theatre last night—produced with what must be one of the highest ships that has ever adorned a "Pinafore" revival, even though the Hippodrome presentation of some years ago may have offered something a little wider. Not even the fact that it is a "Pinafore" fitted to the ample Century, however, keeps it from being a generally noble revival.

In fact, the capaciousness of the Century stage makes possible such an entrance for Sir Joseph Porter as that Admiral never has enjoyed before. With sailors swarming both decks and rigging, with the Admiral's well-known female relatives covering most of the rest of the stage, with a marine band added to the ensemble for good measure, with flags flying and Jack Hazzard waiting in white sideburns—all this and more precedes that melodious entrance. Sir Arthur Sullivan probably would grumble a little at the fact that Sir Joseph is first greeted with "God Save the King," but as staged at the Century it is all highly effective.

It is "Pinafore" on a grand scale and dotted with celebrated names, most of whose owners contribute in generous margin to the success of the evening. The ample Fay Templeton, looking astonishingly like May Irwin, returns to revel in the rôle of Little Buttercup and to handle it with all of her old skill. Marion Green is a superb Captain Corcoran and William Danforth as good a Dick Deadeye as can be expected—it is a rôle vastly overrated so far as its comic potentialities are concerned.

Then, too, there is Tom Burke as Ralph Rackstraw—better by far than he was in "The Mikado" a year ago. Mr. Hazzard's Sir Joseph is what all the crusty old "Pinafore" lovers would be likely to describe as un-Gilbertian. He is not quite meant for this sort of thing. Marguerite Namara, likewise, is not quite an ideal Josephine; last night, at all events, she seemed a bit overconscious of her vocal powers.

It is an excellent chorus as far as the singing goes, and that, of course, is 90 per cent. of the battle. Last night's audience seemed to be having a generally good time.

APR 7 1926

'THE MIKADO' REVIVED IN SPLENDID FASHION

A Spirited and Lavish Production Warmly Greeted—Lupino Lane Delights as Ko-Ko.

THE MIKADO, by William S. Gilbert and Arthur Sullivan. At the Forty-fourth Street Theatre.

The Mikado of Japan	William D[illegible]
Nanki-Poo	Tom Burke
Ko-Ko	[illegible]
Pooh-Bah	Stanley Forde
Pish-Tush	[illegible]
A Noble	[illegible]
Yum-Yum	Marguerite Namara
Pitti-Sing	[illegible]
Peep-Bo	Elsa Petersen
Katisha	Sarah Edwards

It is a lavish, spirited and generally excellent production of "The Mikado" that was seen at the Forty-fourth Street Theatre on Saturday night, the first of two Gilbert and Sullivan revivals that are coming to town overnight, so to speak. It is a matter of five and a half years since the last important production of "The Mikado" in New York, and that, as any Gilbert-and-Sullivanite will tell you, is too long. Far too long.

The outstanding points of this revival, which was so vociferously greeted by its first audience that it ran until 11:15—a late hour for "The Mikado"—are the Ko-Ko of Lupino Lane, the Mikado (familiar but excellent) of William Danforth, the Yum-Yum of Marguerite Namara, the quality of the ensemble singing and the general scale of the production. It is "The Mikado" on a semi-"Student Prince" scale, but you do not feel that its size is doing violence to tradition. It still is "The Mikado."

The casting of Lupino Lane as Ko-Ko is distinctly an innovation. Probably his performance was not Gilbertian—in the sense, for example, that Mr. Danforth's Mikado is Gilbertian—but it was vastly entertaining. He has bent the rôle to his own talents, which are primarily acrobatic, but he has been wise in not trying to indulge in acrobatics save where the rôle might conceivably be enhanced by them. Vocally he is something short of remarkable, but his performance was a constant delight.

The real Gilbertians, of course, had to wait until the second act for their moments of keenest enjoyment. Mr. Danforth's singing of "My Object All Sublime" was unquestionably the high mark of the evening. Miss Namara was at all times a capable Yum-Yum, reaching her height, of course, in "The Moon and I." Stanley Forde was a variable Pooh-Bah—at times excellent, at other times less so. Elsa Petersen was an alluring Peep-Bo and Sarah Edwards at least a satisfactory Katisha.

There remains Nanki-Poo, sung by Tom Burke. Mr. Burke is a concert singer, and it is the opinion of this reviewer that he should never, never be allowed to act in Gilbert and Sullivan.

This single defect, however, does not keep "The Mikado," in its present production, from being excellent entertainment. Its second act, in particular, offers as grand an hour as ever the collaborators put together. It is a [illegible]

ENGLISH TENOR COMING: IS INSURED FOR $500,000

(Special Correspondence of The World.)

STAGE ON WHEELS FOR OUTDOOR OPERA

Built in Sections, It Will Be Rolled Into Place at the Polo Grounds.

Mr. Burke has a repertoire of sixty-five French, Italian and German operas. Among the famous conductors under whose direction he has at one time or another appeared are Toscanini, Serafin, Bavagnoli, Albert Coates, Sir Thomas Beecham and Giorgio Polacco.

POLO GROUNDS HOME OF OPERA FOR 3 WEEKS

Stoneham Lets Patrons of Music Have Field for Time Giants Will Be on Tour.

The Polo Grounds are to be turned over to a new opera association for three weeks this Summer during the absence of the Giants on tour. Charles A. Stoneham signed a contract to this end yesterday. Tom Burke will be the impresario and A. Ralph Steinberg the general manager.

Mr. Stoneham is giving the field and grand stands gratis, together with the necessary attachés, such as box office men, gate-keepers and ushers, and the large electrical equipment necessary for night performances, with the understanding that the association will furnish an [illegible] series of opera performances, both comic and grand.

The opera association, as yet unnamed, is sponsored by a group of wealthy patrons of music so that opera may be given for the people at prices ranging no higher than $1 a seat. An orchestra of sixty pieces, a chorus of sixty and the best soloists and conductors available are promised. Plans as to repertoire, casts and other details are to be announced in the near future.

IRISH TENOR RIVALS CARUSO.

TOM BURKE IN OPERA DEBUT

Young Irish Tenor, Unannounced, Wins Ovation in "Rigoletto."

Thomas Burke, so the new name ran on hasty street posters, or plain "Tom" Burke in the house bills, made an opera début both unexpected and unannounced beyond the Manhattan's doors last evening, when Tito Schipa was unable to sing in the Chicago company's first current performance of "Rigoletto." Mr. Burke, a young Irish tenor, had appeared here in concert and private recital, his new venture was to operagoers a total surprise and its result as unguessed as a [illegible] on the confines of Ulster.

The popular [illegible], coupled with the luck of [illegible] own "début rôle" of the Duke, reacted in the young man's favor. He was welcomed by an audience which had filled all but the last orchestra rows and the standing spaces and the greeting was spontaneous, cordial and encouraging. There should be other occasions for critical review, but fortunate the tenor who wins a first audience with the "Donna è Mobile." He both acted and sang easily, and his ovation "held up the show."

Edith Mason was a mature Gilda, singing more evenly than hitherto, while George Baklanoff's giant height and dramatic declamation recalled the Renaud tradition in Verdi's title rôle of the hunchback jester. There was a restored scene for him and Lazzari, as the assassin, in act two. Miss Pavloska was the Maddalena, and Nicolay the Monterone, a rôle the late Gilibert once raised also to greatness on this stage. Mr. Polacco conducted discriminately the gripping dialogue and the honeyed airs.

CAST QUITS OPERA COMPANY

Burke, Tenor, Objects to "Outsiders;" "Pinafore" Canceled

"Pinafore" will not be given at the Polo Grounds July 22. Tom Burke, tenor, resigned as President of the Municipal Opera Company, formed a few weeks ago for the purpose of giving opera at the Polo Grounds.

According to a statement, Mr. Burke's withdrawal is due to his opposition "to business methods exercised by outsiders who elected to control the business management of the company."

The entire cast, including the technical and musical directors, also has left the organization.

A "Tom Burke Company" has been formed which will make short tours, beginning in August, giving opera in cities throughout the United States.

TENOR BEATEN IN CABARET

Burke Tells Police, Goes Back; Is Beaten Again

TOM BURKE MAKES DEBUT.

Irish Tenor's Concert at Saranac Yields $80,000 for Charity.

Special to The New York Times.

SARANAC LAKE, N. Y., Sept. 24.—

A Dejected Burke after the Hippodrome Debacle.

Burke Practices on Tour in U.S.A.

(c) Bain News Service, New York.

APEDA
N.Y.

PRICE OF PROGRAMME 6d

ROYAL OPERA
: : COVENT GARDEN : :
Lessees: Covent Garden Opera Syndicate, Ltd.

THIS EVENING'S PERFORMANCE

Friday, July 6, 1928, at 8.15

Mascagni's Opera

CAVALLERIA RUSTICANA

In Italian

Turiddu	TOM BURKE
Alfio	ARMANDO BORGIOLI
Lola	OLGA DE FRANCO
Lucia	ENID CRUICKSHANK
Santuzza	DUSOLINA GIANNINI
Conductor	VINCENZO BELLEZZA

Followed by

Leoncavallo's Opera

PAGLIACCI

In Italian

Nedda	ROSETTA PAMPANINI
Canio	AURELIANO PERTILE
Tonio	GIOVANNI INGHILLERI
Beppe	NELLO PALAI
Silvio	ARISTIDE BARACCHI
Conductor	VINCENZO BELLEZZA

LINDEN BROWN AND CO., LTD., CRAVEN STREET, W.C.2

Comfortably Ensconced in his Cadogan Square Residence.

Luisa Tetrazzini, Tom's Sweetheart of Song,
for whom he had Great Admiration.

AN UNDIVIDED PAIR.

MISS TURNER'S SANTUZZA

"CAVALLERIA RUSTICANA"

In Italian.

Turiddu	Tom Burke
Alfio	Armando Borgioli
Lola	Olga de Franco
Lucia	Enid Cruickshank
Santuzza	Eva Turner
Conductor	Vincenzo Bellezza.

Followed by

"PAGLIACCI."

In Italian.

Nedda	Rosetta Pampanini
Canio	Aureliano Pertile
Tonio	Giovanni Inghilleri
Beppe	Nello Palai
Silvio	Aristide Baracchi
Conductor	Vincenzo Bellezza.

As for over a generation so now, there is no separating "Cavalleria Rusticana" and "Pagliacci." They are an undivided if not an indivisible pair. Of course, they have on occasion appeared separately, but they have always come together again, perhaps to their mutual advantage.

Moreover, they twain have a drawing capacity that shows little sign of fading. Last night, when the pair was revived for the first time this season, there was a very large audience, just as there has been in most seasons, from those of the peripatetic companies who on occasion visit London to the "Grand" season at Covent Garden.

A point of interest arose in the performance under notice in that three of the principal singers in "Cavalleria Rusticana" were members, if memory serves, of one or other of these peripatetic companies, and now find themselves greeted amongst the "élite" in a crowded house in this highly successful "Grand" season. These singers are Miss Eva Turner, Miss Enid Cruickshank, and Mr. Tom Burke.

MISS EVA TURNER AGAIN.

Miss Eva Turner, who set the town by the ears as the Princess in "Turandot" the other day, again sang superbly, if now and then a little hardly, as Santuzza. Her voice has a glorious ring in it, a clearness and a roundness that are beautiful to hear. Her singing of "Voi lo sapete" was remarkable, and certainly a bunch of laurel leaves was added to the wreath metaphorically offered to her last week. Miss Cruickshank made of Lucia a sympathetic old lady, and Mr. Tom Burke sang and, moreover, acted with far more conviction than often before he has shown. His singing of the brindisi was capital, and his voice seemed steadier than before, as one noticed in the serenade sung before the rising of the curtain. If Mme. Olga de Franco could rid herself of her excessive vibrato her very French Lola would have been more acceptable, but, nevertheless, she was in the picture, as was M. Armando Borgioli as Alfio. M. Bellezza conducted and produced a performance that was somewhat subdued, though it was none the worse for that, since it had at least a semblance of refinement not often associated with this blood and thunder story. Incidentally the intermezzo, which used constantly to be repeated, passed last night without a hand.

As to "Pagliacci," of this, likewise, a very lively performance was given, very lively and very Italian, as is befitting. In Mme. Pampanini was a Nedda of great temperament and fine voice. Just why she lay prone upon the stage, reclining upon a rock, in the first scene deponent knoweth not, but she sang emphatically well "Oh! che volo d'Angelli," and she acted with a good deal of conviction. So also did M. Pertile as Canio, though he did on occasion so force his voice as to raise the pitch of the notes; and he was a terrifically hard-working and hard-singing Pagliacco. A great outburst of applause greeted the singing of the Prologue by M. Inghilleri, who throughout was a capital Tonio, and the Beppe of M. Nello Palai and the Silvio of M. Baracchi were likewise good. M. Bellezza again conducted, and as before derived a certain refinement from the score, which is by no means always in evidence. R. H. L.

SINGERS IN SICILIAN MOOD.

MISS EVA TURNER'S BRILLIANCE.

"Cavalleria Rusticana" and "Pagliacci," which from their long-founded association have been called the ham and eggs of opera, were sung last night at Covent Garden with full-blooded Mediterranean passion—although a number of the singers were British Islanders.

Thus the soprano and tenor in "Cavalleria" were both Lancastrians—Miss Eva Turner and Mr. Tom Burke. One might spend a whole winter at Taormina and never see anything so Sicilian as their duel.

Santuzza must have emerged black and blue, so often and so fiercely did Turiddu grip and twist her by the arms and force her down on bended knee.

For a time it looked as though Italy were to be out-Italied; but in "Pagliacci" Mr Aureliano Pertile, the tenor,

Miss Eva Turner.

regained the challenge cup in the tournament of passion. "Vesti la Giubba" has been sung in a thousand different ways, but Mr. Pertile's tears of pain were his own.

DRAMATIC OUTCRIES.

His singing, like Miss Eva Turner's, made one marvel afresh at the human voice. In both there was an element of the stridency which is more admired in Italy than elsewhere. But both singers are great technicians and know just how far they can safely go.

Miss Turner and Mr. Pertile together could challenge a full military band and come out smiling. With both there are passages that are more astonishing than beautiful, but both are marvellous singers. Mr. Pertile's dramatic outcries were nearly terrifying. Miss Turner's blazing phrases—so bold and brilliant and dead certain—were, of their sort, the most remarkable known in these latter days at Covent Garden.

There was a rumour a few years ago that the senior partner of the firm of *Cavalleria Rusticana* and *I Pagliacci* was shortly to retire and new blood, in the person of *Gianni Schicchi* was to enhance still further the fortunes of the famous partnership. The rumour, however, has proved premature, and though *Cavalleria Rusticana* has undoubtedly aged, it is still capable of supporting its slightly younger but still active colleague at Covent Garden and causing enthusiastic breaches of the decorum proper to that august house. *Verismo* came upon the operatic stage before music had grown far enough out of its romantic period to match these quadrilateral and triangular dramas of real life, and we feel the discrepancy nowadays, but these operas provide us with opportunities of hearing the singers who have already made successful appearances in other operas. Miss Eva Turner, for example, is equal to the best Italian of them all in this full-blooded, full-throated music, and two other English singers, Miss Enid Cruickshank and Mr. Tom Burke, showed again last night that they, too, are masters of the broad and powerful style of Southern *cantabile* singing.

I Pagliacci is altogether stronger meat, and it was sung by a cast of singers who are quite first-class in this *genre*. From the Prologue (magnificently sung by Signor Inghilleri) onwards the crude story gripped—one advantage incidentally in a change of partners would be relief from the preoccupation with the not very edifying theme of sexual jealousy. But Signor Pertile's sheer intensity raises the opera to the heights of tragedy, and that is what no amount of conviction can do for *Cavalleria Rusticana*, although Signor Bellezza and his colleagues played and sung it as though they believed in it utterly. Signorina Rosetta Pampanini's voice combines richness of tone with a fine ringing quality that matched the male voices and provided a grateful contrast to the ear. In the play within the play she made a pretty thing of her imitation 18th-century music. The team worked well together, and the result was to show that there is still life in the long-established concern. Still, the question of new blood might once more be considered.

ARTISTRY OF MR. TOM BURKE.

FINE SINGING AT COVENT GARDEN.

"Daily Express" Music Critic.

"Rigoletto" was distinguished at Covent Garden last night by the singing of Mr. Tom Burke, the Lancashire tenor, who, as the Duke of Mantua, proved that he appreciated the delicate distinction between the artist and the artisan in music.

Mr. Tom Burke.

He kept the faith primarily with his art and secondarily with his composer, and one felt that his whole performance was the outward and audible symbol of his artistic conscience.

His voice seemed rather repressed against its sonorous Italian background, and his intonation, in the pianissimo passages, was not always faultless; but he sang throughout with skill and discretion. His duet with Mme. Fregini in the second act lingers in the memory as a piece of highly rarefied ecstasy.

Fig – aro! Tom Playing the Fool.

Nome she rose to a climax of vocal excellence, especially in the sustained high notes at the end which were thrilling.' But of Baklanoff's *Rigoletto* the critic had this rather amusing comment to make. 'His performance pales in comparison with some of his great predecessors. He constantly forgets he is lame and runs upstairs like an antelope when he suspects that his Gilda has been captured by the wicked Duke.' Tom used to joke that he felt like singing out "Hey, mate, you've got a gammy leg" but it didn't fit the music!

The opera was conducted by Maestro Polacco, Edith Mason's husband, and hailed in America as second to no living master of the baton.

The 'shy man' of Lionel Powell's publicity 'blurb' was fast disappearing. For Burke was not only a star of the first order he was very prominent in the social life of New York, developing an appetite for high living, late-night parties and 'Rye' whisky; often seen in the company of beautiful women and attracted numerous camp-followers of the parasitic variety. On one occasion at a party he was shot in the leg by a jealous husband because he sang to his wife as they danced. Luckily for him it was only a superficial wound but a painful indication of the gun-happy society at this time. Hostesses vied with each other to have the handsome tenor at their parties. Being uncluttered matrimonially, with Marie away in Australia and South Africa for long periods, was the cue for female admirers to make him the target of their advances and Tom never made any secret of the fact that he thrived on female adoration.

His fame brought him the friendship of many famous people in the business and theatrical world, including Julius Fleischmann, the Yeast Magnate with whom he spent many weeks on his fabulous yacht. Jimmy Walker, the mayor of New York and composer of popular songs, was another great friend. To please him Tom would sing one of his latest songs whenever they met at a party. Not the sort of songs included in the Burke repertoire but Tom sang them just the same – one in particular *Will you love me in September like you did in May* became a popular hit. Al Smith, the Governor of New York, made Tom an honorary Inspector of Police – the ex-miner had well and truly made his mark amongst the influential socialites and dignitaries of New York as he had done in London making him a natural target for the social-climbing brigade who threw parties to impress their friends. In the early days he was good-natured enough to think it a great compliment until he realised that he was simply being invited along for the hostess to flaunt him in front of her guests – and of course to sing without a fee. At last Tom decided that enough was enough. At the house-party of a well-known titled lady he put his little plan into action. "How many songs would you like me to sing?" he asked the hostess. "Oh, as many as you like, Mr Burke!" she replied, all smiles. Tom sang only three. Previously he would have gladly rendered song after song for he never tired of singing. But after the third he gravely approached his hostess and explained that it was his practice not to accept his usual fee at such occasions, instead if she cared to give him a cheque he would see that it was safely handed over to the charity of her choice. He used this dodge several times until his 'fame' spread and there was a distinct falling off in invitations. Instead, he found he was being invited to parties for his own sake and not being used as a pawn to impress people of influence and their fawning satellites, and at these he was more than generous with his renditions.

Quite by accident he stumbled on one of the best con tricksters in New York – not an American gangster but a demure English young lady related to the peerage. She was in the habit of giving cocktail parties every Friday afternoon and because of her rank as well as her infinite charm there was never any lack of attendance at these jolly affairs. The mystery was how she did it, for everybody knew quite well that the whole family was very hard up. Yet she lived in a sumptuously furnished house on Fifth Avenue, had several servants, entertained on a lavish scale and never seemed to lack anything.

Tom was a regular guest at her house parties. One day he happened to be in the district early in the day and called at her house. The butler showed him in to an embarrassed reception from his hostess. Noticing that all the chairs, tables and furniture in general bore white tags he was curious to know what they meant. The girl took his arm and sat him down on a settee. "You have caught me in a very embarrassing situation, Tom," she explained. "I suppose the time had to come when one of my guests would arrive too early. Still, I'm glad it's you for I feel I can trust you being English like myself. This is a little dodge I've worked many times with great success when hard up, and I'm hoping to pull it off again very shortly. You see, I spend rather lavishly and as people seem to like my company and don't mind coming along and accepting my hospitality because I happen to be amongst the nobility with a small 'n', I think they ought to help pay for the privilege. We English are not all as silly as some of these Yanks believe us to be! They're not the only racketeers around.

"You know old - - - - (mentioning a well-known American millionaire who would have done anything to rub shoulders with the English aristocracy), well I wrote and asked him to come along good and early. You see, when he sees all these tags and things he is bound to ask me what they are and I shall look sad and melancholy, dabbing my eyes, and explain that unless I can raise 2,000 dollars within a few hours the people from whom I obtained the furniture will forcibly remove it. Then, Tom, I shall smile bravely and – if it does not come off again I shall be very surprised. It has never failed yet. So you see, Tom, you'd better slip into the library for he will be here any minute. You'll hear me give a performance worthy of any actress or opera singer!"

Sure enough, the performance was a masterpiece and the millionaire wrote out a huge cheque to cover the cost of the furniture a dozen times over.

'Not a very commendable performance,' wrote Burke in his memoirs. 'Not what one would expect from an English Lady. Still in some ways I sympathised with her because I have seen the lengths to which some people will go to get an introduction to a titled person. They deserved to be conned for many of this type are simply parasites of the upper bracket. I saw life in many of its bizarre forms in the America of the early 'twenties. But what disgusted me most of all was the treatment of the blacks. It mattered not how clever or useful they were to society at large they were kept under – in my own profession it was sad to see singers of great talent passed over repeatedly because they happened to be black. Paul Robeson and Marian Anderson, a truly wonderful contralto, never got the opportunities they deserved which is despicable to my mind. This state of affairs was and still is a great loss to American and world opera.'

Burke and money never remained together for long. He was a sucker for a hard-luck yarn and his good-natured personality made him a target for begging pot-shots from theatrical and social scroungers. At the time it seemed wise to him to invest most of his earnings. On the advice of 'friends' he entered the quicksand market of stocks and shares and was made to regret it. With Tom it was not easy come, but was certainly easy go.

His relations with the press were not always amicable but without doubt he was always good for a story. It was his private life that made the best copy, particularly the incident when celebrating his birthday with friends at a night club. Finding the place to be very hot he decided to go outside for a breath of air. Once out of the place he heard a voice say, "That's him – get him!" whereupon six 'heavies' jumped on him and proceeded to give him a good beating, leaving him on the ground bruised and bleeding. They then picked him up and flung him down a flight of stone steps. Tom picked himself up and hurried to the nearest police station. The inspector on duty wasn't over concerned and when Tom got very annoyed he told him to return and he would be met by a party of policemen. But on arriving back at the night club he walked straight into the gang again; once more they gave him the 'works'. This time, however, Tom managed to knock one of them out and dislodge a few teeth here and there before wilting under the onslaught. Mercifully, they left him groaning on the ground and drove off in a huge car. The police arrived after the assailants had left and made it quite plain to Tom that it was little use him making a complaint. He was lucky to be alive. He had been mistaken for some well-known gangster. It was better to forget it. It was very apparent to Tom that the so-called guardians of the law were afraid of the gang. Once his anger had abated and his wounds began to heal he decided that the less said the better and quietly choked on his indignation. A sensible decision in such violent times with daily killings the rule rather than the exception.

The tenor was feeling decidedly sick so he went to Atlantic City to recuperate, providing a particularly witty reporter with the opportunity for a smart piece of journalism in *The Morning Telegraph*:

'**TOM BURKE, TENOR, VERSUS TEX GUINANS**

And Burke is now in drydock Atlantic City for sundry repairs to person.

Happened of a Sunday Night

Tom Burke famed tenor arrived today to recuperate from a visit to Tex Guinans Night Club – or is it a Ju Jitsu Academy? It was Tom's 35th Birthday and the Boys made sure he got a present to remember the joint by. Did they just!

Burke, so the story goes, and there's a battered nose, bruised face and seven missing teeth to back up his story, was badly beaten up in Tex's club and then, to make sure of it, was beaten up again. What is worse is all this happened of a Sunday Night. What a load of guts this singing guy has.

Long Time Between Fights

The tenor was with a party of seven people quietly enjoying the entertainment – there had not been a fight all evening. But after all it *was* Sunday. There had not been a fight, in fact, since the time Lawrence Meck said Billy Moore, son of the famous 'Dinty', bounced a bottle on top of his head. The next event, which can accurately be described, is the arrival of Burke at the police station to report he had been beaten up. The police inspector was not frightened so he told Burke to go back to the club. He did, and he came right back to say he'd been beaten again. He went home to sleep on it if possible.

It is understood that no complaint will be made about the attack. Burke will probably remain here several days while his nose and face heal, although there is some doubt about his teeth growing again.'

Working and living in Chicago could be a very dangerous existence in the almost lawless America of the day. Gang warfare was on every street corner and everything seemed to happen to Burke who bore a charmed life. After night-clubbing it at the swish Chicago Trianon he hailed a taxi in the early hours of the morning. The cab had hardly gone fifty yards when bullets rattled it like a shower of hailstones, killing the driver. The cab hit a wall and Tom flung himself onto the floor until the firing had ceased frightened to move a muscle. When he felt reasonably sure that the gunmen had fled he examined the driver. It was obvious nothing could be done. The golden rule 'never interfere in Chicago' had been pumped into him by his colleagues and remembering this wise advice he hurried away from the scene, making his way back to the hotel by devious routes. Next day the papers revealed the cause of the outburst. A taxi war was in progress between rival companies and drivers were settling it by the gun. The passengers were a secondary consideration as was all human life in the violent city of Al Capone and Bugs Moran.

ACT VI

Amongst his many musical colleagues Tom was on very friendly terms with Louis Graveure, the Belgian tenor. At least that is the name and nationality music-lovers have been led to believe as correct. In actual fact his story is quite amazing, as many opera buffs are aware, and here is the version told by Tom Burke:

'It was during my time in New York that I met Wilfred Douthitt, or I suppose I should say Louis Graveure, that fine English baritone who turned tenor and at the same time turned into another being altogether. It is one of the most amazing stories ever told.

'Douthitt started his career in England as a baritone and achieved some small success but, like many more of us, he probably realised that as long as he stuck to an English name, and as long as he remained in his own country, he would remain unrecognised. True, he was "getting on", if one can say that being the first man to play principal boy at Drury Lane is an achievement for one who aspires to operatic fame. Then he went to the States, where he played in *The Lilac Domino* with a beautiful girl named Eleanor Painter, and it was rumoured that Douthitt and Miss Painter were to be married. This is significant in view of after events. He was playing under his own name then you must remember.

'The war broke out and it was then that Douthitt apparently decided that the time was ripe for carrying out an extraordinary disappearing trick. He announced that he was going to Canada to join the Canadian Forces for the purpose of going to France. This was in 1915, and from that time to the present day Wilfred Douthitt has never been seen – at least in that name.

'A few months elapsed and then one day Louis Graveure was announced as giving a recital in New York. He was described as a Belgian *tenor* and it was stated that he was a nobleman – a count no less! The recital came off and two of the songs which Douthitt used to sing with certain mannerisms, which were unmistakable, were included. The next day the papers rang with the story that Graveure and Douthitt were one and the same. Graveure had grown a beard but friends knew there could be no mistake. He was the same man. Douthitt was approached many times but was always charmingly evasive. His wife, too, was badgered by reporters and when asked had she seen Douthitt lately replied, "Yes, frequently – almost every day." Yet so far as the outside world knows, Douthitt disappeared way back in 1915 and has never been seen since. He was probably wise to change his name and identity, for he has certainly gone further than he would have done if he had stayed over in this country in his own name. Of that much I am quite certain. Sometimes I think I should have done the same. I always resisted the temptation; in fact, there was no temptation as I wanted to stay plain Tom Burke. Imagine Will Hay billed in opera – forgetting that he is a comedian for the moment – he wouldn't go far. Neither does my own name, it seems, lend itself to the idea so many people hold about opera – in their minds there is an aura of mystique about it which is added to by performers with foreign names. And of course if you are a Belgian count you are made!'

It was not uncommon for singers to alter their names – and certainly a foreign-sounding one does seem to appeal to the opera fraternity. But Burke, in spite of his plain name, was a huge success during the 'twenties, despite his obsession that English singers, especially with plain names, were overlooked. It is interesting to reflect on the success of three female singers all with very 'English' names Eva Turner, Clara Butt and Ada Allsop – certainly no mystique there.

Tom Burke, as those who knew him well will agree, was a man who always led with his chin, as they say in boxing parlance. He acted on impulse and not always in his own best interests. But to pick a deliberate quarrel with no less a person than Jack Dempsey, the heavyweight champion of the world, was biting off more than even the impetuous tenor could chew – or so it would seem. Dempsey was then at the zenith of his fame and popularity, and a very welcome guest at the most select and exclusive gatherings. The prohibition racket was in full swing and racketeers seemed to make it a point of honour to make sure that these elite functions were well catered for with liquor, the consequence being that many people who did not normally drink, except for the odd glass of wine, would make pigs of themselves on the unaccustomed 'hooch' – the custom, born out of scarcity, was to drink as much as possible in as quick a time as possible in case of a raid, with inevitable results. At one such party, Burke was in the company of one of the best-looking women in town and feeling particularly proud and slightly tipsy. It follows that he was a little jealous when she became the lure for men wanting her to dance. Whilst being served with refreshments, he overheard Dempsey making a remark which was clearly audible to Tom's partner. He saw her face turn red and with that he got his 'Irish dander' up although not quite sure what the boxer had said. "What did he say to you?" he demanded. The girl quickly regained her composure and wanted to forget the incident.

"Oh nothing," she replied. "Forget it, only that he would like to kiss me more than any other woman in the world."

"Oh did he!" ranted the furious tenor. "I'll show him!"

"But he *is* Mr Jack Dempsey, Tom!"

"I don't care a - - - who he is!" sang out Burke in a most untuneful tone and, with that, marched up to Dempsey to demand an apology. The incorrigible tenor had smouldering fury in his voice and the Irish American was taken aback.

"Look here, you," said Tom, dwarfed by the champion's superior height. "You may be the champion of the world, but you don't get away with insulting remarks to a friend of mine."

Dempsey gazed down half-apologetically, half-kidding, at Tom's clenched fists, then giving him a light-hearted clip on the ear he put his huge arms around Tom's back and said, "Aw, Tom boy, I wouldn't have offended the little girlie for the world."

"But you said you'd like to kiss her," retorted Tom not quite appeased.

Jack hugged him hugely like a bear. "Of course, I would. And I told her so. I told her I'd sooner make love to her than any other woman in this room – wouldn't you – you son-of-a-gun? She is so lovely, Tom, that I had to tell her but you demanded an apology and I'll give her one." And the boxer strode over to the embarrassed girl and graciously told her that he was sorry and had meant no offence.

In later years Tom used to love to recount this tale of how close he was to becoming the world champion – or how far!

It was the beginning of a great friendship between the two. Indeed, popularity as a singer brought him many types of admirers. Some could be a nuisance, especially when they were would-be tenors who thought he had some kind of magic wand capable of turning them into Carusos overnight.

"If I can't sound like Caruso then I'll settle to sound like you, Mr Burke," wrote one of them. There was no answer to that, but many presented themselves in person at the stage door or at his hotel. If he had been unscrupulous there was a small fortune to have been made out of gullible singing fools. On one occasion Tom decided that 'art for art's sake' could take a back seat for once; this was because of a most pesistent man who had contacted him several times asking for singing lessons. One evening he propositioned the tenor in his hotel lobby, "I'm throwing a party, Mr Burke. You're welcome to come if you wish, only I want to do the singing. I've got plenty of dough and I want a lesson now – the party is tomorrow night. And, with no disrespect to you Mr Burke, I want to sound like Richard Tauber." He handed over a wad of notes. "Better make it snappy though, my train leaves in an hour."

After a crash course, the budding Tauber left the hotel beaming with smiles convinced he could sing the Austrian off the face of the earth.

But the sword swallower was the most bizarre of them all;

a character straight out of the pages of a Damon Runyan short story – 'Harry the Horse' of the brash, gaudy theatrical world of third-rate vaudeville; a fast-talking, over-dressed, big-mouthed Jack-of-all-trades who had made a fortune out of travelling around with a bunch of freaks. Sword swallowing was his speciality. When he retired he became a regular concert goer and happened to hear Tom sing in Chicago. So impressed was he that he decided there and then to come out of retirement and take up concert singing. He approached Tom for lessons. "I want to make a come-back, Mr Burke," he explained, "And I guess it'll be as a singer. I'm tired out with circus stuff and vaudeville acts. I guess I'll have a change. Maybe I'll go over to your country and do a tour – take in Covent Garden – who knows? I want to sing and I don't care a hoot how much it costs – name your fee, Mr Burke."

Tom attempted to tell this super optimist just how difficult it really was to reach a standard whereby he would make a living professionally. The sword swallower scoffed, "See here, Mr Burke, I've done the lot. I've walked ropes with the best. Gone over falls in a barrel, swallowed swords a yard long, thrown eggs twenty feet in the air and caught them in my mouth without a crack – and as for juggling balls of soot, well I've perfected the art on the vaudeville circuit. You ask around, Mr Burke – Denver City, Detroit, Dallas – you ask around. I've been all over so I don't reckon as learning to sing is going to beat a guy like me, Mr Burke – no siree!"

Tom was stuck for words, but in between more self praise from the showman he managed to tell him that it would take years of special exercises to repair the damage done to the muscles of the larynx by swallowing swords and it would be at least ten years before he could sing well enough to go on the concert platform. "Aw!" snorted the man in disgust, "You're just like the rest of 'em. You're in so you don't want anyone else to get in. Well be damned to you. I'll get there, you see, in spite of you. And next time you sing I hope you choke, you English bum."

A rider to the tale is provided by Tom who wrote, 'I have not seen his name at Covent Garden yet, but one never knows, especially if he's got the sense to adopt an unpronounceable foreign name.' As always, Burke could never resist a dig at the 'Garden' administrators. The 'bee in his bonnet' on this subject had become a hornet. In the American slang of which he was fond, he was beating the gag into the ground and seemed to forget that subsequent success at Covent Garden depended not only on having an unpronounceable name but on keeping one's tongue firmly in check.

Whilst on the subject of pronunciation, Tom's first meeting with Mae West is worth recording. He had only been in America for a short time and wasn't familiar with the 'lingo'. They met over cocktails. The outrageous possessor of the famous bust persisted in addressing him as 'Mr Boicke'. Thinking she was mistaken over the name he naively explained that it was Burke and not Boicke, actually spelling it out for her. "Oh I see now, Mr Burke," she answered. "Tell me, when do you start woicke?"

But opera had its funny moments also. The Chicago Company were playing in Detroit, Tom singing the tenor lead in *Pagliacci*. They had arrived at the part where the donkey is brought on. Suddenly to the amusement of everyone the donkey set up such a braying never before heard on the operatic stage. Even the singers began to laugh. He-haw, he-haw, he-haw, it carolled blithely and the singers dried up. The whole theatre was rocking with laughter. The man who had led him on tried to coax him off but the donkey wouldn't budge one inch. It was his evening and he wasn't departing the stage without a struggle. The man tugged harder but the animal stuck its feet firmly to the stage and pulled back. The opera was held up and it finally took several members of the chorus to remove the donkey, but not before a tug-of-war with its forefeet well out and its hind ones striving to get a grip of things. At last it was off but the opera could not continue until all concerned had had a jolly good laugh. Afterwards the Company were told that a circus donkey used in comedy routines had been substituted for the usual one. One cannot help but wonder if it was the revenge of the sword swallower?

For a very brief period Burke renewed his acquaintanceship with Enrico Caruso. This was shortly before the great tenor's premature death due to a burst blood vessel. Tom's liking for Enrico verged on idolatory so his joy new no bounds when Caruso appeared as a guest artist in operatic roles. Tom was in his company after a performance when the tenor, a prolific caricaturist was sketching the members of the cast. It was his custom to present every artist with whom he appeared with a caricature of themselves. In the company was a bass of the opposite personality to the tenor, a severe man who took everything with the utmost seriousness. He was very displeased with the drawing, considering it an insult. Caruso was most upset and, thinking that he had insulted the whole company, took them all out on the following morning to a celebrated hatter's where he bought a hat for every member. He insisted, however, that everyone wore the same coloured hat – grey.

'I never saw anything as funny,' wrote Tom, 'than the arrival that night at the theatre, everyone wearing a hat of the self same shape and colour . . . He was a great clown and loved to play practical jokes. He was a great smoker, too. Fifty to sixty cigarettes a day besides innumerable cigars. It is rather a funny thing that smoking is considered bad for the throat, yet I know of no great singer who is not also a great smoker.'

This was correct in Burke's own case also for he was very fond of cigars, though he became an avid snuff-taker in his later days.

Like his friend Caruso, Burke was the constant prey of beautiful women, many of whom could be most unscrupulous – the original Broadway Gold Diggers. Though the soul of discretion in print on this particular subject, he revealed one incident that had a tragic ending, unveiling yet another side of human nature and, in particular, the infatuation some women have with a voice which is just as true today.

'I was a guest at a most fashionable party. I had been introduced to one of the most beautiful girls I had ever seen and was dancing with her to the strains of a waltz played by Paul Whiteman's Band. It was *Roses of Picardy* and as we waltzed past the band Paul called out "Sing it,

Tom," On the spur of the moment I sang as we danced, and never will I forget the expression of my partner as I gave voice to the beautiful refrain. Every eye in the room was turned towards us but it was the eyes of this girl which fascinated me. I am not telling this story in a spirit of vanity, but in that girl's eyes there was something akin to adoration. I know now as I knew then that it was simply the infatuation of a voice. The dance came to an end with the end of the song. There was an intense silence followed by instant demands for more.

'We became very good friends and I was invited to her home. She was one of the young belles of New York and I was a greatly envied man. Soon, however, I began to notice a change in her demeanour. She became more serious and one morning I received a letter which put me in no doubt about her feelings.

'In this letter she told me it was not just my voice, but I'm certain there was nothing more than that behind any infatuation she had. I stopped visiting her house but from time to time we met, as we were bound to do, at parties to which we were both invited. On these occasions it was simply a shake of the head and a greeting and then as far away from each other as it was possible. Apparently this lovely girl who I had been so proud to know, could not forget my voice and there were times when I hated to sing when she was there because I could not help but see that wistful look in her eyes.

'I heard afterwards that she had told her parents all about it, and they decided to send her over to Europe for a time to get her out of the way in the hope that she would forget all about me. She sailed one Friday morning. I knew nothing of her departure, and it was a queer trick of fate when I received a telegram summoning me to the Free Trade Hall in Manchester to start an English tour. This was the very day after she had sailed. I sailed for home the very next day, fulfilled my engagements and then went to London to sing there. Imagine my amazement when almost the first person I met was this girl whom I had thought to be three thousand miles away.

'I knew that I must make it very clear that there must

never be anything of a romantic nature between us. We talked it over very dispassionately and sensibly. She was a very fine sensible girl and not one of those neurotic, stupid girls one so frequently meets.

'She smiled when we said goodbye, "In love with a voice, eh, Tom?" she remarked, repeating what I had suggested was really the case. She agreed to go back home and sailed within the next few days. Less than a fortnight afterwards I read of her death. It came as a terrible shock. Death after a short illness it said and that was all. But I often wonder what was the nature of her illness? She was so vibrant, vigorously healthy that it seemed impossible she could die so young.

'Poor Caruso. I wonder how many incidents of this kind occurred to him? And he did so love the ladies – as, I hope, most of us do. I have known him come to me and confess that the most 'bee-utifule' girl in the world was in love with him and how could he escape her pursuit?'

Years later he told a pupil that all he had to do to get a woman was to sing to her. The sexuality of present day singers is by no means a new phenomenon as today's generation seem to imagine.

The singers of old had their moments too. *Come Into the Garden Maud* sung by a sensual singer such as Burke could readily have been taken to imply 'Hop into Bed with Me Baby!', in modern parlance, by an infatuated camp-follower who travelled from concert to concert certain in the 'fact' that he was singing for her and her alone.

Philadelphia was a favourite city for Burke for it was synonymous with success to the tenor who was rated very highly by its concert audiences. To appear at the Stanley Theatre during Anniversary Week was an honour for an artist. A newspaper of the time ran the following article:

> 'Burke has great versatility in his singing. "I find", he told this paper recently, "that the public is most pleased by variety in song. The operatic arias are liked by many, but other music lovers would sooner hear simple ballads – my operatic training inclines me to the aria but I delight in singing the expressive song and it is always a pleasure for me to hear the responsive applause of an audience when I have sung a song like *Mother*

Machree.

"I am always glad to sing in Philadelphia. Audiences here are discriminating and that is especially pleasing to a singer. He knows that when he is applauded there must be something meritorious in his work – and such knowledge is gratifying. Indeed, throughout America there is a high standard of musical taste in spite of all that may be said about the American's penchant for jazz." '

Although Burke did not comment on this occasion he detested jazz and made no secret of his feelings, describing it as 'Negroid noise'.

Between engagements, and to counteract the excesses of late-night parties, he would work out at gymnasiums, often with well-known sportsmen. Two of his particular friends were Tommy Burns, the boxing champion, and Eugene Sandow, reputed to be the strongest man in the world. Visits to race-tracks, ball games and riding lessons from leading jockeys took up the time when he wasn't travelling between engagements and rehearsing.

Those five years spent in the States after the nervous breakdown were probably the happiest ones of his life, although he could not have known it at the time. And yet in another respect they were wasted years. True, in analysis he could claim to have established himself as a concert singer on the first-class celebrity circuit but in operatic circles he had not made a great impression, even though he could regard his performances as highly successful. The competition was fierce in the tenor division. To be a member of Mary Garden's Chicago Opera Company was an achievement in itself, but being one amidst such a wealth of talent made for sporadic engagements rather than regular appearances. In between he had to take work where he could find it. The truth is that in England he stood out like a shining torch, in America he was one of several and one is forced to ponder on the wisdom of remaining in the U.S.A. for so long. To do so is to reach the inevitable conclusion that he would have fared far better had he taken the lyrical operatic roles offered to him before his departure to the States – had he done so he would have consolidated his reputation in Europe and eventually become the target for La Scala Milan and the Metropolitan in New York. It is not idle speculation to say he could have conquered the musical world.

That he never sang operatic roles at the 'Met' was a bitter disappointment but in view of the in fighting that went on in the mecca of American opera it is hardly surprising that a Britisher could not get an engagement at this time. The Municipal Opera Company of New York is not an organisation that evokes many memories today, even in the city itself. What seemed a brilliant idea, conceived with such enthusiasm, turned into a damp squib. Indirectly Burke was the cause of its brief life and, in one sense, its dramatic climax. Whenever the chance presented itself he would speak impassionately on his pet themes of opera and the masses and the engagement of native artists. Even in America he still held the view that the plum engagements were offered to non-English speaking singers first.

This experiment in musical philanthropy came about in an unusual way. Burke was introduced to a hugely successful business man, one Ralph Sternberg, who sympathised with Burke's views when he went on to voice the sense of injustice aroused in him by the indifference and, in many cases, opposition he had seen manifested towards English and American singers in their own lands unless they had won recognition first in Europe and the mere pittances, compared to the stipends paid to singers of alien citizenship, when they were employed. Sternberg was greatly taken by Burke's sincerity in this matter and introduced him to a lawyer by the name of Frederick W. Spurhing. He, in turn, listened to the tenor's case and at the close asked Tom a direct question.

"Tell me, Mr Burke, what do you feel ought to be done to right the wrong you feel so keenly?"

"Give the people a show," replied Burke. "Give grand opera in English a show, give grand opera singers who want to sing in English a show, give the men and women who want to compose grand opera in English a show, give people who want to hear grand opera in English a show to hear it. What Gilbert and Sullivan, Balfe, De Koven and Herbert have done in light opera Americans and Englishmen can do in grand opera if the chance is given to them and they are properly supported."

"But how are you going to give them a show?" persisted Sternberg.

"By educating the masses of music lovers and arousing their interest in grand opera and singing in their native tongue – in short, by putting on grand opera in English."

The plan appealed to Sternberg as a form of philanthropy well worth a trial. Spurhing was very interested and the triumvirate was formed – Burke as President of the opera company, Sternberg General Manager and Spurhing as Legal Adviser and Counsellor.

Enter then the New York Municipal Opera Company to a barrage of publicity with Tom Burke looked upon as a man with a mission; a pioneer for his principles motivated by the same fighting spirit as the trail blazers of the Old West. In typically American fashion, the whole 'show' was to be on an immensely lavish scale. Charles Stoneham, the owner of the 'Giants' baseball team, was approached and willingly agreed to let the Company stage productions on the Polo Grounds in the open air – completely free of charge. Seemingly Tom had stumbled on yet another amazingly philanthropic man about whom the press waxed eulogistically:

> 'Stoneham will do far more than just loan Mr Burke and the Opera Company his grounds, he will provide free of charge the necessary attaches, such as Box Office Cashiers, Gate-keepers and ushers and the ground's electrical lighting equipment for night performances. He will provide the space in which to store the stage, and motor-trucks to transport it to the spot in the playing field where it will be set up. Burke is planning a spectacular and Stoneham will back him to the hilt.'

Tom had found two fairy godfathers. Seemingly he was on the pig's back. Inspired by this solid mass of benevolence, he aired his own dreams to a press greedy for news of this fascinating venture into culture for the masses: 'The purpose of the Municipal Opera is not merely to give seven weeks of opera at the Polo Grounds this summer. It guarantees to produce each season one American opera composed by an

American citizen, the work to be presented to be selected by authoritative and competent judges from the compositions submitted. A scholarship will also be founded in one of the leading universities which will enable the winner to devote himself to the study and composition of American Operatic Music.'

Ever the clutcher for unreachable stars Tom merrily planned a series of light works to commence the season; light operas by Herbert and Balfe to test the temperature of taste before expanding into heavier and grander productions. A stage on wheels was manufactured 120 feet wide and 60 feet deep, the roof fitted with flies, light bridges and all the panoply of a playhouse designed for massive productions catering for the appearance of 250 people at one time on stage. A chorus of a hundred singers was recruited from musical conservatories and opera schools and a whole army of technicians and, as befitted such lavishness, an orchestra of sixty musicians.

But the bubble of moonshine burst before it could even prove that it was indeed the unsubstantial dream-child of Utopian visionaries, as forecast by the 'level-headed' citizens of the New York financial world. The trills of the coloratura soprano and the ebullient longings of the tenor were never heard on the sacred air of the baseball stadium. Rows over the management became the order of the day, the proposed philanthropy was not being turned into expendable cash as quickly as Burke expected or desired. Disgusted with the whole venture which had turned sour, he quit as the President taking with him the entire cast of singers as well as most of the technicians. Exit the New York Municipal Opera Company. Instead enter *The Tom Burke Opera Company*, overtured by an enthralled press in quotations from its Principal who forecast nationwide tours of light and grand opera – a People's Opera Company. Already Burke had been assured of a Broadway run. Where the tenor was finding the finance they did not know and he was not forthcoming with the information. *But*, they hinted, he had found backers.

For a time the venture was successful, although keeping strictly to a diet of Gilbert and Sullivan which he found very digestible fare for music lovers on tour. The Broadway run did come off, but lack of finance eventually closed the Company. The tenor's managerial ability and business acumen were light years behind his ability as a singer. More, Tom was a free-lance singer, glad to accept the employment he professed to detest – *REVUE*. To be considered by the theatrical press as 'the finest tenor in vaudeville today' was not the ultimate acclamation in his personal dream world. But with nearly all his money tied up in investments which he hoped would, in the not too distant future, turn him into a very wealthy man, he took what the agents had to offer, aware that any illusions he had about singing exclusively in Grand Opera were so much pie in the sky. The tides of fortune ebbed and flowed, concert tours, one with Marion Talley, H.M.V.'s 'American Melba', and the fulfilment of his most prized ambition – to perform on the stage of the Metropolitan Opera House. A concert performance only but nevertheless he had fulfilled his ambition and was a resounding success. The ghost of the Hippodrome debacle had been laid many times since that fateful Sunday evening in 1921 but this Metropolitan appearance screwed it down securely in its coffin.

More offers of operatic engagements came his way as a result, but fate commanded that they were not to be fulfilled.

'. . . I was in better voice than ever and the public were over-generous to me. It seemed as though I were truly set to really make my mark in opera when something happened which caused a sudden upheaval in all my plans and future. I was in bed one Saturday morning when a cablegram arrived from a London man offering me the opportunity of returning to London with the promise of engagements, the first of which was to sing at the Free Trade Hall, Manchester.

'Can I ever describe the urge that came upon me at that moment? The longing to see my loved ones, and the yearning to be back in England even though it meant giving up my operatic engagements in the States.

'It was 8.45 a.m. when I received that cablegram, and in order to reach England in time to sing in Manchester I had to catch the *Leviathan* at 11 o'clock. I was out of that bed like a shot and on the telephone to my lawyer. I told him to book my passage, get the necessary slip from the Income Tax authorities saying that I had duly paid all the taxes demanded of me, and see that my permit to leave the country, together with my passport, were OK.

' "You must be mad!" he exclaimed over the 'phone.

' "I may be mad," I replied. "but I'm sailing on that boat."

'I flung some clothes into my trunks and then discovered I had barely time to catch the boat. I got into a taxi, and dashed off, just in time to hear the blast of the syren announcing the departure of the ship. I skidded up the gangway just before it was pulled in and, without overcoat or baggage, just got aboard in time.

'I did not care. I was going home. For seven years I had not set foot in England, and only those who have experienced an exile of this kind can ever appreciate what it means. That voyage seemed like an eternity, and I remember that when I saw the white cliffs of England looming in the distance I burst into tears. We are an emotional race, we Irish, but again – why not?'

ACT VII

Tom was hardly back on English soil before he was providing good copy for the newspaper men. One paper blazed the headline:

> '**TOM BURKE A JOCKEY!**
>
> Mr Burke's ambition to ride a
> Grand National Winner
>
> Having achieved fame as a singer, Mr Tom Burke noted British tenor, is seeking fresh worlds to conquer and has fixed his attention on the Turf.
>
> "It has always been my ambition to ride as a jockey in the Grand National," he said on his return to England on Saturday from America where he has been singing with the Chicago Opera Company. "I've been training," he added, "to get down to the proper weight and have reduced so much I now weigh under 12 stones. If I'm lucky I'll ride the winner next year." '

This was no idle boast or show of flamboyancy. Burke was sufficiently sure of his own abilities at whatever he undertook to believe he could actually win the National. Like many of his dreams it never reached fruition for he did not compete.

This 'giving off the mouth' was a habit he caught in America, and one is struck by the similarity between Burke's extrovert personality and that of the bizarre showmanship personified by the sword-swallower and showman extra-ordinary. Maggie Teyte of the golden voice and caustic tongue used an Americanism when she said of him, "Tom

Burke was so bum of himself like all tenors."

Another paper printed the following article:

> ' "Take it from me, boy, England is the best place to live in."
>
> So said Tom Burke, the Lancashire tenor, to a press representative on his return from America.
>
> "I hope I have come to stay for ever. I left America because I got nostalgia."
>
> Those who lament the non-financial success of opera in England will find some comfort in his statement that in Chicago, though opera is amazingly patronised, they lose between £70,000 and £80,000 a year. "They justify the loss on the ground that opera is an essential form of education," said Mr Burke.'

On the subject of broadcasting, Tom was adamant that he would not broadcast on artistic grounds. "Broadcasting and cinemas are ruining concerts in America. I am afraid that it will be the same here and in other countries. I will definitely not sing over the air." A statement particularly interesting in view of subsequent happenings.

Percy Pitt, Burke's conductor in several operas, thought differently. He had pioneered operatic broadcasts in 1923 and had this to say in *Music Masterpieces* a magazine of which he was the Editor:

> 'Naturally, there was anxiety in certain quarters at the beginning that broadcasting might have the effect of depleting our audiences. It was argued that if people could hear opera amid the comfort of their own homes there would be little inclination to make a journey to the opera house.
>
> But events quickly proved that box office receipts were to benefit rather than otherwise. Many people came to Covent Garden for the first time after hearing opera on the wireless. They were frank enough to say they had never heard opera before, and had enjoyed it so much that they desired not only to hear it but to see it. The practice resorted to later of transmitting single acts instead of complete operas had the effect of stimulating interest.
>
> Listeners who had heard a single act of an opera on the wireless were so impressed that they bought tickets for the purpose of

hearing the remaining acts. One woman came and purchased a number of operatic libretti in order that her invalid brother could follow the works as they were broadcast.

There is no doubt that broadcasting, by advertising the beauties of opera, has helped it. The benefit, in fact, has been mutual, for operas are always among the most popular features of wireless programmes.

The foundations of great things were laid during those early days of 1923. If it has been possible to carry on the form of pioneer work that was begun then, the credit is due to a large extent, if not wholly, to the interest taken by Mr H.V. Higgins, chairman of the Grand Opera Syndicate, whose far-seeing policy and broad-minded outlook enabled him to realise what inestimable benefits were being conferred upon the community at large by the popularisation of wireless transmission as far as theatrical entertainments are concerned.'

Once again the outspoken tenor was airing views contrary to those of Higgins. The very first operatic broadcast took place on January 8th, 1923 when two acts of *The Magic Flute* were given. In view of the historic interest of the occasion, I give a list of the artists who took part in the performance under the conductorship of Percy Pitt: Gertrude Johnson, Sarah Fischer, Raymond Ellis, Walter Hyde and Robert Radford.

The Albert Hall, London, on a Sunday in May, 1927, was the scene for Burke's return to concert singing in the capital. It was one long triumph. He was called upon to give so many encores of items that the number it was first intended he should sing was doubled. The *Morning Post* was only one of the papers waxing ecstatic about the tenor's return to the English concert platform:

'The great charm of Mr Burke's singing is his diction. One can hear every word even in the vast Albert Hall. He sings, too, with conviction and phrases like a musician. He has a real tenor voice of unusually beautiful quality.'

- - - - - - -

'When he could feel himself back on the operatic stage for a moment in voluptuously singable phrases by Massenet, he let himself go and sang in a way that made one hope that the rumour that he is to appear at Covent Garden in the course of the season opening tonight, will not be allowed to remain rumour only.'

Uncredited review.

- - - - - -

'The Albert Hall unusually crowded for a brilliant afternoon, simply roared its applause, insisting on many encores and Burke responded generously. One encore was *La Mattinata* by Leoncavallo and with the first notes from the accompanist the applause started again. Then there was a request from the Royal Box occupied by St. Dunstan's men. Finally, the tenor was obliged to come forward and make a speech.

Daily Sketch.

Tom's partner at this concert was the welsh-born contralto Leila Megane. Wherever he sang now such reviews had positively guaranteed a full house. Almost within a few weeks he had restored his position as the leading English tenor and the leading European houses were vying with one another for his services.

Covent Garden, however, did not appear to be anxious to clutch the returned tenor to its bosom and he made only one appearance in the 1927 season which began in May, and this as a substitution for tenor Dino Borgioli who, from all accounts, was having a bad patch voice-wise. Tom grabbed the opportunity eagerly. Herman Klein, that opera oracle and doyen of critics, found the Lancashire tenor a decided improvement on Borgioli. The opera was *Rigoletto*, always a good vehicle for Burke's dramatic qualities, with Alexander Kipnis and Maria Ivogun. Burke certainly had admirers amongst the elitist publications for he was a particular favourite with the *Times*:

'A voice that will ring round the house and coo the gentlest love-song, at once a clarion and a dove, makes a duke irresistable to the Gildas and Maddalanas of the stage and conquers all audiences. His brilliant singing made a perfect foil to Signor Stabile's powerful Rigoletto and Mm Ivogun's silver-tongued Gilda.'

But it is quite obvious that the old bogey – nerves – was at it again, for not all the reviews were so kind. Wrote 'F.T.' in an uncredited clipping:

'*Rigoletto* was repeated last night at Covent Garden with Mr Tom Burke appearing in the part of the Duke. There are some good points about Mr Burke's singing; his diction is good, his mezza voce at times agreeable, while his top B at the end of *La Donna e Mobile* nearly brought the house down.

On the other hand, his voice lacks true expression. He might have been singing *Bella Figlia de l'amore* to his mother-in-law. Further, he seemed to take insufficient trouble with recitatives, reserving all his energies for the arias.'

And again:

'Mr Burke was obviously extremely nervous. The result was a certain tightness of the throat and a disposition, in a tiny degree, to sing flat. But he soon became so much at ease that the power and beauty of his tone reasserted themselves.

Mr Burke sang in Act I worse than I have ever heard him sing, and in the rest of the opera better than he or any other British tenor has ever sung in my recollection.'

The *Daily Mail*:

'It is certain that though he seemed a trifle nervous last night, the mellowness and the peculiar lyrical qualities of his voice will stand comparison with any other tenor voice we have heard this year. Above all he does not suffer from the "long note complex" which often mars performances otherwise highly praiseworthy.'

There can be little doubt that the inconsistencies reported in press notices, particularly in opera, were the direct result of anxiety – neurosis, in his day simply called 'nerves'. His closest friends have told me that he admitted there were times when he went through sheer hell. It is hardly surprising, then, that Burke took to the bottle to bolster his confidence. To condemn is easy. How many top opera stars in the world today take tranquillizers one wonders? A glass of whisky was the Valium of Burke's day. Stories about Burke being an alcoholic are completely untrue. Drink was never his master. A latter-day pupil recalls a social gathering when the tenor was discussing singing with some of his pupils. One of them rather tactlessly raised the subject of drink in connection with Jussi Bjorlings death, saying it was a terrible shame that such a superb singer should take to the bottle. Tom quietly told his pupil that he could have no conception of the tremendous responsibility a singer of Bjorling's fame has to carry. Fame, he explained, can be fatal to a person not equipped emotionally to cope with it. Rather nicely put in his place, the aspiring vocalist asked Tom did *he* ever drink before a performance. "Always!" was the blunt reply and that was the end of the discussion.

Whilst in America he was unaware that a battle of words had been taking place in the press on his favourite subject. Hugh Walpole had declared that British singers were inferior to foreign artists. Beecham was furious. He wrote a scathing condemnation and declared that Britain had the finest singers in the world. Truth was, he declared, they were not given the chances to prove this in their own country.

True to form, Burke was soon backing up Beecham in the *Daily Dispatch*, and this only two days before he was due to sing at Covent Garden which makes a mockery of a statement made by an American reporter who referred to Burke as 'a very diplomatic young man.' Journalism gone mad, indeed. In the statement to the *Dispatch* he came down heavily against the repeated policy of employing foreign artists:

> 'It should be possible to stage an opera at Covent Garden with an all-Empire cast, which would outshine any in the world. I would cast *Aida*, for example, as follows:
>
> Eva Turner — Foster Richardson
> Tom Burke — Harold Williams
> Norman Allin — Madame Austral
>
> The opera should be conducted by Sir Thomas Beecham and I guarantee that such an opera would create a furore in this country. But I can never see it being produced. Even if the public

recognise the merit of British voices, the people responsible for the operas have yet to recognise it.

In my opinion my name, because it is typically English has been a great handicap to me in this country. I am tempted to ask why it is that Alfred Piccaver is the rage in Vienna and why Eva Turner, the greatest living dramatic soprano, is not brought to England to sing instead of charming audiences in America.'

Noble sentiments these may well have been, but seeming to ignore that in his own case he had fared very well. It had been his own decision to go to America.

Between this sole performance in *Rigoletto* and the opening of the new season in 1928 he was kept busily employed singing opera in Paris, Berlin and Vienna and following on was an extensive concert tour of Britain which took him to Leigh and a joyous reunion with Josephine. The national 'dailies' made great play of his homecoming and origins.

PIT-BOY SINGS TO HIS OWN PEOPLE

"Our Lad"

"Come on, Tom lad, show us what tha's made of" growled a gruff voice last night from the back of the Co-operative Hall in Leigh.

Said Mr Burke, "I shall know nearly every face in the Hall, and every one of them knows me. Many of them will have known me since I was a boy. It is a glorious experience, but a highly nervous one. I shall try not to look at any of them."

The applause rose to a thunderous climax as 'Our Tom' walked on stage. Prominent business men and colliers, freshly washed from the afternoon shift, clapped side by side; Lancashire housewives and mothers stamped their feet in excitement. They would have cheered him if he had told jokes or stood on his head. To speak to elderly people in Leigh is to fully realise the pride the folk of this little town, noted more for grime than culture, felt for the local boy who conquered the world of music by sheer determination.

Then all was deadly still, the tenor's knuckles showing white as he clenched a handkerchief in his fist – suddenly a volley of chords from Percy Kahn at the piano and the audience was swept away in the enchantment of *Andre Chenier*; then a succession of arias. Burke announced to great applause that he had been asked to sing *Turandot* in Rome and, as if to celebrate the honour with his friends, sang *Nessun Dorma* from the opera. At the finale he received a long standing ovation – a fitting amen from his own people.'

During this visit, which he made sure was a reasonably lengthy one, he found time to put the local amateurs through their paces in rehearsals for a musical comedy, and once again rekindled his association with St. Joseph's Church where he caused quite a stir by singing incognito in the choir. But most of all he enjoyed helping his father on the piggery and smallholding in which Vincent Burke was now established thanks to the financial help of his singing son. Tea, Lancashire style in the parlour, was a great treat and he declared that it was the happiest week in his whole career. And plain bread and jam was just as tasty as any other food, no matter how exotic.

Be that as it may, Tom had got the taste for good living and was living life to the full in a style befitting an international celebrity, comfortably ensconced in a fashionable Mayfair address, complete with butler and a Rolls Royce; an elegant sanctuary of rest whenever his engagements allowed him to use it.

Not that Burke cared for resting. Instead, he drove himself hard professionally and socially. All-night parties, often in the company of his great friend the Prince of Wales, were not the ideal recreation for a man who needed to be in sparkling form with a clear head the next day.

The *TOM BURKE TOUR* continued on its financially successful way and was only terminated by more operatic engagements in Italy, Spain and Vienna – this period of his career is hazy due to the destruction of operatic archives by bombing, but for certain Tom sang with Tetrazzini amongst other celebrated prima donnas of the era.

Burke now had the world at his feet and proceeded to play with it like a football. He was earning enormous fees for his services, but he could never keep money for long and lavished it on new found 'friends' and his female admirers.

The Caruso image was still a halter around his neck. Drink had become his prop and a reputation for unreliability was not, in the long run, to make him a favourite with concert-booking agents and impresarios.

Marie arrived back in England to play Julie in *Showboat* at Drury Lane, which enjoyed one of the most successful runs in British theatrical history, her singing of *Bill* being one of the highlights of a wonderful show. The appearance of Paul Robeson and his show-stopping *Ol' Man River* contributed to spotlight Marie Burke's name as one of the first magnitude in the world of musical comedy. Besides Robeson, Marie's other co-stars were Edith Day and baritone Howett Worster.

During 1928 a decree nisi was granted to Marie on the grounds of her husband's adultery with a woman in a London hotel. News of the divorce acted adversely on Tom's career, prudish public opinion expected exemplary behaviour from its idols. A reported 'affair' with an American actress added to his notoriety in the public's eyes. The playboy image was very much abhorrent to impresarios who adopted a Victorian hypocritical stand as self-appointed guardians of the nation's morals. Crass hypocrisy, for many had actresses as mistresses.

Artistically, Burke was on top of the tree and certainly couldn't be dissatisfied with the doyens of Covent Garden when selected to play Turriddu to Eva Turner's Santuzza in *Cavalleria Rusticana* in June and July of 1928. This all-Lancashire partnership – Oldham and Leigh – caught the public imagination and was held up as an example of all that was good in British art. If the handicap of plain English names did exist then it was given the lie by the reception Turner and Burke were given both by the public and the critics. The *Times* said of Eva Turner: 'Her voice is more like a superb instrument than a human organ' and Burke 'Exhibited much of the southern style.'

The *Manchester Guardian* wrote:

> 'Both works (the other being *I Pagliacci*) were given the eloquent apology of exceptionally great performances. In Mascagni's work both the principal parts were taken by British singers who, while

finding no permanent work worthy of their powers to do at home, have recently helped to make opera in Italy what it is.

Tom Burke's voice rang out soundly and smoothly even in the most strenuous passages assigned to Turriddu and was free of the cheap effects with which one has had occasion to reproach this singer at his concert appearances. The stage is obviously his true sphere.'

The 12th July, 1928 saw him again renewing his partnership with Margaret Sheridan, once more in *La Boheme*. The opera which had projected him into stardom in a single night was, ironically, the one in which Burke made his farewell to Covent Garden. It was his swan song at the Royal Opera House.

Yet the voice was better than ever. An article written by Leslie J. Thorpe, the celebrated accompanist, in 1928 makes fascinating reading to lovers of tenor singing:

'When Caruso died, seven years ago, the musical world was robbed of one of its leading figures, as Caruso at the time of his death was certainly the most famous tenor in the world; and it is interesting to lovers of vocal music, both operatic and ballad, to speculate who is the greatest tenor singing today. Beginning at home, two names immediately occur to me – John McCormack and Tom Burke. . . '

He continues by naming other tenors – Tito Schipa, Martinelli, Charles Hackett, Lauritz Melchior, Joseph Hislop, Alfred Piccaver, Miguel Fleta, Fernand Ansseau and Jan Kiepura – but terminates by saying:

'With such a selection of wonderful voices it is certainly difficult to say who is the finest singer today, but in my opinion two of the singers mentioned are finer and more finished artists than the others spoken of. Bear in mind that I have accompanied scores of fine singers. They are John McCormack and Tom Burke. McCormack the wonderful ballad singer, and Tom Burke the great operatic tenor, and to decide which is the finer singer of the two is a difficult matter.'

This was no glibly given opinion. Thorpe was a connoisseur of the first order as well as having claim to accompanying such eminent exponents as Caruso, Charles Santley, McCormack, Pareto and Albani, amongst a host of others.

Almost concurrent with this article the *Daily Mail* ran a popularity poll of the world's tenors. Burke was placed number one. In the light of such great esteem one would assume that the Columbia Gramophone Company cashed in on the tenor's fame. Such is not the case for he made only a handful of recordings for them after his return from the U.S.A. It is possible that by recording for other companies under a pseudonym he angered the company; the fact remains that the listening public were denied the chance of collecting regular issues by the tenor. The dearth of his art on wax is another cause of the obscurity into which he has fallen. What a shame that such a voice as Burke's was not recorded for posterity anywhere near as abundantly as the voices of his contemporaries, and it remains a puzzle that he should have to go to the lower divisions of the recording business to make records. A mere drop in the vast musical ocean represents the Lancashire man, whilst other great singers recorded prolifically – Peter Dawson, Richard Tauber, John McCormack, Norman Allin are just a few whose contributions filled up considerable pages of catalogue space – yet this source of income, which surely must have been very considerable had he recorded regularly for one of the premier companies, was denied him. In consequence lesser tenors were heard far more frequently and became better known to the tens of thousands of gramophone addicts. This, coupled with his obstinacy over broadcasting, was akin to castrating the hard-earned fame of opera and concert tours. Soprano Miriam Licette in an article 'Wireless and the Opera' wrote in 1927:

'I think it will be generally admitted that opera in this country is not in the healthy state it ought to be in. Large numbers of people have never heard an opera, a condition of affairs that would be difficult to equal in any other country.

They are appalled by the mere mention of the name in many cases. It is not surprising, therefore, that operatic companies are continually beset by financial anxieties and find it a hard struggle to exist.

Yet consider that the outlook is more hopeful at present than it has been for a long time. Public taste always tends to reach a higher level, and this in itself must have its inevitable effect. But there is also a factor at work which is going to have a very powerful influence in the future.

I think it may easily be that broadcasting will affect all forms of musical activity in a way that we little dream of at the moment. Already one age-long illusion has been shattered, the illusion that nobody wants to hear good music. I suppose we may assume that broadcasting programmes would not consist so largely of music if no one wished to hear it.

I have had a rather extensive experience of broadcasting, and of the keen interest of listeners. Often enough I receive letters of appreciation, and I believe other artists do. I have generally found that there is exceptional enthusiasm for operatic items. Many people have heard them for the first time through the medium of the wireless, and have been astonished to find that they could enjoy them.

Gradually, too, the attitude of aloofness on the part of musicians is being abandoned. Today there is only a mere handful of artists who do not broadcast, at least occasionally, It all makes for the best interests of music.'

But Burke could be extremely stubborn and had his own views on the subject and would not broadcast.

Terry O'Neill was the name Burke adopted to record what he referred to as 'pot-boilers' for Edison Bell and Crown (Woolworth's) labels. For Picadilly he used the pseudonym Pat O'Sullivan, for Parlophone John O'Grady – the Irish influence in these names being very obvious; several of these 'pot-boilers' – sentimental ballads – were written by the tenor and some were published as sheet music. Possibly the most successful was a song described as 'the most beautiful ballad of the year' – *I Heard You Sing* (recorded as O'Grady). This was a poem written by Tom and set to music by Harry Soloway, the violinist who toured with him on the concert circuit. Others included *That Old-fashioned Cot in Kildare*, *When You Come Home to Rest*, and *I Loved Her Best of All*. But he never made a name for himself as a songwriter. In 1929 he transferred to the Dominion label to record several numbers, which leads directly to the question: Were Oreste Di Bernardi and Tom Burke one and the same man? Many collectors think they were. When Burke heard one of the Di Bernardi recordings on the reverse of one of his Dominions he was annoyed at the suggestion that it was his voice. He went into a long winded description of Bernardi's phrasing as compared to his own. So who was Di Bernardi? One must realise that in the 'twenties and 'thirties name changing was a common practice. Singers who recorded 'exclusively for Columbia', for instance, often altered their names to earn royalties with lesser companies. Frank Titterton, a prolific recording artist, was heard under various guises on several labels, particularly as Francesca Vada. But Di Bernardi was not him. My money is on Lappas, though the voice is not dissimilar to Greek 'tenor' Costa Milona who made scores of records for various companies during the interwar period.

'To my ears the voice has a very rapid vibrato but more than this I'm basing my opinion on the style of singing.' Is the verdict of an international voice-critic who has helped me considerably though wishing to remain anonymous. 'As soon as Burke starts *O Primavera* the singing comes alive as it doesn't with Bernardi. The contrast is marked when you listen to Bernardi on the 'flip' side singing *Torna a Surriento* of Dominion B.32. Tom would have let rip more and made more effect in *Surriento*. Quite a number of unknown tenors (and others) were released during the 1927-32 era drawn from American sources so this is a possibility. Bernardi was definitely not Tom Burke although I have heard that Burke made records under an assumed Italian name. Could this have been in Italy?'

Or was Guido Volpi Burke? An obviously assumed name and a fine voice to go with it. A sample can be heard on Dominion B.25. I feel that Guido Volpi could indeed be Tom – to my auditory senses he sounds much more like him than Di Bernardi does.

Paul Morby, collector and great admirer of Tom, wrote to me: 'One Sunday morning I played the tape down the phone to Tom at his home in Sutton. He was aggressively angry with me at the suggestion; "Paul, you are a fraud. I thought you knew more about singing than that? How could these two voices be me?" I also played him a 10" Green Columbia I had found in the American search – *Kathleen Mavourneen* . . . Pure Tom! He cried on the phone. "That's me Paul. . . I can't remember making it. . . where on earth did you get it? I've never heard it before." Tom was incredibly honest in that way."

It is not impossible that Tom recorded the numbers thinking they were going out under his own name – and he told several correspondents who aided my research that he did record under an Italian name. 'I did all sorts of things in those days,' he said, a rather hazy admission that he wasn't really certain about the details of his somewhat haphazard recording career. For certain he never kept a list of recordings.

The practice of putting two different singers on the one disc was by no means unknown in the 78 era, but it seems strange that this should have been acceptable to Burke at a time when his star was very much in the ascendancy. One would think that it would have been very much in Dominion's interests to run the Burke name for all it was worth. He was undoubtedly their star artist so why lessen this prestige by coupling his name with unknown singers like Di Bernardi? Singers are notoriously unreliable regarding their past recordings anyhow, and Tom particularly so, for he was never one for keeping diaries of his engagements and, in fact, in his later life didn't possess any of his original records. So, as Sherlock Holmes would say, "The problem is a three-pipe one, Watson," and an intriguing exercise in musical detection if these old Dominions can still be found.

During the period 1927 to 1930 it is hard to know where truth ends and legend begins for there have been many stories told about the tenor's often outrageous behaviour. My sources are Burke's own personal friends which he made in the twilight of his life, loving nothing better than listening to his adventures over a bottle of wine. Taking the advice of a tenor friend of Burkes at this juncture I will 'forget the facts and print the legend'. One of the favourites is the tale he often recounted of an operatic incident involving an eminent English baritone who enjoyed a long and successful career. Burke's flirting with the ladies of the chorus annoyed him and before the start of the opera he chastised Tom as if he were a naughty schoolboy. The tenor kept his mouth tightly sealed and the baritone felt that he had made his point of view firmly understood. There would be no more nonsense with the chorus ladies. Or so he thought, but he didn't know the incorrigible ex-collier's reputation for always getting his own back and resorting to basic crudity to do so, if necessary. On stage the baritone was warbling blithely. Burke was standing behind him clutching a sword. After his aria the baritone bowed but as he did do felt a pointed object prodding his seat and heard the words, "Mind your own business, see. If you don't I'll shove this bloody thing up your arse!" The next second Tom was singing a tender love song to the heroine. The baritone never interfered again.

While rehearsing for *La Boheme* in 1928 Sir John Barbirolli very pointedly stopped the orchestra twice during Burke's singing.

"Are you stopping because of me?" the tenor enquired, bluntly.

"Yes," said the conductor.

"Oh, I see," answered Burke. "I've got to have a rest sometime, I'm not a machine. I could come down there and do your job but *you* can't do mine," and with that he stormed out.

The conductor reported the incident to the producer who had the unenviable job of soothing a heated situation. The maestro was not pleased when told that the audience were paying to hear Mr Burke sing and that he was an accomplished singer who would be perfect on the night. Burke was pacified and the conductor reluctantly agreed to continue even though he felt his authority had been usurped. Burke's final riposte, "Ugh! I never had this trouble with Toscanini." must have been a hard pill to swallow for the Italian was a noted firebrand. Burke had the greatest regard for Toscanini and his remark was the truth – birds of a feather. . . ?

The second incident concerning royalty is another legend which has become synonymous with the tenor's name, recounted in so many differing versions that one begins to wonder if it did actually take place at all. That an 'incident' did occur is true enough, as far as I can ascertain, and I have good reason to believe that this version is the most accurate. Burke was a guest artist at a private concert given in the presence of royalty at Covent Garden. It was an 'Invitation only' affair. He was to sing *On With the Motley* from *Pagliacci*. The concert was not a costume affair but Tom decided to put on his Pagliacci costume to sing the aria. When he arrived on the stage he was the worse for drink. Yet he sang magnificently. After his performance he bowed rather tipsily to the audience, sang an encore, then looked up at the Royal Box and enquired, "Where's the King?" There was an embarrassed deadly silence. "Oh, there he is," announced Burke and, pointing to himself called out, "I'm the King. The King of song." The incident didn't ruin the tenor as most people imagine, but it was yet another nail in his own private coffin at the 'Garden' and the bad publicity allied to that he had already acquired made him *non persona grata* to the administrators and many theatrical agents. Unquestionably, His Majesty was not offended for who sang the National Anthem at the 1930 Royal Command Performance – Tom Burke!

It is well known that this sort of outrageous behaviour was not unusual in the operatic world yet it was unacceptable from a British artist. What the establishment would accept from temperamental artists such as the volcanically eruptive Theodore Chaliapin it would not condone in a native singer. Yet Burke was a lamb compared to the tantrum-throwing Russian. Quite definitely, exhibitionism was considered the exclusive province of the foreigners. The British operatic world was not ready for the irascibility of Tom Burke. In the words of one of his best friends, tenor Alexander Hood; "You didn't meet Tom – you experienced him."

It was almost as if he had a commitment in life which demanded of him total dedication to being the outstanding person in any crowd. Yet to use the hackneyed cliché 'life and soul of the party' would not be entirely correct because of his delight in causing acute embarrassment amongst company. He loved to shock people and revelled in the reputation he had aquired. As if he felt he had a God given right to be indiscreet and that his career was guaranteed not to falter whatever he did or said. Influential ears took note. Later on when he needed friends in his fight back many turned a blind eye to his misfortunes.

The 'Irishness' of his character has often been blamed for his downfall. Yet there have been scores of completely stable Irish artists; likewise, there is a large percentage of Irish people who are non-drinkers. Nevertheless, there is little doubt that Burke inherited the 'devil may care' trait of some of that nation's sons and he was always proud to claim that he was an Irishman. A friend challenged this, stating that he was born in England and was therefore English. "Rubbish!" roared Tom, "If I'd been born in an aeroplane would that make me a ruddy sky-ite?" Certainly he was a confused personality, an enigma; an arrogant know-all to some people, yet the very essence of kindness and affability to others, and undoubtedly the arrogance in his complex make-up manifested itself in the presence of authority. Hardly surprising, then, that he made enemies in his own profession, and yet I am convinced that he was subjected to jealousies within the profession which contributed to his subsequent relapse into comparative eclipse.

In 1929 he was touring in *Dear Love*, a musical play which finally landed at the 'Palace' theatre in November. In Birmingham Tom was struck down with a severe dose of Laryngitis which necessitated several weeks rest. On the subject of musical comedy he had this to say: 'I don't like the draughts waiting about in corridors, going and coming off the stage. Musical comedy is not my favourite sort of work." Favourite work or not, Covent Garden had ignored him and there were no concerts booked.

News soon travelled on the concert grapevine and today it is hard to realise the straight-laced attitude of many promoters who were apprehensive of the effect any 'bad publicity' would have on the sense of outrage and public humbug, especially at Sunday concerts. Basso Malcolm

McEachern, Jetsam of the wonderful vocal team 'Flotsam and Jetsam', was struck off the engagement list of a concert manager for making an audience laugh on a Sunday. 'It was in North Wales (not Llandudno),' wrote McEachern, 'That I committed this "offence". I had scored a triumph at the concert, and although I gave four encores the audience showed no inclination to go home. At last I appeared with my overcoat on, but no one took the hint so, clad as I was, I sang another song. The name of it was *A Chip of the old Block* which has a laughing refrain. It was during the refrain that someone guffawed, and it was Sunday and I was obviously the cause of this outrage, it was ordained that never again should I sing at those concerts. And I never did.'

During the 'twenties and 'thirties this sense of public sanctimony, and the degree of licence allowed to an artist to test it, was a state of affairs that all performers had to keep in mind and a very fine balance between their private and professional lives had to be struck. To disillusion the public was to scandalise them. I know of two eminent artists, one a contralto, the other a baritone, who were banned by the conductor of a male voice choir from performing as guests at celebrity concerts. Their 'sin' was to be seen having a drink during rehearsals.

During an all-night party after an exacting stint on the stage, Burke collapsed while entertaining guests. On arrival in hospital doctors diagnosed a strained heart valve and advised rest for a long spell. But never the man to take advice he was soon back singing and enjoying himself as hard as ever.

Hard on the heels of this illness financial troubles rocked him to the core. The Wall Street crash meant that the large amounts of money invested in America vanished for ever. Not one dollar of it ever was paid to him. Yet he was fortunate compared to tens of thousands of business men and investors who were ruined for life – he had a profession, but the tree of which he had been at the top was shaking violently. A drastic curtailing of engagements meant he was rapidly running out of the money had had earned since his return from the U.S.A.; water off a duck's back is synonymous with the way Tom spent money – he was not yet one of the 'Buddy can you spare a dime' brigade but the time was not far off when he was to be reduced to a pitiful state financially and professionally. But he was still Tom Burke – broke or not. Still regarded as the finest tenor in the land, and as such, invited to sing in the 1930 Royal Command Performance at the London Palladium. He sang the National Anthem at the commencement of a show which included Will Hay, Gillie Potter, De Groot, Jack Payne and his BBC Band and Madame Odali Careno in 'Songs from her repertoire'.

At this particular time Marie had lost track of her ex-husband's whereabouts. He hadn't paid the alimony money so she approached a firm of solicitors. When they discovered that Tom was singing on the Royal Command Show, unknown to Marie they instructed a clerk to call on the tenor in his dressing room. This smart operator congratulated Tom on his honour and shook his hand, at the same time pressing a writ into it.

Tom Burke Receives Two Commands in One Night ran a paper headline the next morning. As if this wasn't enough unwanted publicity rumour had it that Burke was too drunk to attend curtain call at the Finale – part of the legend of the man or not it was not a rumour that was one little bit advantageous to his crumbling career.

ACT VIII

On the 9th February, 1932 the papers revealed the 'plight of the forgotten tenor', announcing that Burke had filed his own petition for bankruptcy. It was cited in the court that he had liabilities of £6,901 and assets a doubtful book debt of £12. He had an unsigned contract with a gramophone company giving him a royalty of one penny on each record sold and a recording fee of £40 per record. This was with the Crystalite Company.

Burke stated that he had lost £250,000 due to the world slump, most of which was in investments in America. In one year he made £27,000 and was paid £400 for a single night's work. When he toured with Melba he received the largest fee ever paid to a British artist for a concert.

"I am bankrupt and on the verge of starvation," Burke told a reporter on the 18th February, 1932 "because English impresarios prefer to give fabulous fees to foreign artists, while they consistently ignore British singers of established reputation like myself. It is now two years since I had an engagement and I feel compelled to speak out and draw attention to the boycott or neglect to which I have been subjected. I also feel bitterly about the BBC. Despite many offers and protests on the part of my late manager, Mr Lionel Powell, the BBC has constantly ignored me. Can it be true that the British public really desires all this negroid noise and other nonsense which masquerades as music and entertainment so largely in BBC programmes? I do not believe it. I strenuously deny that the jazz complex which has overtaken the BBC is an honest expression of the soul of the British race."

In another paper he declared that his engagements had not been sufficiently remunerative to enable him to maintain the social position necessary in his profession. But, he revealed, that he had accepted a week's engagement at the 'Trocadero' Cinema at a salary of £175 gross out of which he had to pay an accompanist, orchestration fees, an agent and other expenses.

But Tom Burke was made of stern stuff and the dream that he would return to the lofty pinnacle of fame despite all the setbacks never left him. He was still a great survivor – an inherent combination of Irish agriculturist perseverance and Lancastrian grit, both born from a womb of struggle, drove him on. At the risk of being called a foolish romantic one can link together the soul of meaning in the song *Invictus*, recorded for Dominion in 1929, with the awareness of his roots which was such an essential facet of his character. The words of the song, to which he gave such meaningful nobleness, are the perfect anthem to Tom Burke:

> In the fell flush of circumstance
> I have not winced or cried aloud
> Under the bludgeonings of chance
> My head is bloody but unbowed. . .
> . . . I am the
> Master of my fate
> I am the Captain of my soul!

It was during this period of depression that he made his debut in films – a not very successful version of *Carmen* which went out as *Gipsy Blood* in England and *Carmen* in the States. The film starred Tom as Don Jose and Marguerite Namara as Carmen, Lance Fairfax as the toreador and Lester Matthews as Zuniga. The musical direction was under the baton of Malcolm Sargent. The film was described as, 'Very artificial, neither good drama or good opera and is thus distinctly unsatisfactory. But while Thomas Burke and Lance Fairfax both sing well they are not well cast histrionically'. Burke made very little money out of the film royalties as it quickly became just another version of *Carmen* and was eventually buried deep in cinema archives.

There are facets of Burke's nature which reveal him as a musical snob. His dislike of 'popular' music is understandable in a man dedicated to classical singing and opera, but for his business judgment to be coloured by this dislike is akin to a drowning man refusing a rope. Immediately after the announcements in the press, Moss Empires approached him with an offer of £100 per week all expenses found, a tour to be arranged including all their Variety Theatres in Great Britain. Steady work on the first class circuit, the chance to reinstate himself with the public; to promote his records which were being released almost monthly – all this he rejected. It was a decision he must have regretted, at times he could be incredibly foolish. His operatic career appeared to be at an end, but he would not settle for second best.

Many famous singers have appeared on the 'halls' – including Madame Albani who, to the amazement of her friends and advisers, determined to undertake a variety tour of England because, she said, she wanted to sing to the masses not just to that section of the public who attended celebrity concerts. Burke could not afford to be musically snobbish and after the single Trocadero engagement he was again out of work.

The BBC inform me that there was no question of Burke being banned as many people claim, an assumption no doubt based on the puritanical reputation of its overlords at the time and Burke's so-called 'snubs' at royalty. Unquestionably the snub he had made earlier against the BBC in print was bound to colour their opinions when it came to employing vocalists. He had shut the door himself.

Later, in March 1932, a discharge from bankruptcy was granted.

Although he didn't record for Columbia again he certainly made a test record for the company in the very early years of the decade. This was a 12" recording of *Berceuse De Jocelyn* by Benjamin Godard, sung in English, with the title *Angels Guard Thee*. The translation was the same as the one sung by McCormack in his recording for H.M.V. with the obligato by Fritz Kreisler. This test record was single-sided and had a plain white label with Columbia's name printed, the title and the singer's name being in handwriting.

Former diplomat Richard O'Hagan was a neighbour of the tenor at the time and the fortunate recipient of the test record. Mr O'Hagan tells me he was quite amazed and delighted at the gift considering it was such a rarity. He is of the opinion that Columbia decided not to publish it because of the McCormack version which was currently in the H.M.V. catalogue. He recalls the record as 'a beautiful piece of singing' but is sad to relate that due to his travelling because of the war the record was mislaid. Unfortunately, this example of Burke's art is lost for ever.

Mr O'Hagan also remembers the tenor's flat at Cadogan Place, London, which included a huge room with a minstrels' gallery at one corner which Tom used as a bedroom. Interesting, too, is his recollection of another Leigh-born man, Captain Vincent Collier of the Army Intelligence Corps, who acted as Tom's private secretary. It was Collier was was responsible for launching Burke on a short-lived, but successful, new career – the formation of *The Human Voice Orchestra*. A unique name for a unique form of choralism. Both were Tom's own ideas, brought to fruition by a request from Lady Furness. She was organising a concert in London for the League of Mercy at the Plaza Theatre. When she ran into difficulties over recruiting artists she contacted Captain Collier who suggested that Tom put on a full choral concert with himself as the solo vocalist. Forming a choir from the thousands of out-of-work singers presented no problem.

Robert Stirk has vivid memories of the venture: 'Tom Burke's formation of a choir went round like news of a gold strike – it *was* to the thousands of out-of-work vocalists due to the slump of the early 'thirties. I was one "prospector" with very little hope because I soon heard that ex-D'Oyle Carte and Covent Garden men were auditioning for the twenty-one places. Still I decided to have a go. Previously I had toured with a minor opera company for a couple of years, mainly in Ireland and Scotland, doing fit-up opera in the country towns. The audition was in a hall "somewhere in London", and what a queue had formed. The news that Mr Burke was forming a choir had an almost magical effect. I felt I didn't stand a chance. A lot of Welsh chaps, too; fine singers. I remember seeing Tom Burke for the first time as if it were yesterday – leaning against a piano, a large cigar in his mouth and dressed in a velvet jacket with a dicky-bow. He had a very imposing presence. I handed him my music and he put it on the piano, then waved me to begin with his cigar. I sang *I'll Sing Thee Songs of Araby*. Amazingly, I wasn't told to stop – some of the hopefuls had only got as far as a couple of bars – and I sang it through. "I must record that, lad," commented Tom. "It's a nice song and you did it justice. Do you want a job?" "Please, Mr Burke, I need the money," I replied. He smiled and said, "Don't we all, lad, don't we all. Be here tomorrow nine sharp."

'The next morning I turned up and Burke put the choir through its paces. He was a hard taskmaster, a musical martinet almost, but he knew how to handle men. He didn't promise anything, but with a bit of luck he hoped we'd get a further engagement. But we had to be good enough.

'The League of Mercy concert was a huge triumph at the Plaza Theatre. The charity benefited to the tune of £6,000 and we were inundated with offers from all over the country. I was delighted, so were we all. I remember one of the choir, a Welsh miner with a lovely voice, almost in tears because he'd found work. Not only work but doing what he loved best – singing in a choir. To him, Burke was the new Messiah.'

Captain Collier had arranged with a promoter by the name of Harvey Vincent Tyldesley for the new venture to have its birth under his management should the League of Mercy concert be a success. Some collectors will rightly associate the promoter's name with a very popular choir of the late 'thirties and 'forties, H.V. Tyldesley's 8 Mastersingers, who recorded for Parlophone. Several members of The Human Voice Orchestra were also in that choir. It is interesting to note that they often sang with Marie in music hall and starred with Patricia in *Lisbon Story*.

The new ensemble was an immediate bait to theatre and concert managements. Once more Burke was inundated with work all over the British Isles. Says Mr Stirk: 'We were a sensation – this may sound big-headed, but it's the truth. We broadcast several times and made a very short film which I don't think was ever released. Tom had bounced back again and for a while we were the talk of the musical world. What a great character he was and he helped me enormously. But there was a gulf between Burke the artist and Burke the man. The trouble was his fits of depression. I didn't realise it at the time but now I am aware of the truth of the matter; in those days nervous illness was considered to be something akin to being a freak. Today he would just be another of the thousands who suffer with nervous tension. Tom took to the bottle to alleviate the black moods. When we were engaged by Paramount Films things looked rosy. We didn't get fantastic money – simply a living wage which meant three meals a day and 'digs' found, but this was a luxury compared to the state of tens of thousands in the dole queues. He was a good boss; a real perfectionist with the choir, but so very lax in his own affairs. He wasn't a boozer in the strict sense – more of a sporadic drinker when he felt he needed a 'lift' – alas, it was the cause of our demise. On a couple of occasions I had to pour black coffee down him to get him to the cinema on time. This was during the days when the huge Wurlitzer organ would rise up from the basement – we would sing between films, songs like *Silver Threads Amongst the Gold*, *That's Why Darkies Were Born* and *Roll Away Clouds*. Tom would do a couple of popular ballads. *You Are My Heart's Delight* sung in German was his favourite. Eventually – I'd say the whole venture lasted about fourteen months – Paramount gave us the sack. It was a great shame. It was a new form of choralism and very popular – no instruments at all, but Tom sang his solos to a piano accompaniment. I recall in one song there were eighteen parts for the twenty-one voices of the human orchestra. If he thought you really wanted to learn he'd spend hours coaching a singer. "Never belittle yourself, lad," he once told me. He was an egotist, of course; he'd had to tell himself he was good as he made his career from being in the pits. I suppose he went too much the other way, but he always praised us. We were the best in the world. He made you feel good. But sometimes we'd notice a change in him before his drinking bouts. The hang-ups, as they call them now, would be coming on and he'd get the bottle out. I remember Captain Collier telling him Paramount were waiting for him at a certain theatre for a meeting. "Paramount can get. . . !" he bawled. But afterwards he'd be as gentle as a lamb, there was a great warmth in the man but the unreliability beat us in the end. I believe he suffered through jealousy of certain other artists but really he was his own worst enemy.'

As far as I can ascertain the end came suddenly at Manchester. Tom was drinking in the old Palace bar – a place of some notoriety – and in no fit state to go on stage.

The 'unique form of choralism' was at an end. On the 27th May, 1934 the following article appeared in a leading 'daily':

> 'Tom Burke yesterday talked to a *Sunday Express* representative in a tiny rented room in South Kensington. For Tom Burke has no home of his own. He has not earned a penny for a year.
>
> "It is only in the last two or three years that things have gone wrong," he said. "I am 38. My voice is in its prime. I was famous at 19 and in the following years made over £250,000. I lost most of it in speculations. Yet I have not made a halfpenny this year! I haven't a farthing in the world and must either live in my father's home or enjoy the hospitality of friends. You ask me why? Listen: It is because I have refused to pander to the stupid ignorance of the British public who will not respect a singer unless he comes from some obscure European country, sings with a foreign accent – and has a name which is difficult to pronounce. In short, because I am British. Were I to call myself Tomaso Burkski and sing in bad English I should probably be overwhelmed with work. Walking through the West End the other night I passed four theatres all employing foreign artists in leading parts. Yet there are hundreds of fine British artists without a meal to eat.
>
> "England has gone crazy over foreign artists forgetting that in the wave of Nationalism sweeping Europe, English artists can't get work abroad. Nearly all the principal roles in Covent Garden opera this season are filled by foreigners – Germans who sing in bad Italian are paid fabulous sums to come to England. Two out of every three artists who played in a recent concert at the Royal Albert Hall in aid of the British Artists Variety Benevolent Fund were foreigners! British artists of proved worth have had to change their names to become successful.

"Edward Johnson, the famous British singer at the Met. in New York, had to alter it to Eduardo Di Giovanni before he was recognised. Another Britisher is known as Leopold Stokowski and is now conductor of the famous Philharmonia Symphony Orchestra. But Burke is not beaten. He is as robust as ever and defiant. I intend to fight. I am down but not out." '

He was becoming a bore. It would seem that everyone was to blame but himself. His persistent references to neglect smacked of persecution mania. True, that foreign artists were given preference was the prevailing state of affairs, but scores of British artists survived and lived well enough. So why should Burke, the possessor of the country's finest tenor voice, be on the 'bread line'? The article is incorrect over the tenor's age; Tom was forty-four, not thirty-eight in 1934. I have indisputable proof that he remained thirty-eight for at least five years! But dropping a few years along the way is not uncommon amongst theatricals. The article's claims hardly stand the acid test of truth and smack of exaggerated journalism for there is no mention of the records released monthly by the Imperial and Broadcast 12 labels (The Crystalite Company). The period 1932–1934 was by far Burke's most prolific period recording-wise. Sales were not astronomic but his name assured regular sales, mostly on a modest scale, but at times reaching quite large figures. At least thirty-five records were produced during this period. Certainly he must have fared better financially had he made them for one of the Premier labels whose marketing and publicity techniques ensured the artist prestigious advertising in the leading gramophone shops throughout the land. Even so, *Tell Me Tonight*, Broadcast 12's answer to the version by Jan Kiepura on Parlophone, had excellent sales. So, too, had *Danny Boy* coupled with *Roses of Picardy*; and even H.M.V. couldn't boast, or didn't boast, that they had 'England's greatest tenor' which was the caption used by Broadcast on many of the Burke discs. Of the Imperial output *My Dreams* coupled with *You Are My Heart's Delight* did good business on the cash registers and the former title is claimed to be Burke's finest recording of the non-operatics; in fact, it is the unanimous opinion of collectors that it is one of the

Tom Burke.
A Portrait showing the Masculine Good Looks so Appealing to Female Admirers, including Dame Nellie Melba.

In 'Manon Lescaut'.

Reproduced by Paul Morby.

The National Anthem

Sung by Mr. TOM BURKE

Programme

Mr. H. PRESCOTT *presents*

1 THE SEVEN HINDUSTANS

Whirlwind Acrobats

2. Mr. TOM PAYNE *and*

Miss VERA HILLIARD

Character Burlesques

Page of 1930 Royal Command Variety Performance.

OPERA STAR A GROCER

"Jazz and Talkies Have Done It"

—Tom Burke

TOM BURKE—one-time Lancashire pit-boy and now one of the greatest operatic stars in the world—is to abandon his art and become a grocer.

"England no longer wants Grand Opera," he says. "Jazz and the talkies have killed it."

So Mr. Burke, who is still a young man, is going in for business.

HIS COURAGEOUS EFFORT

He has been appointed chairman and managing director of a chain of multiple shops in Lancashire.

His career has always been an example of stern endeavour and indomitable determination to succeed.

When he was working down the pit he used to sing on Sundays in the choir at Leigh Parish Church. The beauty of his voice attracted attention throughout the North of England.

Tom Burke

He was sent to Milan to study music, and for four years no one in England heard of him. He came back famous.

His voice is as lovely as ever. But—no one nowadays, he says, wants Grand Opera.

"People may smile," he said to a *Sunday Chronicle* representative last night, "at the idea of a world-famous star turning grocer. But why should I not do it?

"And I do not propose to end my days teaching singing in some untidy little back room."

NOT TO BECOME A GROCER

Tom Burke, the well-known tenor, is not, as reported, forsaking his art to become a grocer.

He has been appointed chairman and managing director of a new company trading in various towns in South Lancashire as Ronald Gray, Limited.

"His interest in the grocery trade will be more or less of a hobby or a side-line," said a friend. "It certainly does not mean he is giving up singing."

Receiving Order Made Against Tom Burke

TOM BURKE told a representative of the "Daily Express" why he had voluntarily filed his petition in bankruptcy.

"I am bankrupt, not only in money, but almost in spirit as well," he said. "I am literally starving to death in my own country because my own countrymen will not give me a chance to sing to them."

He spoke bitterly when he said that he had not had one offer from a British impressario for a year, and not a single invitation from the British Broadcasting Corporation during the past five years.

"I am boycotted by my own people," Mr. Burke said. "Why will they not let me sing? I have ability—no one has ever questioned that.

"When I opened with Melba at Covent Garden in 1919 in the presence of the King and Queen I was hailed by the critics as the greatest tenor of the day. I solidified that reputation during my eight years in America.

"I am not boasting. This is no time to beat about the bush. My back is against the wall, and I am starving. These are facts.

"I came back to this country in 1927, and although people had forgotten me I re-established myself. Every country in the world calls me 'a great artist' and hears me sing except the one country—my own—where I want to be heard.

"Why have the British Broadcasting Corporation never even asked me to sing? Lionel Powell, my late manager, protested time and time again to them.

"I have no complaint against that except that if they give engagements to foreigners they should give us some too. Less than one-fifth of the artists employed in Britain are British.

"I am prepared to give my services to Covent Garden and the British Broadcasting Corporation for just a living wage.

"The soul of the British public does not lie only in jazz. Cannot I get the chance to sing to them?

"I feel very bitterly about it. Just think what it means to be an outcast, boycotted in one's own country.

"I am not the only one, but my own plight is very real to me."

RECEIVING ORDER MADE.

Notice was given in Friday night's "London Gazette" that a receiving order was made on February 1st against Thomas Aspinall Burke (professionally known as Tom Burke), of Rolands-gardens, South Kensington, professional singer.

The order was made on the debtor's petition. An adjudication order was also made on February 1st, the date on which the petition was filed.

Tom Burke is the famous opera tenor. Starting as a pit boy at Leigh, his reputation spread over the world.

ROMANCE OF NEW CHORAL COMPANY

TWENTY-ONE VOICES

15 AUG 1932

"Daily Express" Correspondent.

EDINBURGH, Sunday.

Britain's most remarkable company [illegible] now touring Scotland. They call themselves the "Human Orchestra," and they are headed by the famous tenor, Mr. Tom Burke.

Sixteen weeks ago Mr. Burke, at the request of Lady Furness, organised a benefit performance on behalf of the League of Mercy. He had little more than a fortnight to arrange the programme, but in that time he heard [illegible] voices, chose twenty-one vocalists, formed his Human Orchestra, and after eleven days' rehearsing he appeared on the stage at the Plaza Theatre, London, with his new company.

The League of Mercy [illegible] the extent of about [illegible], and the success of the new company was such that they were [illegible] [illegible] all over the country.

They have now been singing [illegible] sixteen weeks in the theatres and [illegible] charity shows. They have broadcast three times, and they have made a film.

SECRET OF SUCCESS

The members of the company, who appeared in Glasgow last week, have already taken Scotland by storm. The secret of their success lies in the fact that they are in reality a human orchestra. They have no instruments. In one song alone there are as many as eighteen different parts for twenty vocalists.

Mr. Burke is appearing with his new organisation at the Empire Theatre here this week before returning to England.

"I have got some ex-Covent Garden and some ex-D'Oyly Carte men in the company," he said to me to-night. "They are all men of big experience. It is strange how our London charity show led up to the formation of this company. Our success has been tremendous and our new form [illegible] choralism has been a big hit."

During his week in Edinburgh his programme will include popular and classical songs.

TOM BURKE, a pit boy at Leigh, [illegible], who rose to be world-famous tenor, has made [illegible] town proud.

Next month will play lead part in "Gipsy Love," to be produced by amateur operatic society at Heysham.

In 1919 appeared before the King and Queen with Melba in "La Bohême" at Covent Garden.

Audiences in all parts of the world acclaimed him. Toured America for eight years.

9 MAR 1934

"BRITAIN has boycotted me," he said in 1932. "I am on the verge of starvation because English impresarios prefer to give fabulous fees to foreign artists instead of to their own."

Appointed last May as chairman and managing director of grocery firm trading in industrial Lancashire town, including his native Leigh.

Audiences in London or New York may forget, but Heysham is proud.

TOM BURKE TO STAR AGAIN

3 JUN 1934

A WOMAN'S PLAN TO [illegible] HIM

Tom Burke, the famous tenor whose penniless plight was revealed in last week's "Sunday Express," is not forgotten.

Hundreds of sympathisers from all over the country sent messages wishing him luck.

3 JUN 1934

Many managers and agents wrote to refute the suggestion that he was being victimised because he was not a foreigner.

Mrs. Van der Elst, who heard him sing before the King and Queen at Covent Garden with Melba and Caruso, has decided that Tom Burke shall come back.

She intends to organise a concert at the Royal Albert Hall, in which he is to be the star.

When she read the interview in the "Sunday Express," Mrs. Van der Elst immediately got in touch with Tom Burke and told him of her intentions. He was delighted.

WORLD FAMOUS TENOR

To Play With Heysham Amateurs

Musical Treat Next Week

THE Heysham Amateur Operatic Society have taken a bold and enterprising step by engaging Tom Burke, the world-famous tenor, to take the leading part of Jozsi in the musical play, "Gipsy Love," which is to be performed at the Astoria for one week, commencing on Monday next.

Thus, people in this area will have the opportunity of hearing this celebrated vocalist singing in a part of which he is well fitted to make the most, having played this character in the film version.

The part gives him full scope for his wonderful voice, which will be heard frequently in many numbers, and his singing is bound to be an inspiration and a treat which people in this area seldom get, at least in amateur productions.

Mr. Burke will be supported by a cast who have been undergoing assiduous rehearsals, so that a splendid all-round show is anticipated. Quite apart from the solo singing of Mr. Burke, there are many other splendid musical numbers and the Society this year have been fortunate in recruiting a well-balanced chorus.

Obviously, Mr. Burke will stand out, but the other members of the cast are equally able in their respective roles both from a singing and acting point of view. Opportunity should be taken as early as possible of reserving seats for this unique production which has a woman musical director in it.

AMBITIOUS HEYSHAM AMATEURS

Famous Vocalist in "Gipsy Love"

Tom Burke Repeats Successful Screen Performance

HEYSHAM Amateurs have taken an ambitious step in their presentation of "Gipsy Love," at the Astoria this week, in securing the service of Tom Burke, the famous tenor, to take the rôle of Jozsi, which he portrayed in the film version of this bright musical comedy.

Mr. Burke's appearance has undoubtedly drawn a great deal of attention to the society, and many people who would not otherwise have attended the performance will no doubt go with the object of hearing Tom Burke.

Naturally, his beautiful voice and vivid personality dominates the show, and at the commencement on Monday the other players seemed rather awed by his presence. Throughout Mr. Burke acted and sang with delightful ease, and he first found the audience with "Joy Like a Gipsy Lover," at the conclusion of the first act, when the audience were stirred to enthusiastic cheering. Mr. Burke is not given a great deal of scope for his talents until the last act when with "Gipsy Song" he again displayed the vocal powers that have won fame for him all over the world.

The difficult task of playing against such an experienced actor and vocalist is allotted to Phyllis Masini, whose portrayal of Ilona is done with admirable restraint. She conveys the right atmosphere, particularly in the second act as the disillusioned lover of the Gipsy vagabond.

It is a very smart and pleasant show, and with the wonderful singing of Tom Burke it should receive large support during the week.

UNEMPLOYED ADMITTED FREE.

TOM BURKE AND HIS VOCAL ORCHESTRA

16 AUG 1932

Tom Burke and his Human Voice Orchestra of eighteen members had an enthusiastic reception at the Empire Theatre, Edinburgh, last night. Seldom, if ever, has better male-voice choral singing been heard in the city.

The famous tenor himself sang "You are my Heart's Delight," in German, and "Donna e Mobile," in Italian. The supporting items are also first-class.

"The Night of the Garter," which

Tom Entertains in the film 'Kathleen Mavourneen'.

Courtesy of National Film Archive/Stills Library.

June 26/39

BINKIE STUART

in

"MY IRISH MOLLY"

Original Story by J. F. ARGYLE
Additional Dialogue by W. G. FAY
Screenplay by IAN WALKER AND ALEX BRYCE

with

MAUREEN O'HARA   TOM BURKE

PHILLIP REED   MAIRE O'NEIL

C. DENIER WARREN   FRANKLYN KELSEY   LEO McCABE

•

Musical Director : GUY JONES

Original Song Number "Farmyard Frolics" by CHRISTINE MAKGILL

Production Manager : H. G. INGLIS

Photography : ERNEST PALMER

Sound Supervisor : H. BENSON

Recordist : A. E. RUDOLPH

Settings : DUNCAN SUTHERLAND

Film Editor : F. H. BICKERTON

Camera : R. ANSCOMBE

Assistant Directors : GEORGE COLLINS AND JACK MARTIN

•

Directed by - - - ALEX BRYCE

Produced by - - - JOHN ARGYLE

AN ARGYLE PRODUCTION

Length 6300 *feet*   Distributed by   *Cert "U"*

ASSOCIATED BRITISH

FILM HOUSE, WARDOUR STREET

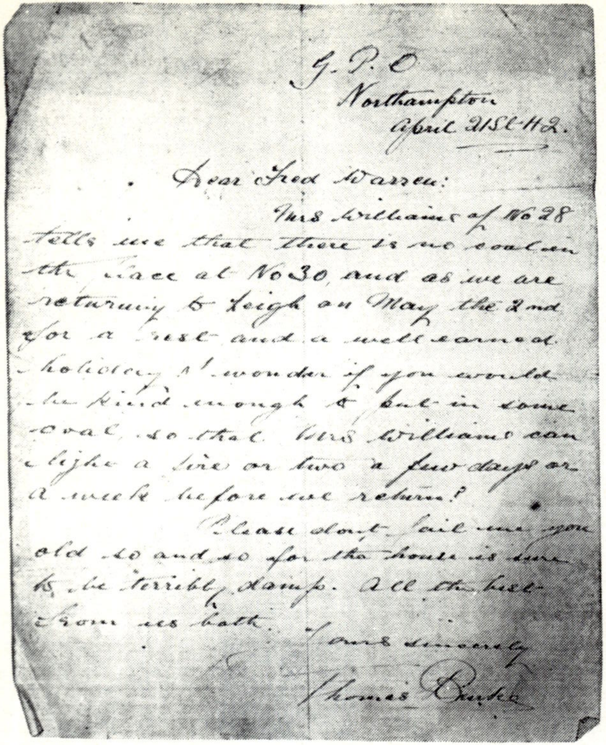

G.P.O.
Northampton
April 21st 42.

Dear Fred Warren:

Mrs Williams of No 28 tells me that there is no coal in the place at No 30, and as we are returning to Leigh on May the 2nd for a rest and a well earned holiday, I wonder if you would be kind enough to put in some coal, so that Mrs Williams can light a fire or two a few days or a week before we return?

Please don't fail me you old so and so for the house is sure to be terribly damp. All the best from us both.

Yours sincerely
Thomas Burke

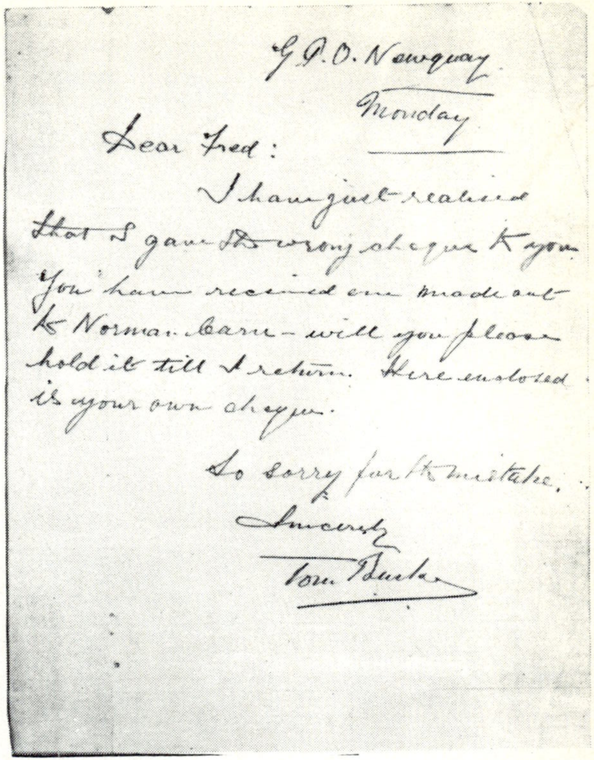

G.P.O. Newquay
Monday

Dear Fred:

I have just realised that I gave the wrong cheque to you. You have received one made out to Norman Carr – will you please hold it till I return. Here enclosed is your own cheque.

So sorry for the mistake.

Sincerely
Tom Burke

Letters from Tom to his Coalman during ENSA days.
An Indication that Burke was not the Meticulous Business Man!

LANCASHIRE OPERA

Founder: Tom Burke

PURCELL ROOM SOUTH BANK
General Manager: John Denison CBE

WEDNESDAY 26 JUNE, 7.30

Starring

DOREEN DOYLE

in

MADAME BUTTERFLY Act 1
LA TRAVIATA Act 2
AIDA Act 3 Nile Scene

Musical Director—Pianist: **GERALD GOVER**

Artists include:
TOM BURKE **NEILSON TAYLOR**
DAVID PARKER **ALEC HOOD**
ROBERT BOWMAN (by permission of the Administrator General of the Royal Opera House)

Tickets 10/6 from Royal Festival Hall Box Office 928-3191

An Advertisement for the Tenor's final Venture which never left London.

Tom with Daughter Jennifer at Rake Hall.

Happy Teacher and Serious Pupil.
Burke Teaching in his Sutton Flat.

Tom in the Twilight of his Life Interviewed on Television.

TOM BURKE
THE GREAT TENOR
WHO PASSED OVER
13TH SEPTEMBER 1969
IN HIS EIGHTIETH YEAR
"I have never heard my music
more beautifully sung." PUCCINI.

finest tenor recordings ever made. Until I heard Burke's rendering I considered Crooks' version to be the finest transmitted to shellac, but definitely it comes second best to this superb interpretation. After hearing it one is left almost shattered by the crescendo of the ending. This is Burke at his soul-stirring best.

Fate had hurled him rudely from his pedestal but to put the blame entirely down to neglect due to his English name could hardly have fooled a press who reported avidly everything the outspoken tenor had to say; nor can the blame be laid entirely on the doorstep of Covent Garden. In 1932 the administrators had decided that the general slump and the consequent prevailing conditions had forced them to limit expenditure. They were determined not to export capital by continuing the practice of engaging foreign singers. The 1932 international season was dispensed with and in its place opera in English introduced. Tom Burke was not included in their plans – ironical that a state of affairs should be forced upon the syndicate he so openly criticised and that he should not be a part of the new procedure he had for so long advocated.

The fact was the Burke copy-book was blotted in indelible ink and from 1934 his career was composed of a hotch-potch of work which varied greatly. The details are not in chronological order but definitely in May, 1934, before the article was published, he had appeared as Jozsi in Heysham Amateur Operatic Society's production of *Gipsy Love*. The amateurs pulled off a superb stroke of business when they approached Burke. The Society's producer did occasional work for the BBC and was well aware of the tenor's plight. Tom accepted gladly, the Astoria Theatre in Morecambe was packed for every performance and the Society were well able to pay him a handsome fee for his services. A highly satisfactory reciprocal arrangement.

Lena Ferrarini wrote to me:

> 'How well I remember going to see *Gipsy Blood* when performed by Heysham Amateur Operatic Society in 1934. It was my first visit to an amateur show and my reason for attending that night was of course to hear Tom Burke sing.

g

I recall that when the audience demanded an encore after some of his superb singing, at a signal to the orchestra – which included my father, a professional musician – Tom Burke swept into *You Are My Heart's Delight* from *Land of Smiles* which was all the rage at that time as Richard Tauber was making musical history with it at Drury Lane. So it was with delight and appreciation I heard Tom Burke render that aria in the middle of *Gipsy Blood* and 'bring the house down!' '

A female member of the cast wrote to tell me that she was aware of Tom's reputation as a lady's man and hardly surprised when he invited her to his dressing-room 'to run over a few songs'. She politely pointed out that as they had run them over dozens of times at rehearsals she was quite happy. After the show she refused an invitation to dine with him at his hotel, and passed the opinion to me that she didn't think 'he was all that good looking anyway!'

But by all accounts a week's wage was more acceptable than a conquest at this period of his career.

Around this time he hit the basement culturally speaking. He professed to take any work that was going and was no longer proud. Albert Houghton of Bolton remembers hearing him sing at the 'Boar's Head' public house in Tyldesley near Manchester. Colloquially it was known as 'Ponky's Pub' – owned by a local character and musical 'genius' by the name of Peter Rothwell who ran a band which called itself 'Ponky's Loonies' and was furnished with weird and wonderful instruments made by Mr Rothwell. The pub was a musical museum of his ingenious creations one of which was a violin made from the jaw bone of an ass. Locally it was noted for its 'turns' performed along with the band. It was at one of Ponky's musical sing-song evenings that Mr Houghton heard Tom entertain as a 'paid turn'. 'My father was full of this great singer who was appearing at Ponky's. The pub was jammed full and he got a great reception. I was too young then to be bothered much but afterwards my father said, "You've just heard one of the world's finest tenors". The thought of what he was doing appearing in a pub didn't cross my mind of course. But it did later as I grew older and collected Burke's records.'

The wheel had turned full circle. The 'minstrel boy' was back where he had started. His humiliation must have been complete. It is always sad, no matter the cause, to see those who have provided so much pleasure for others being reduced to this sort of level. Yet Burke did carry on working, unlike Otto Marak, the fine Czech tenor, who was reduced in 1935 to selling newspapers on a Chicago street corner. Fortunately for him friends and admirers heard of his plight and arranged for his return to his homeland. Tetrazzini finished upon the music halls and died in poverty. Florence Austral, too, was reduced to near poverty in Australia, aided by a fund started by Sir Robert Menzies. Benio Ziegler, a baritone who recorded duets with Tauber, fled the Nazi menace to work as a hatter in London; Joseph Schmidt, the 'pocket Caruso', died of tuberculosis in an internment camp in 1942 at the age of 38. A one-time celebrated English soprano, whose name I am unable to reveal, ended her days as a London charwoman cleaning offices.

Towards the end of 1934 Tom was again being controversial in the press and telling the world he was giving up singing to become a grocer, a statement most people took with the proverbial pinch of salt! He did have some kind of connection with a firm known as Grey's but certainly he never wore a brown overall and sold pounds of sugar as some people seem to imagine.

Burke was a singer and no matter where he sang *this* was his business. "And why shouldn't I become a grocer? Who cares anyway?" was the bitter remark extracted by reporters who questioned the tenor's motives at the time.

Someone did care, said the press two days later. Impresarios and agents had been in touch with Mr Burke to assure him he was not being boycotted. Mrs Van Der Elst, a wealthy patron of the arts and a great admirer of Tom's voice declared that Burke was not finished. He would sing once more at the Royal Albert Hall. 'The tenor was delighted at the news,' said the *Sketch*. As far as I can ascertain from my research, the proposed concert did not materialise; but the promise of one of the impresarios did in May 1935.

It was not widely known to what depths the desperate opera singer had sunk, even so the theatre fraternity were surprised to see his name in lights in the West End. This time at the Princes (later renamed The Ambassadors) in a new musical *Gay Masquerade* with music by Michel Haijos. It was a pleasant, completely escapist gipsy romance – not truly Romany nor was it English or Viennese, yet all three operetta-idioms were jumbled together to produce a play with little originality and no lasting quality.

Burke took his chance with both hands. Wisely his producer, who cast Tom as the Romany Prince Carol, realised that people wanted to hear him sing and implanted no stringent strictures of thespianism upon the notoriously non-conformist Burke who sang his heart out in a plethora of solos and duets, all the time playing the nonchalant role of Carol in the way Burke did everything – differently to everyone else. Do tenors smoke huge havanas while they are singing? Musical comedy buffs would answer in the negative, but Tom not only filled the stage with his delightful notes but also a thick pall of tobacco smoke which those in the back stalls could rightly have mistaken for the smoke of gipsy camp fires. *Gay Masquerade* was a flop. Five days, including one matinee, was the length of its run. The critics were by no means unkind. Burke made a lot of his hard luck himself but on this occasion was a genuine sufferer from that strange unfathomable commodity – public taste. The *Times* liked it, but it made no difference:

> 'This is a good old-fashioned musical comedy, so old-fashioned that it may be said to introduce into the Jubilee a quaint echo of the Coronation. From its gipsy choruses and its brave insistence that Romany life is a song down to its puns and the horrible brown smoking-jacket which someone had persuaded Mr Tom Burke to wear in the preliminary rally on the terrace everything conspires to persuade us that we are living once again in a more leisurely world than this. Even the story has the artlessness, the prettiness, and the familiarity which suggest that it is something revived.
>
> The Countess Kriska, wandering disguised in a white riding habit among the gipsies, gives offence to a sturdy fellow who is cleaning his harness, smoking a cigar, and singing the joys of Romany love. Since this fellow is Prince Carol he speaks his

mind, and she, much taken by his frankness and still more taken by the gipsy dances now going on all about the quarrelsome pair, makes him her estate manager and seals the appointment with a kiss. Hence the musical misunderstandings in the ball-room until it is time for the final duet which is called *My Heart is Yours*.

Naturally the piece pays more attention to singing than to dancing, and Miss Helen Gilliland and Mr Tom Burke, those experienced duettists, are nearly always at the centre of the stage. Their songs are pretty in no unexpected way, and they are sung as we expect them to be sung, though perhaps we do not expect a tenor to smoke on the stage so heavily as Mr Burke smoked in the early part of the evening. His part calls for no realistic details. Miss Nancy Brown brings a pleasantly fresh voice to her gipsy song. Mr Hugh Wakefield is as humorous as a feebly written part will let him be, and Mr Morton Selten is most agreeably of a period when gay dogs had gaiety and doggishness written all over them. The piece may please those who are getting a little tired of chromium-plated fun.'

Madame Moon, one time soubrette and woman of many theatrical parts is now resident in a geriatric hospital. Despite her eighty years and physical handicap she has a memory like a computerised encyclopaedia and speaks with refreshing candour: 'A long London run is the dream of all artists and I saw *Gay Masquerade* as the answer to that dream. Here I was in the West End chosen almost by a miracle from a chorus of a third rate song and dance show. How wrong can you be? I was back in third rate variety, glad to be in work, three weeks after we opened at the Princes. Tom Burke worked really hard to make the show a success, he sang beautifully and his warm and sensual voice ideally suited the Romany theme. During rehearsals he went to great lengths to help the lesser lights with their singing to the detriment of his own acting performance, for he was not a great actor by any means. The show was a flop at the box office but the competition was so fierce in town at the time. Tom knew he had a great voice and he knew the effect it had on women but I found him a most charming man and I would willingly have had an affair with him – what's the use of being coy about it? He had the power of seduction in his voice just in the same way some pop singers have for their female fans today; it's no different and a man would be less than human if he didn't cash in. When the show closed suddenly he was really down in the dumps. His name back in lights for a few days only – then disaster. If anyone needed a long run he did, to restore him to the elite of the profession where he belonged. I can remember that sad day of farewells and Burke saying "To the devil with 'em, I'll be back, just you see." But I don't think he ever sang in London again.'

The competition she speaks of was indeed formidable – Ivor Novello and Mary Ellis at Drury Lane; Paul Robeson in *The Stevedore* at the Embassy; George Robey as Falstaff at His Majesty's and that popular song and dance man Jack Buchanan at the Duchess – these were just a few of the vast array of talent to be seen in London at the time.

Literally Burke took any work that was going. A young and extremely naive agent asked Tom to audition for him. For once he was too upset to be angry and simply walked out of the office.

Music hall and cabaret were both fields he explored with little success and certainly no satisfaction. You couldn't really get much lower down the theatrical ladder than the Metropole, Bootle, a theatre noted for its third rate variety acts and abuse hurled from the gallery, often along with rotten fruit, by an audience composed mainly of Liverpool dockers. When Tom topped the bill at the 'Bootle Metropole Show' he was given a great reception by nasally Bootle-ites yelling for encores with "Give us God's Garden, Tom La!" Tom, with whom *Thank God for a Garden* will always be associated, responded gladly. The 'Met' Bootle was aeons away culturally from the 'Met' New York, still it was good to be wanted. He had become the Mr Micawber of the music world and eternally optimistic that fame and fortune would once more be his.

A cabaret act with a soprano dancing round him and sticking roses in his mouth as she sang *Ciriciribin* while he wore a top hat and tails *a la Tauber* was not a notable milestone in his career either; more of a tragedy that portrayed him in pathetic style. Now he was making himself look foolish.

Though ignored by the concert impresarios for tours, he still managed to obtain Sunday concerts and seaside work; often these were charity engagements organised by town choral societies. That the Lancastrian was still a great tenor was proven to the hilt at these excursions in to the more cultural realms of song. One such concert in St. Helens proved better 'box-office' than a McCormack concert several weeks later.

The term 'very good' is never used by voice critics or the tenor's fellow professionals. Greatness was his lot. But mention of Burke the man usually produced groans and remarks which were far from complimentary, the reverse side of the coin for tales of his preposterous behaviour were legion in the profession. An accompanist who wishes to remain anonymous told me: 'He was a law to himself. He seemed to love to be different. He knew he had this reputation for being a card – sometimes he was hilariously funny, but other times he went too far. Once during the 'thirties we were appearing at an afternoon concert – I think it was Scarborough Spa, when we met Parry Jones the Welsh tenor. They had never been friends and within seconds there was a row. Tom pulled a pound note out of his pocket and handed it to Parry saying "Here's a quid if you'll come outside and we'll sort this out once and for all." Parry wisely ignored him. "Ugh!" Tom snorted to me later "He can't fight and he can't sing either!" I had played for Parry many times and he was a lovely tenor of the typically Welsh type. The amazing thing with Burke was his love of a fight. If Jones had accepted after a few punches that would have been the end of it, Tom would have been inviting him to tea and cakes. There was a lot of the big kid in his make up.

'On another trip to Blackpool by train we were in a compartment with an elderly lady and a young man. The old lady obviously knew who Tom was because they spoke about Leigh. Just before we reached Blackpool Central the man started to talk about the shows and Burke's name came up. We were giving a concert on one of the piers. He then began a tirade about Burke and how he had rejected his parents and spent all his money on pleasure. Tom silenced the old lady with a sign and let the big mouth know-all keep on talking. When we got on the platform Tom asked him if he knew who he was "Don't know you from Adam mate," was the answer. "Oh I see," said Tom "but you seem to know a lot of lies about me. I'm Tom Burke the chap who was bad to his parents," and with that he gave him such a punch that the young chap was knocked several yards backwards into a pile of mail bags. The old lady was hopping mad, "Hit him again Tom lad!" she yelled "I know you were good to your mam and dad. . . hit him again Tom. . . give him a damned good hiding!" We had to restrain the old girl from laying about the chap with her umbrella she was so furious. Tom laughed about it so much he went blue in the face!'

'Some time during the 'thirties' is a rather vague statement but I can be no more accurate than that, though believing it to be close to the end of the decade, when a chance came his way which, had it reached fruition, would have swept away the miseries of work vastly inferior to his talents: the offer to sing *Pagliacci* with the Carl Rosa Opera Company. To tour with the company – opera in English, by English artists – alas, what seemed the ideal vehicle and cultural environment for Burke's artistry and dream-fulfilment were dashed once more on the rocks of his unreliability at rehearsals. It was his last chance to recapture and rebuild his operatic career.

One can only surmise from this point in time. But was it the old bogey 'nerves' – the insecurity – the fear of failure? Or was Burke's personal tragedy the fear of *success*? One must go back to that night in 1919 for the answer. Greatness had been thrust upon him and he could never cope with it – something inherent in his nature prevented him from cosummating the tremendous potential. Whatever the reason, Carl Rosa devotees were denied the great pleasure of hearing this heroic and virile tenor who, to the great loss of English Opera, could never handle fame.

During the 'thirties and very early 'forties he made several broadcasts but they were a mere drop in the ocean compared to the other British artists who furthered their popularity through the media – to recall the names of some of them is to evoke memories of the old wireless golden days when lovers of good singing were provided with a continual musical feast – Gwen Catley, Olive Groves, Joan Hammond, Anne Ziegler, Margaret Eaves, Robert Easton, Robert Irwin, Owen Brannigan, Raymond Newell, John McHugh, Webster Booth, Walter Midgeley, Lester Ferguson and Cavan O'Connor – all names of a bygone era but well revered by those who remember and appreciate the days when the wireless set reigned supreme in home entertainment. Regretably, Tom Burke is not remembered as a radio artist.

An unrepentant ladies man to the day he died, Tom was as often pursued by the fair sex as he was the pursuer. 'Errol Flynn with a voice' is one description of the tenor's romantic activities; but Burke was only an 'also ran' compared to Flynn although well aware of the fascination he held for the opposite sex and made sure that his reputation for having affairs with actresses and chorus girls kept pace with his notoriety as a hell-raiser in the profession.

Asked many year's later if he would change his way of life had he the chance all over again he replied, "Not one little bit baby!" One wonders. . . if Burke the playboy had submerged Burke the artist? But one is left with the indelible impression that his background, for all the aplomb and face against the world he had aquired, could never be completely obliterated; success is so often the father of tribulation. By that wierd chemistry of birthright Burke *had* to have an escape route from himself and his greatness; the gift God gave him in his throat was a potential open sesame to the highest realms of song but it was a gift he was unable to accept without defamation because he never totally overcame or came to terms with his upbringing. One could write thousands of words on the subjects of fame and class but when discussing the subject of this biography and the, seemingly, gross waste of an epic talent one can only try to imagine life in a miner's cottage at the turn of the century and put oneself in the place of Burke the pit-boy who went around hungry for most of his young life, yet was that one-in-ten-thousand who possessed the genius to make himself a world idol – how would we have reacted?

Yet I am certain that had Burke been a stable predictable person his voice would have lacked the thrilling fire with which it was so richly endowed. Likewise Brendan Behan and Dylan Thomas could not have written such wild wonderful prose and poetry had they been different. Their genius was in the very essence of their eccentricity as it was with the Lancashire tenor. He would still have possessed a fine voice but could never have been the Burke who took Covent Garden by storm with the sheer excitement and passion of his vocal gifts.

Even though many years had passed since the divorce, and Tom had subsequently remarried, Marie still felt a keen sense of tragedy at his demise. It was only to be expected. She had shared the hard times of his preparation in Italy and had delighted in his success. One cannot simply detach oneself like switching off a plug. This is convincingly evident in the following story in her own words: 'I had never met John McCormack. I was in a show in Newcastle and he was singing in a concert there. Through a mutual friend he invited me to dinner one evening. Naturally I accepted. During the course of the evening he turned to me and said "You know that bugger of a husband of yours could have sung me off any operatic stage he wanted to – but he was a fool!" and I remember saying to him that if he didn't mind I'd rather not discuss it.'

The singing playboy had no thoughts of marriage but he had reckoned without Pauline Steele-Dixon the daughter of a wealthy paper merchant whose family tree stretched back to Robert Prince of the Catti and subsequently through a lineage of Knights, Earls and Barons and who's residence was historic Rake Hall in Cheshire. The Steele-Dixons were close friends of Rapheal Sabatini the famous author and his wife Ruth. The Sabatinis were closely affiliated to the musical pulse of the nation by virtue of the fact that the novelist's father was John McCormack's teacher of voice. Ruth Sabatini knew many personal facts about the great vocalist passed down from her father-in-law. One being that the Irish tenor had such bad teeth that Sabatini refused to teach him until he had visited the dentist. She was also aware that Tom Burke had a reputation in 'town' for being a rake and a 'man-about-town'.

When Pauline visited London in 1935 Ruth went along as chaperone. Knowing the fashionable clubs and society haunts Ruth took Pauline to one frequented by musicians and theatre-folk for a meal.

She immediately recognised the handsome man sitting at the piano indulging his favourite pastime of 'doodling' and setting his poems to music. Jennifer Skempton, Tom's daughter by his marriage to Pauline Steele-Dixon, takes up the story told to her by her mother: 'Mother saw Tom and asked Ruth Sabatini who he was. She was completely overwhelmed by him although he hadn't as much as glanced her way. "That's Tom Burke the singer. Don't get involved with him whatever you do. He's got a reputation my dear." Mother always made her own decisions and completely ignored the well meant advice. To Ruth's horror she enquired what Tom liked to drink then took a whisky over to him at the piano. I suppose he was well used to such gestures for he had an enormous appeal to women. It was not all one-sided by any means. The ladies idolised him. But in Pauline's case it was genuine love at first sight. Tom politely accepted the drink and was casually talkative but no more. She visited him on several occasions and Tom tried to fob her off. "Go home little girl and grow up" he told her but to no avail. She left home to the horror of her parents who knew of her infatuation for the playboy tenor. She left Tom in no doubt about her feelings for him, telling him that she would not be satisfied until she had become his wife. Mother was a rebel and didn't care for the high-life of society to which she was accustomed.

'What happened next is like a story in a woman's magazine but it is true. Knowing a man who owned a car she arranged for him to take her to where Tom was living between his singing engagements. She pretended that they were going for a trip somewhere and Tom accepted. On the way they collected a couple more friends of Paulines. Little did Tom know that the trip was to Chelsea registry office! Pauline had hijacked him and they were married on 28th December 1935. Tom at that time lived at 1 Elm Park Gardens, Chelsea. He was forty-five and she twenty-two. They toured together and it was six weeks later that Pauline broke the news to my grandparents. They were very upset indeed. Tom was a Catholic, a theatrical and a divorced man. But it was too late. Pauline had got her heart's desire. When I was born it was considered best that I should be brought up at Rake Hall. There and at Ascot I was reared and educated. I saw very little of my parents, except when I was home from school on holidays.

'I can truthfully say I only got to know my father when he finally settled in London. We became very close friends and I often accompanied him to the theatre and concerts. He was a black or white character. You either loved him or hated him. Poor Tom! He loved to be thought of as the devil-may-care Irish man and he was such a wag when he felt like it. My half-sister Patricia and I rather disrespectfully refer to him as 'our father who art not in heaven' and I'm sure he would have been the first to roar laughing at it! That was my father. He loved notoriety.'

Daughter Patricia has her own favourite story of her father, though 'father' is a title Tom did not fit according to its true meaning. Touring with her mother, schooling, and learning the rudiments of her own theatrical career meant she saw very little of him. But despite the gulf of circumstances Tom didn't forget her when she made her debut in a small theatre club in Charing Cross; 'He sent a note round after the show saying "Will you come and have supper with me – signed Your Father" Naturally I accepted and we had great fun – ending up at about two in the morning at Brompton Oratory Taxi Cab Station playing dominoes with the cabbies. How can you be angry or dislike a man like that?'

Although he blamed the 'talkies' partially for his decline he was glad to make three further films after *Gipsy Blood* – all very much with an Irish flavour. Sickly sentiment was the order of the day in many of the British films turned out in the 'thirties – yet often they contained the correct ingredients to appeal and entertain the masses who needed a lift from the depression of the times. All three were begorra-laden vehicles of stage-Irish whimsicality. *Father O'Flynn*, *Kathleen Mavourneen* and *My Irish Molly* never became classics of the Silver Screen but they were productive in song. *Kathleen Mavourneen*, particularly, giving Burke the opportunity to sing a selection of well-loved Irish ballads. *My Irish Molly*, made in 1939, notably of interest because he co-starred with Maureen O'Hara which, in the light of her subsequent fame, is a significant feat. Film archivists are of the opinion that he could have had a successful career in films but for the war.

Spasmodically he had grasped at the straws of fame but could never hold on long enough to cement together the fragments to once more establish his name firmly in the minds of the public. A close friend described him as being, in the 'thirties, a 'musical rubber man'. Trouble was he could never quite bounce back high enough. But a far greater performance than ever Tom had taken part in was being stage-managed – the rumblings of war exploded into world conflict, and Lancashire's Caruso returned once more to Leigh. The career which had turned sour was now virtually over. The man who should have 'ripened' in the 'thirties into the greatest *Othello* in the world entered a long period of almost total obscurity.

FINALE

There is an aloofness about showbusiness which the outside world has come to accept from its members; a gulf between those on the stage and those off it – a great divide which it is difficult to cross. The public find it hard to accept that a theatrical can return to the way of life he or she has left.

Leigh welcomed its famous tenor and his wife back home but it couldn't have been an easy decision for Tom to return. The dreariness of industrial Lancashire must have presented a drastic contrast to the rural setting of Pauline's former permanent home in Cheshire. But if Tom wished to live in Leigh then she was content. One could not expect such a marriage to be perfect. It was not. There were stormy moments and angry 'scenes'.

Pauline could not and did not expect a 'hijacked' husband to be the model of constancy and marital perfection. She imposed no strictures taking him entirely for what he was and accepted that her former life style had been replaced by a share in the tightrope existence of a struggling singer. To many he was regarded as a failure despite his triumphs, and he was well aware that he was one of the 'how are the mighty fallen' brigade with his reputation as a 'hell-raiser' and a rake public property. He was painted in gaudier colours than he deserved and labelled as a 'bloody fool to throw it all away', forced to live with a reputation which far out-stripped his celebrity as a tenor. What people didn't know about him they invented. But Tom was never one for hiding in corners and treated Leigh as if he had never left it. The Burke swagger was still as obvious as ever and his personality dyed with the indelible veneer of the stage. It could never be denied that he had made the town famous. Mention his name even today to a 'Leighite' of the old generation and you will be told proudly that he was the greatest singer in the world and there is no budging them to consider him otherwise.

A Red Cross concert in 1941 gave the town a chance to show their appreciation of his artistry. Once again Leigh Hippodrome was the venue. Walter Jones was his accompanist. He told me:

'I had never met this famous tenor before. We arranged to meet in the Midland Hotel in Manchester. We had tea and a pleasant chat about the programme for the concert. I was very anxious to get to the theatre in Leigh but Tom was so casual, he didn't want to rush off, and as time wore on I felt we wouldn't get there in time.

'When we did arrive the first thing he did was to move some large plant-pots which would have hidden the pianist from the audience. He was considerate like that. The theatre was packed, the concert a sell-out and he was immensely popular and still the idol of Leigh. The audience called for encores. "Give us *Aida*, Tom," one chap called out. "Yon mon wants me to work!" he quipped to me. I suggested Percy Kahn's *Ava Maria* as Leigh is such a Catholic town, but he said, "Play *Mother Machree*." I put two pedals down to create a harp effect in the playing of the arpeggio. Tom walked off after one verse and I followed. "Don't ever do that again if you play for me," he told me. "It reminded me of Josephine." There were tears in his eyes. A lady told me afterwards that she was Tom's sister and Josephine was their mother of whom her brother had been extremely fond. As a Celt myself I understood. There is a very fine line between laughter and tears.'

Several unconfirmed reports exist about his activities in the early war years. His concert appearances were now sporadic and mainly given to help the war effort. 1942 was almost completely taken up by working for ENSA – that much maligned and immensely popular form of wartime entertainment for the services – singing in countless venues all over Britain, suffering the seemingly endless journeys on cold trains and nights spent in station waiting rooms, all for £8 a week. It was a very welcome contract for the

Burkes who found life in Rutland Street, Leigh, a round of struggling to afford necessities such as coal. The devoted Pauline much preferred to travel with her husband than living alone in Leigh. The house was looked after by a kind neighbour and young Jennifer was sent to the hopefully safe sanctuary of her grandparent's estate.

After ENSA there was a spell as a steward in a golf club. Several people remember him taking bets as a self-appointed 'bookie's runner' for his own book-making business. In those days only licenced book-makers were legally allowed to function but most of them employed 'runners' who gathered up bets in pubs and clubs and, in the main, a gentle blind eye was turned on these daily transactions. Tom did his own 'running' and is recalled as a distinctive well-groomed figure standing at the bar of the local hostelries frequented by his patrons. On more than one occasion he was hit by an unexpected winner and couldn't pay immediately. The lucky punter had to wait until he was in funds once again. But these ventures were only phases, means to an end to make enough money to maintain a reasonable standard of living.

People who knew him in his pomp recall with sadness how during this period he began to drink heavily and to lose pride in his appearance. It was anything for a 'quick buck' for he turned his hand to all manner of employment, including singing in working men's clubs. One such club – Astley Working Men's Club – actually offered him a pound for a night's work. Tom kept the letter and would show it to friends he made in London in later days. As an exponent of basic crudity when he felt it appropriate, even his expletive armoury would be sorely stretched when referring to the letter! Though this now seems a ludicrous fee to offer a famous singer, it must be realised that the standard fee for a club 'turn' was from thirty shillings to two pounds. Someone extraordinary, say from another county (which added to the mystique) would be paid three or even four pounds. How long he sang at these venues is not known, but certainly he performed for a short time in the Manchester area. Towards the end of his life he could even laugh at the chaotic state of concert presentation in club land. Impersonating concert chairmen has become a very popular act with many comedians who served their apprenticeship in these licensed venues. It is not generally believed that such characters actually existed and still do, yet I can vouch for the fact that many I have heard have been funnier in reality than the comedians impersonating them. A favourite tale of Tom's was about a chairman in the Manchester area noted for his often hilarious remarks. One night a xylophone player, simply billed as NELLY, was announced in this fashion: "And now, folks, thar's going to hear Nelly knock 'ell out of these bits of wood with two 'ammers." And, again, after the clapping had subsided for a baritone, he said: "That were reet enjoyable. But next wik I've booked a good 'un."

There was never any regret apparent in Burke's behaviour. He was far too proud for that. One confession he did make was to a very close friend: 'My wife and I went to her parent's home, Rake Hall, in Cheshire. They were out. I went in to the garage where I saw a beautiful car. I lost my cool and kicked the tyres shouting to Pauline "I had a car twice as big as this once and a flunkey to drive it. Now look what I've got, a bloody match box on wheels!" '

The 'bloody match box on wheels' was a baby Austin. A car which caused Pauline to remark "Have you ever seen anything more like an elephant getting into a snuff box?" Her husband was fifteen stones heavy at the time, his old keenness for keeping trim and fit had left him. Gerrard Warren recalls seeing Tom getting into the tiny car 'with all the aplomb of the celebrated opera star getting into a Rolls Royce – he never lost his aura of majesty, even in his bad days.'

As the decade progressed it became increasingly obvious that he had grown disenchanted with singing. His life-blood had seeped away and it showed. He was a man without a mission any more. Those who knew him intimately feared that he was losing his will to live. They knew that life without music was no life at all to him. Whereas before he loved to tell friends about his career and discuss singers, he now wanted to forget. All the momentos of the Golden Years had gone, his own collection of 78's he gave away and all he possessed were a few personal photographs and six records of his boyhood hero Caruso. But such a master of singing technique couldn't be allowed to rot. At this period there was a dearth of good teachers and it seemed the natural step for an ex-opera singer to become a teacher. Many years before he had vowed that he would never teach and there could be no more obstinate man. Fortunately for him, he was pestered by persistent would-be pupils and in the end agreed to take on a tenor who had sung with Carl Rosa. This was the start. The late Rowland Jones of euphonium fame was one of his earliest students and certainly his most successful in the sphere of opera. Jones had played with the Black Dyke Mills Band before moving to Bickershaw colliery near Leigh as a clerk. His ambition was to be a tenor singer. Eventually he forsook the euphonium – of which he was considered to be the country's finest exponent – for the concert stage before finally landing the plum engagement as leading tenor with the Sadlers Wells Opera Company.

Tom was notoriously testy about any reference to his fall from the palmy heights of international opera. Foolish indeed was the man who reminded him of it. There was an almost brutal frankness about the man, but one wonders just how deep his love of playing the unrepentant reprobate really went. There were no excuses about his life of wine, women and song. In fact he was often heard to brag about it – yet if someone in his company made the remark that there had been too much of the wine and the women and too little song he would grow very annoyed. Only Burke himself made such personal references. So one wonders if deep down in the soul of the singer there was not a well of regret that his consummate art had never received the recognition it might have done? He was far too great a musician not to be racked by disappointment at the lack of acclaim awarded him by all but those who remembered him for the wonderful bard he had once been.

The mid 'forties saw an attempted come-back in *Madame Butterfly* with Joan Cross on Radio. The soprano recalls the occasion: 'Tom Burke was delightful company, but he was notoriously nervous and didn't do himself justice.' Lord Harewood recalls the soprano telling him that she had never heard such a sound from a tenor as he made, particularly at rehearsals, but by the time the broadcast was due he was not so confident as he had been earlier. Nervous or not, the fact remains that Burke gave opera addicts a whiff of what the international standard had been before the war. The come-back never materialised and now he concentrated on teaching full time.

An advert for the School of Voice appeared in the Manchester Evening News and was typical Burke bravado. One can imagine him waving two fingers at the world as he wrote it:

TOM BURKE, WORLD'S GREATEST OPERA SINGER.
VOICE PRODUCTION – ITALIAN METHOD. OPERA CLASSES
EVERY SUNDAY 3 to 6 PM. IN PREPARATION *LA TRAVIATA*.

Even his beloved Enrico had to take second place now as Tom once more was being bum of himself, as Maggie Teyte had so aptly put it. Today it would be called an ego trip. But whatever it did for his ego it certainly filled his appointment book and soon his prowess as a teacher spread throughout the North of England.

Southport tenor Tom Lannigan sang an audition at his Leigh studio around about this time: 'He listened and at the end said, "Small frame, big voice. I'll take you as a pupil," then, putting his thumbs behind the lapels of his jacket, he asked me very seriously, "Who do you consider to be the world's greatest operatic tenor?" I felt like a school kid in the Headmaster's study. I thought for a second then said, "Gigli I suppose." Burke shook his head. I tried again with Tito Schipa. Again the shake of the head. I tried Martinelli, again a vigorous shake. Then, pointing at his own chest with a finger, he said, "Me, Laddy! I'm still the greatest."

'I went home and told my wife about meeting this extraordinary conceited man. It was real Mohammed Ali stuff.'

This super-exaggerated self praise was his way of boosting his own sadly deflated image and a self-respect which was reflected in the increased pride he began to take in his appearance. The old aplomb was returning, the bitterness disappearing. A new future through his pupils loomed ahead.

An indication of the respect he still commanded within the profession was shown by the visits of international vocalists to his Leigh studio whilst on provincial tours. Many sought advice on voice problems.

Another pupil recalls hearing a beautiful baritone voice as he waited for his own lesson: 'The singing was superb. I felt so inadequate, being a baritone myself that I almost went home there and then. When I went in I said to my teacher, "Tell me, Mr Burke, surely that man must be the best baritone you ever taught. He's great." "I didn't teach him, lad," said the maestro, "that was Paolo Silveri and he came over from Manchester to sort out a little problem he's having. Burke still commands a bit of respect, lad." '

Every pupil I have spoken to about his alleged drinking habits confirms that he was never the worse for liquor whilst teaching. Occasionally he would take one of them for a drink but it was only a glass or two of beer. Very occasionally he would go to Manchester Studios to broadcast in variety programmes, but apart from rare local concerts he seldom sang in public. There was still the odd engagement at clubs in the Manchester area, taken to supplement his income from teaching. More satisfying work were the charity concerts in Leigh. These were notable for the fact that all the vocal artists were his own pupils. As well as being the principal singer he conducted the orchestra, comprised of members of the Liverpool 'Phil' and the BBC Northern Orchestra. Burke the complete musician was revealed during these vastly entertaining and successful events.

Violinist Stewart Basle is now in a twilight home for musicians, but despite being in his ninety-fifth year he remembers these concerts: 'Many of the musicians from the big orchestras lived around Manchester and some of us would go over to Leigh on Sundays to rehearse with Tom. He had a room over a hotel. I was quite amazed that he was such a fine conductor; in fact, like Tauber, he was not only a beautiful singer, he was a very competent musician. I've played with many singers who were musically hopeless as regards to reading scores. Burke was an all-rounder and had he not been a vocalist, he would have become a fine conductor or achieved fame on any instrument he set his heart on mastering. With the baton in his hand he seemed carried away into some kind of fantasy land where nothing, only music, mattered.'

He even took his pupils on tour to North Wales resorts under the banner of the 'Tom Burke Opera Stars'. Operatic concerts were given at Colwyn Bay, Rhyl and Llandudno. Tom paid all the expenses out of the fees but there was nothing left to recompense those artists who had to take unpaid leave from work in order to perform. It was brought home to him that even in Wales Grand Opera concerts were not the current musical taste. Artistically the venture was highly successful but a flop financially. It is amusing to read the programmes of these concerts because of the blatant deception adopted by Burke who was determined that he would present to the public foreign singers, or at least English singers with foreign-sounding names. Any name that could be altered to sound Italian or French was changed. He was determined that his pupils were not going to suffer in the way he had claimed pre-war British singers had suffered by way of their names. Two examples are Richard Boardman who became Ricardo Bordeaux and Eileen Gallagher – Mari Galli.

Mari Galli, now Mrs Darwell, probably knew the tenor better than any other pupil during his stint as a teacher in Leigh. She first saw him back in the early 'thirties when she was a young girl. To her he will also be 'the maestro': 'Maestro was forming a choir from local people and my father took me to hear them rehearse in a schoolroom. It was to sing at a concert featuring him, Anne Broadhurst and Olive Groves. They were doing the *Four Seasons* by Vivaldi – he wanted the wind and he got it! He was like an autocrat – a sergeant-major of the choir. It was an all-male part. "You keep quiet! You keep quiet!" Cutting them out one by one until he got the sound of the wind murmuring. I was frightened to death of him then but I remember saying to my father that if ever he came back to live in Leigh I wanted him to teach me to sing – which he eventually did.

'As a teacher he was a martinet who wouldn't settle for second best. As long as pupils were willing to learn he would teach them – even though they had no aspirations. He wanted above all to preserve the Bel Canto style of singing and pass it on to would-be teachers. He could swear in a most refined way and was a great snuff-taker. He had a tremendous respect for the human voice as the perfect musical instrument. You couldn't say "I'd like to sing *One Fine Day*, Mr Burke." He wouldn't let you. You mustn't lift an operatic aria out of context. You must learn the opera first and know the story and why the aria was written. Get inside the character. He never judged a voice by its range. It was the timbre of the voice which classified it. He had such a wonderful understanding of a potential pupil's physique, facial structure and speaking voice that he could classify the voice without a note being sung. He could talk like a doctor about the body in relation to the lungs and diaphragm. I remember him once telling me, "Everything you can absorb from life, from music, writing, literature, art and experience of life, goes into your voice. A limited horizon will hold you back." '

His style of teaching voice was based on the method devised by Enrico Sedie an Italian baritone, and celebrated teacher in Paris during the early part of this century. Sedie claimed that his methods provided the voice with a flute-like beauty of tone rather than volume. With this style the voice is held under very firm control so that strong tone comes without shouting or forcing. Burke would tell his pupils that the modern-day breed of roaring Italian tenors could clearly do with a course of the Sedie method because they were clearly past masters at wearing out their voices in a few years. 'Sing like a bird. It has no resonating chambers yet see how far it can be heard'.

Of the 'roaring tenors' Burke would often cite Mario Lanza as a typical example and was of the opinion that Hollywood had ruined a potentially great voice by over exploitation. "I could have made him into a superb tenor" he often boasted. In the 'fifties it was Lanza who annoyed Burke and many other Caruso worshippers when he claimed that the tenor he had portrayed on film had flaws in his voice. This was sacrilege to Tom and what he had to say in private one can only guess at but it certainly wouldn't have got into print! The heat of the moment gone, he wrote a polite but pertinent letter to one of the 'dailies' that was published under the column's heading: *They Don't Agree about Mario Lanza.*

Dear Sir,

It would be interesting to hear the record which Mario Lanza claims to possess wherein Caruso is supposed to crack on top B flat; presumed to be made when Caruso was 29, which would be in 1902.

In point of fact, Caruso was famous at the age of 27, having created a sensation in Milan in that year. Further, he sang for the first time in England in 1902, being already famous, with Melba and Journet.

I have in my possession six records made during 1902, there is no semblance of any cracking on top B flat, but there is a plethora of top C's, and a beauty of tone never possessed by any tenor before or since.

Yours sincerely,
TOM BURKE,
30 Rutland Street,
Leigh.

P.S. I would appreciate it if you would publish this letter in order to acquaint your readers, young and old, with the true facts about Caruso, whom I loved, and who was my idol.

Mrs Darwell became very friendly with Tom and Pauline who, she recalls, was known to Tom as George. Although not a practicing Catholic she feels that deep down Tom was proud of his Catholic birth and wanted her to know that his marriage to 'George' was a true one in the eyes of the church. His first marriage to Marie could never be recognised by Rome. When he married for the second time in a registry office his in-laws objected on the grounds that they wanted their daughter to have a church wedding. After applying to the ecclesiastical courts Tom was allowed to re-marry Pauline in a Catholic church, the service being conducted by an Army padre.

'I felt that they both wanted me to know that they were in fact properly married. It was important to them both.'

Away from the teaching studio Tom was very fond of watching Rugby League football as a keen supporter of Leigh. This interest not only centred itself on the terraces. The scheming side of the tenor's character was once again weaving dreams – this time of a Pools System on the fashion of the

Football Pools, with Rugby League instead of Soccer. I have not been able to find out if he was the pioneer of the Rugby Pools, now very popular in 'League' areas; certainly he was amongst the very early operators after the Second World War. Pupils acted as agents and the venture was reasonably successful for a short time. Gradually it became too large to handle and he left it to the larger, better financed, firms to monopolise.

In 1952 he opened the 'Arts Club' – a unique venue for the town, and once again Tom's ideals were running away with him. In fact, it was simply a licensed club but in the inaugural speech at the Club's opening he claimed that it was to become the town's Cultural Centre for Art – whether in the form of singing, poetry, dancing or drama. Fred Yates was made a member by his old friend. 'There's been a lot of rot spoken about the Club. It was something new in Leigh, possibly the only privately owned club in the town. People thought there was something sinister about it. Actually Tom was a stickler for the law. When the last bell went that was it. He once told me he tried to run it on the lines of the 'Eccentric's Club' in London of which he had once been a member. I believe the reason for closure was something to do with the Club not being correctly licensed. It was a very respectable place in my opinion.'

Whatever the cause of the closure it was an overnight sensation in the town. Two dozen policemen in four cars and a van raided the premises.

Tom decamped to Ireland the very next day and stayed holidaying there until the rumpus died down. The Club was officially closed when he returned in time for a court hearing. This was the end of life in Leigh. The Burkes moved to London to a bed-sitter in Earls Court which daughter Jennifer recalls as a 'seedy place'. It was all he could afford. From here Tom continued his teaching and had hardly settled into his new home before he was gathering the press reporters around him for more gems from the Burke fantasy world.

'Tom was a great dreamer,' says daughter Jennifer. 'Always jumping from one scheme to another. He couldn't remain still. He saw himself as a messiah of the opera world – he dearly loved opera and wanted to spread it throughout the country. He could never quite understand why everyone else didn't share his love of music and culture.'

Several interviews were given to the press who heralded the formation of 'The Tom Burke Opera Group'. Popular tenor John McHugh was associated with the proposed scheme in the early period but lack of finance was the stumbling block. When Burke opened a school at Weekes Studios it was under the patronage of Dame Margot Fonteyn. Many well known singers took lessons, including American tenor Lester Ferguson and Doreen Doyle who sang under the nom de chanson of Dorinda Lastrada, a name given to her by Tom.

Since moving to London Pauline's health had deteriorated rapidly and in 1958 she died of an incurable disease. After her death Tom was very depressed and lonely. His pupils rallied round and between them helped him over this period, forming a bond which lasted until his death. He was fortunate in his friends. They steered him from the consoling whisky bottle to rekindle his participation in music. Dinner wine became his drink now and he was an avid snuff taker. Tenor Tony Jackson told me, 'All my opera scores are covered in Tom's snuff. He was a magnetic person. He inspired devotion. He formed a clique of music lovers and pupils and many became his close friends. We were almost like disciples. When he moved to Sutton I remember helping him decorate his flat. At practical things he was hopeless. I only heard him sing when he was an old man. Even so, he spoilt me for any other tenor. He was a spine-tingler and he used to tell me how he could feel his audiences being thrilled as he sang. "Sing for yourself," he would say. "Please your own self and you will please the audience. When I was singing I was in ecstasy, I experienced a delightful pleasure when I sang. And always sing to the person on the back row of the 'gods', not the woman in the front row of the stalls." But I saw both sides of the man. He could be very blunt and crude when inclined and extremely embarrassing at times. I know he made enemies and he once told me "Put me round a table with my enemies and I'll sort the b- - -s out one by one." But when he was in one of his delightful moods he could be so warm and encouraging and kindness itself. Strange, but he often boasted about things which were not really important – like his strength and boxing ability – but seldom mentioned the great triumphs he had had.'

But though Tom struggled to inspire and teach he never discovered the world-beater for which he craved. "I want to give the world a really great singer" he once said. "I have produced very good ones but never a great one." He was well aware that greatness often springs from the most unexpected sources and now launched a most ambitious scheme to encourage the emergence of international talent and he didn't stop at singing: for five shillings a week he advertised three nights training in voice, drama, opera, films and television or any other medium the pupil wished to explore. His plan involved forming a group in which notable dramatists, actors and instrumentalists would give of their time free to act as coaches. In addition, as a display cabinet for his scheme he intended to hire a local theatre to stage productions which would be supervised by professional producers and viewed by top theatrical agents. 'My dream is to help the poorer kids. The lower income bracket youngsters who nurse ambitions in their bosoms which they know they can't fulfil. But why can't they? I did and so did many other of the famous singers, all you need is someone to give you a chance. Five bob a week is all I ask. Let's see if it will work. I will approach the job in the proper manner. Never put the cart before the horse. There is too much emphasis put on acting in opera teaching today. The BBC, unable to find a British tenor, chased all over Europe for a Herod to sing *Salome*. What a sad indictment of our system of vocal teaching!

'Yet in London opera students are paying ten guineas for an hour's teaching – how to sit, how to stand, where to put their hands and so on. I learned how to sing first, the rest followed. I suggest that we learn the first essential for singing, i.e. the technique of tone production.'

Sincerity shone like a bright torch in all the tenor's activities concerned with the perpetuation of the English tradition of classical singing. His devotion was lavished unstintingly and unsparingly but like many citizens of Utopia his dreams were punctured by those with their feet firmly planted on the ground. The people of influence and money. The free help was not willingly forthcoming. Once more the dream-boat was sunk.

Many stories of the 'maestro's' often outlandish personality have been subscribed by his pupils, all of whom were extremely fond of him yet agree unanimously that he was a man of the most complex moods. You had to accept him for what he was. To be in his company could be an embarrassment to say the least.

Once whilst discussing singing over a bottle of wine in London a stranger joined in the conversation. Tom gave him his head as if to test what the fellow knew about the subject. For a while he aired his views on various singers until Tom stopped him with the question, "What do you do for a living, by the way?"

"I'm a plumber, why?"

"Only that you talk like a bloody plumber! I am a singer, but I know damn all about ballcocks and lavatory chains, so I never discuss them in public."

When he wanted to put someone in their place he wouldn't hesitate to use the strongest language if he felt like it.

On another occasion a pupil was having morning coffee with him in a coffee-shop close to Weekes' Studios. Three women singing teachers were making loud derogatory remarks about Maria Callas. Tom saw red, strode over to their table and told them that the three of them put together could never sing half as good as Callas. Still fuming, he downed his coffee and stormed out of the café.

The fact that his remarks might at times prove upsetting was never a worry to him. At a rehearsal night with the pupils one of the females was standing so close to the piano stool he could hardly raise his right elbow. After trying to adjust his stool and free his elbow unsuccessfully he suddenly gave up trying and said to the woman, "Madam, how do you expect me to play the piano when you persist in riveting the base of your navel into my elbow!"

In tenor lore it is understood that the larger the testicles the larger the voice. The mother of a girl pupil told me how her daughter came home one evening to recount how her teacher had reduced her to a state of acute embarrassment.

She had a pretty but weak voice about which Tom was always reminding her, continually pleading with her to 'sing up'. One day he could stand it no longer and whipped round on his stool and bawled, "For heaven's sake, girl, get yourself a pair of balls!"

Daughter Jennifer remembers visiting her parents at Leigh whilst on holiday from school: 'I was very young then, but I distinctly remember Tom bawling at a rather coy young lady who, according to him, put no feeling into her singing. "For Pete's sake, go and have an affair!" he yelled. She was very upset and kept bleating, "Oh, Mr Burke. . . Mr Burke. . . really, Mr Burke!" He was a shocker alright but the women folk idolised him. He had a Svengali effect on them, especially those who were very close to him. As an example of this, I remember my own mother, Pauline, who was very sick at the time, waiting for him in the street outside the bed-sitter. The weather was freezing cold. She was worried because he was late for his dinner.'

A pet aversion was misuse of the English language by a pupil. During his Lancashire teaching days he made it clear to his pupils that he expected them to speak perfect English, to practice doing so, and to avoid using colloquial slang. A tenor with a tolerable voice continually aggravated Tom by his excessively broad dialect. One day at his lesson he announced, "Mr Buck to-neet I'm gooin' 'ave a do at our Ada." That was the last straw, the tenor never 'had a do' at *Aida* and Tom told him he was a teacher of voice in the singing sense and not a professor Higgins who taught people to speak correctly. He advised that he sought an elocutionist then returned in a year. He also was intolerant of pupils with exaggerated opinions of their voices. 'But by the same token,' says Tony Jackson 'he would never ridicule someone who was musically hopeless. He advertised in the paper to form an operatic group and I remember a dear old lady coming to the hall Tom had hired for auditions. She was the sort of old woman you'd imagine sitting in an armchair by the fire surrounded by cats. She sang and the voice was almost non-existent but Tom played for her all the way through, thanked her for coming and promised to let her know his decision. He was most charming and not at all pleased at the others who had been secretly pulling faces and sniggering behind her back. "Poor soul, she's done her best, one should never ridicule anyone for trying," was his serious comment. On the other hand if she had come in a patronising way telling him how lucky he was to have her he would have told her to shut up after a couple of chords.'

Where other famous tenors were concerned he could be very disparaging but one can only smile and consider his remarks pathetically amusing, for as he grew older and more feeble he became jealous of their reputations and bitter in the light of his own downfall. Of Tauber he would say, "A damned good shouter". On Crooks "O.K. for ladies' soirées" and on Welsh tenors in general, "They sound like ducks' arses – very wet". Mention of Gigli was enough to raise his blood pressure to bursting point. Though he admitted he was a first-class tenor he disliked him for personal reasons and the Italian wasn't the only artist with whom Burke had had disagreement and rows.

But in his heart of hearts he was a great admirer of Tauber – 'A superb recitalist'. Burke's frankness is shown vividly in the sleeve-notes of the LP *Aurelanio Pertile Vol. Two* produced by Paul Morby: 'Two English singers have graciously allowed me to quote them about Pertile in those London seasons. Dame Eva Turner who sang *Aida* with Pertile in 1928 (and many times with him in Bologne and in other Italian houses) used the vivid phrase "Of all tenors he was the most exciting to go over the top with". On June 1928 there was a Cav. and Pag. at Covent Garden. Eva Turner with Tom Burke in Cav. – Pampanini and Inghilleri with Pertile in Pag. "Tell me about Pertile", many times I insisted to Tom Burke in the decade before his death. "You said you used to watch him from the wings". "I never liked the voice". . . was the answer of the Lancashire tenor in his 70's but with a memory like a computerised encyclopaedia. "He didn't go in for tone and cantilena like Caruso did. . . and like the rest of us struggled to do. I felt he used to hypnotise the audience by nailing them to their seats. He used to want to do so much more with his performance than words and music actually asked him to do. No – I didn't like the voice – but next to

Chaliapine he was the greatest actor-in-voice I ever heard".' And Tom would never back down, Paul told me in a letter. Neither did he appreciate admirers who told him he had a gifted voice, "God had a part in it," he told an old friend "but he left me a lot of really hard work to do."

The rapidly aging tenor needed people. In order to counteract loneliness and depression he spent hours on the telephone running up bills he couldn't afford to pay. His Birthday parties were always happy musical affairs often catered for by his own cooking – Italian cuisine which he had learned in Italy. One pupil recalls having a meal with the tenor: 'He wouldn't take no for an answer, he was such a head-strong man. He loved Italian food and insisted on cooking chicken Italian style. I don't think he took the innards out. I saw him put the bird in the pot then fill it up with white wine, red wine – you name it, he put it in. Then he put all sorts of herbs in, I've never tasted such a dish in all my life – it was horrible! He thought it was great and I hadn't the nerve to contradict him. When his back was turned I emptied half of it in the waste bin.'

Studying the dictionary was another way of passing the time when not engaged in singing and planning for his dream-fulfilment – a touring opera company to take opera to the provinces. His mastery of the English language ran his mastery of music a close second, possessing a style of letter writing distinctive for its ebullience and prolific usage of words the recipient often had to look up in a dictionary himself. Very fond of using the word *colourist* in his writings, it is a word which ideally sums up his own character in all its facets. He was a life-colourist supreme.

For a period he struggled gamely on with a book *How to Sing*. It was never completed. In this he gave his views on the vocalists of the golden era of singing – prior to the 1930's – as well as laying out his own method of voice production. The reading public and vocal aspirants are the poorer for the non-publication of a book which, if only for the fact it was written by such a master of both the voice and the pen, would surely have possessed something of the flavour of the man himself despite the awful title.

The original manuscript, unfortunately, was destroyed but

in it he extolled the virtues of Emmy Destinn whom he considered to be the greatest singer in the world; '. . .She was better than Melba. In fact Melba was overrated,' wrote Tom. Spaniard Graziella Pareto he adored not only as a singer but as a woman. He was her Nadir in *Les Pecheurs des Perles* and her great admirer when she performed with the Chicago Opera Company. Another idol from those Chicago days was Chaliapine and he could hold an audience spell-bound recounting stories about the Russian basso-profundo who was beaten regularly by a drunken father. Singers from such like backgrounds, and from poverty, make the finest singers he would claim and there are many examples to supplement his belief.

Ricardo Stracciari, he considered to be the master of mezzo-voce, the art of swelling a note and letting it die away. This technique, of which Burke himself was a master, was the ideal armoury for a baritone in the great roles of Verdi in which Stracciari specialised.

Other great favourites included soprano Ebe Stignani and basses Christoff and Kipnis. Of the English brigade he had great regard for fellow tenor Alfred Piccaver who became the idol of the Vienna Opera; colonials Harold Williams and Peter Dawson he admired greatly and considered Norman Allin to be the 'king' of the basses.

A girl pupil inadvertently started him singing the praises of contralto Sigrid Onegin. Tom who had sung with the contralto in the U.S.A. on her highly successful coast-to-coast tours was amazed to find that she possessed an LP of Onegin. His own contraltos never heard the end of it – no one had ever sung contralto like Onegin according to the maestro and he almost wore the record threadbare in demonstration of her coloratura technique. 'We grew sick to death of listening to him extolling her virtues,' a contralto pupil told me. 'She was the greatest. But then any singer who sang with Mr Burke was the greatest. He was a great lavisher of praise, made you feel good. He believed in encouragement and if you were one of his pupils you were the best, too. He was a great believer in parents praising their children.'

It is hardly surprising that he preferred the old guard

of singers to the more modern generation. In an interview with Frank Granville Baker, Tom had this to say on the subject:

'I think there is a basic weakness in all opera today, wherever you may go to hear it, and it is that the old school of singing – and the old style of singing – has gone. In technical terms, there is no head voice in present-day singing: it is all pushed forward, into the mouth or the nose. The result will sound too plummy one moment, too nasal the next, and then too harsh.

'Now this is not just a matter of opinion. From gramophone records we know beyond any doubt that actual voice production was far better in those days. These recordings were made under what we would now term primitive conditions, but they nevertheless show that many of the voices of 50 years ago were not only magnificent in quality but also were superbly produced. These singers had their voices under such perfect control that they could do so much more with them than singers can do today.

'I've just said that poor voice production today causes uneven singing. Now let me add to that – it also causes monotonous singing. Bad production makes the voice sound rough when it should be smooth, and it also prevents the singer from varying the sound when it should be varied, by the *colouration* of the voice. In my opinion there is no colouration at all today so far as most singers are concerned.

'Callas is a great colourist, and for me she can do no wrong on the stage. She knows how to portray through the voice the characterisation she is playing. This is the truly operatic use of the human voice, the creation of chracter and drama through singing. It is the reason why all Callas' performances, in spite of her occasional harsh notes, are so wonderfully moving.

'There are two other singers who rank with her in this respect. Christoff is also a great singer of our time. Even if you don't understand the language he is singing in, and therefore can't follow what he is saying, the meaning is all there in the voice. The same applies to Gobbi, but apart from these three I don't know any singers today with a sense of vocal colouration to match that of the great singers of the past.'

If modern singing didn't please him he didn't hesitate to say so in blunt terms. Once when leaving his beloved 'Garden' after an opera he was asked by the voice-coach, "Well, Tom, what did you think about the singing?"

"What singing?" asked Tom. "I never heard any bloody singing."

Daughter Jennifer recalls an opera visit with her father: 'The singing wasn't up to his standard and he simply fell asleep. He was like that, if he didn't approve he made no bones about it. He was snoring loudly and I had to keep knocking him to waken him. I was greatly relieved when the opera was over.'

As a protest against the standard of present day singing he would blatantly walk out in the middle of an aria.

A tremendous fillip came when it was arranged that John Hassel Recording Studios would re-issue the old 78 rpm recordings on modern microgroove records. It was Tom himself who christened the label – V.I.P. What was there to lose anyway? He had aptly been described as 'the last survivor of the Golden Age of Singing' so why undersell himself now? The first releases – four 'extended play' 45 rpm discs – were immediately successful, sought after eagerly by connoisseurs. Three Long Play records followed which are still in print. Some of the unjustness of obscurity has been righted by these recordings which perpetuate the God-given voice of the finest tenor produced in the British Isles.

Shortly before Burke's death, towards the late 'sixties, he was given further an accolade at a lecture by Giovanni Martinelli who was showing operatic films at the British Film Institute. Unknown to Tom the Italian had a film of him singing when he was still a young man. The audience were so thrilled that they stood up to cheer Burke the old spine-tingler with the power to captivate and galvanise an audience most of whom were not born when the film was made. Tom would have been less than human had he not been visibly affected and deeply moved by this wonderful moment. After the clapping had subsided, Dame Eva Turner stood on a chair to announce that the singer was present in the hall. Tom stood up to tumultuous applause, then went to the platform to embrace Martinelli. Two giants of the operatic meridian reunited after all those years – a momentous occasion indeed.

So the popular theory that Leigh's famous singing son passed into a complete void of nonentity is nonsense. The last few years were undoubtedly some of his happiest.

Sydney Winstanley met Tom at a lecture the tenor gave to the Verdi Society in Liverpool. He recalls his amazement that he should be the subject of an article by Sydney for the *78 Magazine*, and his surprise that collectors avidly sought his records. The lecture was given during Tom's visit to the city with the *Tom Burke Opera Company* who peformed concert-opera at the Crane Theatre. A local paper had this to say: 'Those of us old enough to remember the great singers of the '20s and '30s will have no trouble in recalling Mr Burke's glorious voice. Always a controversial character Mr Burke proved to the Verdi Society the truth of the maxim "a leopard never changes its spots". He is *still* outrageous. His descriptions of voice production techniques at times bordered on the acutely embarrassing. But forgetting his obvious glee at making his audience cringe, he knows his Verdi and can hold an audience for hours with his stories of singers and opera.'

The reference to embarrassment stems from Burke's over done comparisons between vocal strain and constipation. The very next day he suffered a heart attack and was hospitalised in Liverpool.

Typically, he continually ignored the doctors' advice not to sing and taught as vigorously and enthusiastically as before. Lord Harewood not only remembers him for his glorious voice but as a great character:

'He had a great gift of blarney – in fact, I at first thought he was Irish-born! – and used to bull-doze one when we met.

'He did not sing at a party of mine but he did once ask to introduce to me a young tenor whom he thought greatly gifted. This turned out to be Kenneth Macdonald, whom I had never heard but who sang rather well in the big room in the house I lived in at that time. George Coop, the old coach and prompter, came to play, and it only became obvious after I had heard Ken in two or three arias that the point really was that Tom Burke himself wanted to sing. He asked if we had a score of *Manon Lescaut* – he could not very well offer to sing *Tosca* as Ken Macdonald had just sung the first aria – and when we produced it, behaved as if looking for something to choose and then sang quite a number of excerpts from it. It must have been quite carefully prepared as I was turning over for George Coop and noticed from looking at the printed page that everything was being transposed down a semi-tone, something I should not have realised if I had not been looking! But the sound was gorgeous, and he must have been well into his seventies.

'He said he would like to sing at Covent Garden but I do not remember any mention of Maria Callas, though it would have been typical of him to have suggested her.'

His Lordship's last sentence is written in reply to my question about yet another 'Burke' story that he demanded to have Maria Callas as his partner if he sang at the 'Garden'!

Plans had formulated for launching his cherished desire to take opera to the provinces. The *Lancashire Opera Company* was formed and given its baptism in two concerts in London and one at Hastings. Alexander Hood acted as promotion secretary, but he soon realised that opera was not wanted in Northern towns; Councils considered it a 'financial risk' – culture was on its way out; even Leigh refused to stage Burke's venture. But the desire to 'go on the road' with opera for the masses never left Tom. Financially he had no hope and there were no backers. Secretly, several of his closest friends were pleased because they saw the worry and organisation as an encroachment on his already fragile state of health. His insistence on taking singing roles worried them, especially as this was in direct opposition to medical advice. But on the 9th May, 1968 a leading 'daily' had this to say:

> 'Back to the concert platform is coming Mr Tom Burke, Lancashire tenor. He will sing 'just a few bars' at a London

concert to promote his new Lancashire Opera Co. "I want the world to know what wonderful singers we have in Lancashire. People know all about the famous football teams we have in Manchester and Liverpool, but find it hard to believe that we have any cultural merit." He hopes to interest more young people in opera "because it's a wonderful life and anyone who is great in opera can be great in anything." He hopes to give singers from the provinces a greater chance to make their names in opera. He is seeking to bring true quality back to opera singing. "There isn't the emphasis there was on quality in my day and as a result very few opera 'greats' are being produced." '

The irrepressible and quixotic Burke was giving it to them again. The same flowing sentiments. Noble, but part of his Never-Never-Land. He would adamantly deny that the vast majority of people preferred Manchester United and Everton to *Tosca* and *Madame Butterfly*.

Acting as his own promotion agent he handed out leaflets advertising his concerts to people queuing outside Covent Garden. It is unlikely that anyone recognised the stout man with the dicky-bow or realised that queues six times larger had waited in pouring rain to hear *him* sing. Some took him for a religious crank dishing out tracts and refused the hand-bills.

The proverbial church mouse wasn't much worse off than Burke at this time. Illness had drained him of the little money he had saved. The fairy godmother in the shape of a benevolent sponsor didn't appear and his vision of provincial opera was not fulfilled in his lifetime. His, however, was not the only voice crying in the wilderness for *Opera North*, a Leeds-based enterprise has recently formed and is successfully producing opera in venues throughout the North of England. This company is fulfilling the ideals cited by Burke in an article:

'In this country, at the moment, there is really no opportunity at all. What is essential if we are to have any appreciable number of good singers, and what I have been advocating for years now, is that all our big cities should have their own opera centres. If we had a system of municipal opera there would be an incentive to our composers too, and we might at last develop a strong national opera. We need companies in all cities such as Birmingham, Manchester, Leeds, Liverpool, Nottingham, Bristol, Glasgow and Edinburgh. These companies could interchange from time to time so that audiences wouldn't always have to hear the same singers and there are sufficient singers at the moment who can't be absorbed into Covent Garden and Sadler's Wells to make a basis for such municipal companies.

Here would be the ideal training ground for a whole school of opera singers, who would be able to develop their abilities, both vocally and dramatically, in the same way as young artists have always been able to develop in Italy and Germany. These centres would inevitably produce some singers good enough to graduate to Sadler's Wells and Covent Garden, while established stars from the London companies would be able to make guest appearances at the provincial houses. Also, it would be possible for the secondary singers of the London companies to be tried out in leading roles in these smaller houses.

This is also the only way, as I see it, of ever building up a healthy opera public. At the moment only people living in London can go to the opera at all regularly. The rest of the country is starved, apart from the occasional visit from a touring Sadler's Wells company, so that whole generations grow up without knowing what opera is. There must, I am convinced, be thousands of young people who would develop quite a taste for opera if only they had the chance to hear it at the right time. Municipal opera is the primary need in this whole business of establishing opera on a healthy footing in this country.'

His teaching only served to allow him to maintain a very modest standard of living. He was glad of any fees he could get for the odd lecture and broadcast. As he grew older he changed his views. The purist attitude was unprofitable. A nagging fear of illness plagued him because he feared he would be unable to afford medical fees. He could never quite understand that he could be treated free as a National Health patient. "I've always had to fight like hell for anything I've had in life," he told a fellow patient in hospital.

A well-known tenor once heard a 'pathetic voice' in the flat at Sutton. As the student was leaving 'Maestro' lavished exaggerated praise on him. The professional challenged him when the pupil had left and called him a 'so and so hypocrite'. Burke shrugged his shoulders and said, "And why not? I've struggled for years to promote the very best in vocal art. What have I produced? Not very much. I've got to live like anyone else – if they think they're Callas or Caruso then why not, what's wrong with that?"

Amateur musical comedy baritone Percy Brooks was aware of this when he approached Tom to give him a few lessons for his role of the Mountie in *Rose Marie*. 'I knew his reputation as a character so I was prepared for anything. He took me on and sat down to accompany me in *Rose Marie*. He heard me out politely then turned on the stool and asked me very seriously if I was singing to a woman or a pound of cold tripe! I answered, "A woman, Mr Burke," just as seriously and he smiled and said, "And making love to her? Well, to my ear you sound more like an insurance man trying to sell her an endowment policy and not being very confident about it." And with that, we changed places. I played and he sang, and what a difference I noticed, not just because of his fine voice but because of the convincing virility of it and he was 77 then. The show was a success and I got great applause for singing *Rose Marie*.'

In 1968 another illness reduced Burke to an old man in looks and spirit. He was now obviously failing. Says Tony Jackson: 'But the old spirit was very much alive and he was as outrageous as ever. He detested fuss and people telling him what to do. I remember a nurse talking to him as if he was a child. ". . .Come on now, Mr Burke – we must do as we're told, there's a good boy." Tom turned round on her and boomed, "You know what you can do my good woman? You can kiss my royal Irish arse!" '

Back home again he was teaching as hard as ever and delighting in playing mine host to his clique of friends. The 12th September saw him in great form entertaining in his flat. As always at Burke's parties, the wine was flowing and the singing uninhibited with Tom, sick man though he was, bursting into the odd phrase from opera. As the evening grew late it was obvious he was very tired. His friends offered to clear up the flat but Tom asked them to go home so he could go to bed. They left him comfortable, ready for sleep.

The next day daughter Jennifer found her father ill. She called an ambulance to take him to hospital. A doctor had been alerted to meet the ambulance and in the true dramatic tradition of opera the tenor died in the doctor's arms. "Trust Tom to think of a new twist. He would have preferred a blonde soprano, but he had to settle for a doctor." Quipped a close friend. Somehow it sums up Tom Burke – he was his own man and he liked people to know he was different. There will be those who say he tried too hard.

Once more the popular stories are refuted. Contrary to tales told in Leigh the Lancashire town's great tenor did not die unknown. His funeral was attended by his circle of friends and pupils, the coffin smothered in red roses by Doreen Doyle who had been so kind to him. It is true to say however that his passing was not mourned in person by the celebrities of the musical profession. Burke was laid to rest in Wallington Cemetery, Surrey. All the leading daily papers carried an obituary notice.

Tom Burke was a magnificent singer but – when all is said and written – Tom Burke was a man.

CURTAIN

THOMAS BURKE – Performances at The Royal Opera House.

1919

12 May	*La Boheme* with Melba – 1st perf. at ROH after the war. Cond. Beecham.
15 –	the Duke in *Rigoletto*. Cond. Mugnone.
17 –	*La Boheme* with Melba. Cond. Pitt.
21 –	*Rigoletto*. Cond. Mugnone.
27 –	*La Boheme* with Margaret Sheridan. Cond. Pitt.
30 –	Pinkerton in *Madame Butterfly* with Eme Destinnova (Emmy Destinn). Cond. Mugnone.
31 –	*Rigoletto*. Cond. Mugnone.
5 June	*La Boheme* with M. Sheridan. Cond. Pitt.
9 –	*Rigoletto*. Cond. Mugnone.
19 –	Conte D'Almaviva in *Il Barbiere di Siviglia*. Cond. Mugnone.
28 –	(Mat.) *La Boheme* with M. Sheridan. Cond. Pitt.
31 July	Gala in aid of Housing Assoc. for Officers' Families: *La Boheme* Act III with Melba. Cond. Mugnone.
1 Aug	*La Boheme* with Jeanne Brola. Cond. Mugnone.

1920

10 May	*La Boheme* with Maria Kousnezova – 1st night of the season. Cond. Beecham.
12 –	Nadir in *I Pescatori di Perle* with Graziella Pareto. Cond. Beechem.
18 –	Nadir in *I Pescatori di Perle* with Graziella Pereto. Cond. Beecham.
27 –	Nadir in *I Pescatori di Perle* with Graziella Pareto. Cond. Beecham.
29 –	Des Grieux in *Manon Lescaut* with Ida Quaiatti. Cond. Coates.

31 – *I Pescatori di Perle*. Cond. Beecham.
2 June *Manon Lescaut*. Cond. Bavagnoli.
11 – *Manon Lescaut*. Cond. Bavagnoli.
18 – *Il Tabarro & Gianni Schicchi* – 1st performances in England. Cond. Bavagnoli.
21 – *Il Tabarro & Gianni Schicci* with Dalla Rizza. Cond. Bavagnoli.
24 – *Il Tabarro & Gianni Schicchi*. Cond. Bavagnoli.
1 July *Il Tabarro & Gianni Schicchi*. Cond. Bavagnoli.
10 – *Gianni Schicchi*. Cond. Bavagnoli.
12 – *Il Tabarro*. Cond. Bavagnoli.
20 – *Il Tabarro*. Cond. Bavagnoli.
26 – *Il Tabarro & Gianni Schicchi*. Cond. Bavagnoli.
31 – *La Boheme* with Miriam Licette – last night of the season. Cond. Bavagnoli.

1927

6 June The Duke in *Rigoletto* with Maria Ivogun, Marieno Stabile. Cond. Fornarini.

1928

13 June Turiddu in *Cavalleria Rusticana* with Eva Turner, Duschina Giannini. Cond. Bellezza.
21 – Turiddu in *Cavalleria Rusticana* with Eva Turner, Duschina Giannini. Cond. Bellezza.
6 July Turiddu in *Cavalleria Rusticana* with Eva Turner, Duschina Giannini. Cond. Bellezza.
12 – *La Boheme* with Margaret Sheridan. Cond. Barbirolli.

FILMS OF TOM BURKE

GIPSY BLOOD

B.I.P. British 'U' Cert.
Romantic Drama with singers.

Marguerite Namara	Carmen
Thomas Burke	Don Jose
Lance Fairfax	Toreador
Lester Mathews	Zuniga

Directed by Cecil Lewis from Prosper Merimee's story *CARMEN*.

FATHER O'FLYNN

Certificate 'U'.
Distributors: Butcher's Films.
Directed by Wilfred Noy.

Tom Burke	Father O'Flynn
Jean Adrienne	Macushlah
Robert Chisholm	Nigel
Henry Oscar	Westmacott
Denis O'Neil	Flanagan
Ralph Truman	Fawcett
Johnnie Schofield	Cassidy
Dorothy Vernon	Bridget O'Loveley
Billy Holland	Muldoon

Ethel Revnell and Gracie West, Stanley Kirby; Sherman Fisher Girls.

MUSICAL. Ireland. Jailbird's daughter adopted by priest, loves squire's son.

KATHLEEN MAVOURNEEN (77) (U)
U.S.A: **KATHLEEN**

Argyle-British (Wardour)
P: John Argyle
D: Norman Lee
S: (NOVEL) Clara Mulholland
SC: Marjorie Deans, John Glen.

Sally O'Neil .... Kathleen O'Moore
Tom Burke .... Mike Rooney
Sara Allgood .... Mary Ellen O'Dwyer
Jack Daly .... Denis O'Dwyer
Talbot O'Farrell .... Dan Milligan
Denis O'Neil .... Mat Cooney
Fred Duprez .... Walter Bryant
Pat Noonan .... Sean O'Dwyer
Jeanne Stuart .... Barbara Fitzpatrick
John Forbes-Robertson .... Pat O'Moore
Lucan & McShane; Rory O'Connor; Sean Dempsey; Frank Lee's Tara Ceilidh Band.

MUSICAL. Ireland. Waitress rejects rich man for singing stevedore.

MY IRISH MOLLY

Principal Characters:

Binkie Stuart .... Molly Martin
Maureen O'Hara .... Eileen O'Shea
Tom Burke .... Danny Gallagher
Phillip Reed .... Bob
Maire O'Neil .... Mrs O'Shea
C. Denier Warren .... Chuck
Maureen Moore .... Hannah Delaney
Franklyn Kelsey .... Liam Delaney
Leo McCabe .... Corney

Sparkling new songs and famous old melodies including:

My Irish Molly
Londonderry Air
Ireland, Mother Ireland
Eileen Alannah
Farmyard Frolics
The Irish Emigrant
Off to Philadelphia
Come Back to Erin

DISCOGRAPHY

78 rpm RECORDS MADE FOR COLUMBIA

Number	Matrix	10" Purple Single-sided	
X246	69959	*Invictus*	1920
X247		*For You Alone*	
X310	–	The above titles coupled on Double-sided 10" Purple	1920
X249		*Lorraine*	1920
		7100 Series 12" Purple Single-sided	
7199	76366	*Recondita Armonia* (Tosca)	1920-21
7200	76367	*E Lucevan le Stelle* (Tosca)	1920-21
6345	–	The above titles coupled on Double-sided 12" Purple	1920-21
7201	76405	*La Donna e Mobile*	1920-21
7202	76506	*Questa O Quella*	1920-21
7346	–	The above titles coupled on Double-sided 12" Purple	1920-21
7203	76414	*M'Appari* (Flotow)	1920-21
7204	76402	*Chiudo gli Occhi* (Massenet)	1920-21
7205	76599-2	*Che Gelida Manina*	1920-21
7222	76547	*Celeste Aida*	1920-21
7347	–	Above titles coupled on Double-sided 12" Purple	
7225		*Donna Non Vidi Mai* (Manon Lescaut)	
7233		*Dear Old Pal of Mine*	
7244		*The Minstrel Boy*	
7348		Above titles coupled on Double-sided 12" Purple	

10" Light Blue D/sided 'D' Series

D1593	29021	*E Lucevan Le Stelle*	
–	WA6143	*Nessun Dorma*	1927
D1594	A5659	*The Minstrel Boy*	
–	A5693	*Thank God for a Garden*	1927

12" Light Blue D/sided 'L' Series

L1951	WAX2865	*My Dreams* (Tosti)	
	WAX2881	*O Vision Entrancing* (Esmeralda)	1927

UNPUBLISHED COLUMBIAS 10"

Love Went A'riding (Bridge)	A5658
A Dream (Bartlett)	A5701
On With the Motley (Leoncavallo)	A5817
E Lucevan (Puccini)	A5818
Vesti La Giubba (Leoncavallo)	A6142
Recondita Armonia (Puccini)	A6144

UNPUBLISHED COLUMBIAS 12"

A Dream (Bartlett)	AX2874
Che Gelida Manina (Puccini)	AX3041

Recorded in The Scala Theatre with Orch. conducted by Hamilton Harty. These details also apply to A6142.

78 rpm 10" DOMINION RECORDS Circa 1929

Torna A Surriento – Oreste De Bernardi (Classic series 1444-1) — Tenor B. 32

O Primavera – Tom Burke (Classic series 1473-1) — Tenor B. 32

Vesti La Giubba (*On with the Motley* – Pagliacci) Orch. Acc. Leoncavallo. — B. 15 (1471-3)

Sea Rapture (Coates) Orch. Acc. — B. 15 (1472-1)

The above recorded also on Red Label C. 314.

Ombra Mai Fu (Largo – in Italian)	B. 35 (1627)
Invictus (Huhn)	B. 35 (1628)
Cast Thy Burdens	B. 23 (1528-2)
There is no Death (Coates)	B. 23 (1529-2)

The 'B' prefix Dominions bear Blue labels.

ELECTRIC IMPERIAL 12" 78 rpm Recorded: 1932-34

Number	Matrix	Title
Z 117	(156)	*My Dreams* Weatherly-Tosti
–	(157)	*You Are My Heart's Delight* from the Land of Smiles Lehar-Graham-Herzer-Lohner
Z 120	(160)	*Serenata* Toselli
–	(161)	*The Song of Songs* Moya-Lucas-Vaucaire
Z 121	(172)	*The Two Grenadiers* Schumann
–	(173)	*Queen of My Heart* Comedy Opera – Dorothy Cellier
Z 125	(T I 175)	*For You Alone* O'Reilly–Geehl
–	(T I 176)	*On With the Motley* Vesti la Giubba (from the opera *Paliacci*) Leon-Cavallo-Weatherly
Z 131	(T I 181)	*Ich Liebe Dich* (I Love Thee) Grieg
–	(T I 182)	*Elegie* Gallet-Massenet

Z 136	(T I 189-2)	*One Alone* from The Desert Song Harbach-Hammerstein 2nd-Romberg Tom Burke with chorus
–	(T I 190-2)	*Maire My Girl* Casey-Aitken Tom Burke with chorus
Z 141	(T I 201)	1) *Because* : D'Hardelot 2) *Until* : Teschemacher-Sanderson
–	(T I 202)	*Silver Threads Amongst the Gold* (Danks)
Z 126		*Somewhere a Voice* (Tate) *The Shade of the Palm* (Stuart)
Z 128	(T I 179-2)	*Serenade* (Student Prince) *Lover Come Back to Me* (New Moon)
Z 134	(T I 184-2)	*When I'm Looking at You* (Stohart) *Only My Song* (Lehar)
Z 137	(199)	*Love Everlasting* Friml
–	(200)	*Macushla* MacMurrough
Z 144	(T I 209-2)	A. *O Sole Mio* (Di Capua) B. *The Minstrel Boy* (Moore)
–	(T I 210-2)	*Excelsior* (Balfe) W. Foster Richardson

ELECTRIC IMPERIAL BROADCAST TWELVE
(English), Recorded: 1931-34, all 10"

Number	Matrix	Title
3219		*Billy Boy* (Trad.)
–		*Stormalong* (Trad.)
3251	1209X	*Nightfall*
–	1208X	*Masquerade*

3264	1231X	*You, Just You* ('Wild Violets')
—	1230X	*Tell Me Tonight*
3279		*Rosa Mia*
—		*Smilin' Thro*
3287		*Don't Say Goodbye*
—		*Ich Liebe Dich*
3291		*Her Name is Mary*
—	A1302-2	*Play, Fiddle Play*
3305		*Ah, Sweet Mystery of Life*
—		*Adois, Goodbye* (Fernandes)
3312		*Dance, Pretty Lady*
—		*Come Out, Vienna*
3316		*My Gypsy Rhapsody*
—		*Maria, My Own*
3326		*Roses of Picardy*
—		*Danny Boy*
3333		*Sunrise to Sunset*
—		*I Cover the Waterfront*
3342		*Throw Open Wide Your Window*
—		*Reflections in the Water*
3346	A1409-2	*Gypsy Fiddles*
—	A1408-2	*My Moonlight Madonna*
3354	A1442-2	*Parted*
—	A1441-2	*Song of Songs*
3362		*Sing, Gypsy, Sing*
—		*My Song Goes Round the World*
4012		*Love's Last Word is Spoken*
—		*Un Peu d'amour*
4021		*Vesti la Giubba* (Pagliacci)
—		*La Donna e Mobile* (Rigoletto)
4024		*My Song for You*
—		*Love, Forever I Adore*

4035	*One Night of Love*
–	*Smoke Gets in Your Eyes*

The labels for the Broadcast 12, 10", are mostly Red with Gold lettering, but some of the later ones appear with a Black label.

AMERICAN COLUMBIAS

536D	*I'm Sitting by the Style, Mary*
	Snowy-Breasted Pearl
33027F	*Minstrel Boy*
	Danny Boy (sung by Barbara Maurel)
3307F	*Kathleen Mavourneen*
463D	*Killarney*

RECORDS UNDER PSUEDONYMS

As Terry O'Neil

Edison Bell 7"
When You Come Home to Rest (Burke)
That Old Fashioned Cot in Kildare (Pedgar, Burke)

Edison Bell 7"
I Loved Her Best of All (Burke)
Thank God for a Garden (Del Riego)

As Pat O'Sullivan

Piccadily 10" Yellow Label
That Old Fashioned Cot in Kildare (Pedgar, Burke)
Ave Marie (Not Burke)

As John O'Grady

Parlophone E. 606 10" Matrix: 1743-2
Just a Little Fond Affection
Ramona

Parlophone E. 5979 10" Matrix: 1744-2
I Heard You Sing (Burke, Soloway)
The Blue Danube (Strauss) Violin obligato H. Sliberman

Undoubtedly there are other 78's under these pseudonyms. The CROWN 7" label featured Terry O'Neil but no details are to hand. Terence O'Neil, generally thought to be Burke, who recorded for Edison Bell in the early 'thirties, was a music hall singer in his own right. Definitely not Burke's voice.

Burke often told friends that he recorded under Italian names. It is possible he did so in the U.S.A. and quite likely he did so in England on minor labels. It is not beyond possibility that the 78 you possess of an 'unknown' Italian tenor is indeed Burke.

The 'Silver Masked Tenor' who recorded for R.C.A. and was subsequently reproduced on H.M.V. was definitely not Burke as some people suggest. Nor was he McCormack. Without doubt this was Joseph White, father of tenor Robert White.

The publisher would be glad to hear of any recordings not listed under the Burke name or pseudonyms which may come to light.

45 rpm EXTENDED PLAY

VIP/EP 100 *For You Alone* (O'Reilly & Geehl)
Invictus (Henley & Hahn)

VIP/EP 101 *The Minstrel Boy* (Thos. Moore, arr. H. Hughes)
Thank God for a Garden (Teresa del Riego)

VIP/EP 102 *Recodita Armonia* from *Tosca* (Puccini)
Nessun Dorma from *Turandot* (Puccini)

VIP/EP 103 *Questa O Quella* from *Rigoletto* (Verdi)
La Donna e Mobile from *Rigoletto* (Verdi)

(Above now deleted)

THE LONG PLAY RECORDS

VIP/ 104 MONO **THE LAST OF THE GREAT**

E Luceuan Le Stelle from *Tosca* (Puccini)
Celeste Aida from *Aida* (Verdi)
Chiudo Gli Occhi Dream Song from *Manon* (Massenet)

Vesti La Guibba from *I Pagliacci* (Leoncavallo)
Che Gelida Manina from *La Boheme* (Puccini)
Nessun Dorma from *Turandot* (Puccini)
My Dreams (Weatherley and Tosti)
O Vision Entrancing from *Esmerelda* (Marzials and Goring Thomas)
Kathleen Mavourneen (Trad.)
Lorraine (O'Reilly and Sanderson)
Sea Rapture (Coates)
**O Primavera* (Tirindelli) Piano G. Coop.

*(This recording is of special interest to Burke collectors for it was recorded when the tenor was 71 years old)

VIP/LP 106 **THE MINSTREL BOY**

The Minstrel Boy (Moore, Arr. Hughes)
Invictus (Henley & Hahn)
Killarney (Balfe)
For You Alone (O'Reilly-Geehl)
Silver Threads Amongst the Gold (Danks)
Thank God for a Garden (del Riego)
On With the Motley from *I Pagliacci* (Leoncavallo)
Questa O Quella from *Rigoletto* (Verdi)
La Donna e Mobile from *Rigoletto* (Verdi)
Recondita Armonia from *Tosca* (Puccini)
Because (D'Hardelot)
Until (Teschemacher-Sanderson)

VIP/LP 102 **A TOAST TO TOM BURKE**

Queen of My Heart (Cellier)
Ich Liebe Dich (Grieg)
Maire My Girl (Casey-Aitken)
The Song of Songs (Moya-Lucas-Vaucaire)
Serenata (Toselli)
Elegie (Gallet-Massenet)
The Two Grenadiers (Schumann)
Excelsior (Longfellow-Balfe)
O Sole Mio (Di Capua)
Donna Non Vidi Mai (Puccini)
One Alone from *The Desert Song* (Romberg)

Tell Me Tonight (Spolainsky)

The LP's are available from V.I.P. RECORDS, 21 Nassau Road, Barnes, London SW13 9QF, and all specialist record dealers.

V.I.P. RECORD LP REVIEWS
by Sydney Winstanley

VIP/LP 102

Apart from *Donna Non Vidi Mai* from *Manon Lescaut* and *Tell Me Tonight*, all the records used are Imperial 78's. Very good copies were used so there is little evidence of wear or ticks.

Queen of My Heart is a delight. *Maire My Girl* is very well sung, with scrupulous diction but without reaching the very high standard set by McCormack. The *Elegie* is very well captured and illustrates this tenor's great strength in handling descending phrases. *O Sole Mio* is very Italian in approach and actual sound. *Tell Me Tonight* is powerfully sung with Burke at his most thrusting and insistant, in fact it is very operatic and he is in fine voice. The Puccini Aria is taken from an early Columbia (7225) and I suspect it was not recorded at the correct speed: at this period the voice was much lighter, but here we have it transposed down approximately a semi-tone and the effect is not quite right.

VIP/LP 1104/5

My Dreams and *O Vision Entrancing* are very well recorded. *Kathleen Mavourneen* was never published in Europe but it did appear in the Columbia U.S.A. catalogue during the period when Burke was a great success over there. The interpretation is quite different from McCormack's and poles apart from the delightful record by Patti, but it is a valid version of this lovely song and he ends the record with some of his most delicate work.

O Primavera was a song Burke loved. Splendid though the 1929 78 is it is tame compared to the 1961 version offered on this record: some of the top notes are huge in proportion, delivered with thrilling power. A testimony to Burke's technique which preserved his voice unharmed after years of use. Most singers in their 70's are dreadful and here, to be frank, we have a ruin, but like the Coliseum, a magnificent ruin! Operatic items on the LP show the best and worst of dubbed LPs and of Burke.

Nessun Dorma is well recorded and is my favourite version of this frequently recorded aria. I have versions by Valente, Cortis, Gigli, Martinelli, and Lauri-Volp: and Burkes' stands up very well even in such exalted company.

We are in speed trouble with *The Dream Song* from *Manon*, also it was under rehearsed; a wayward handling of a delicate piece – not recommended. *Vesti La Guibba* is taken from a very poor 78 copy (Dominion) – a good version of the aria but this copy should not have been used. The *Tosca* is well done and like *Celeste Aida* seems to be the correct speed. The latter is a good transfer.

VIP/LP 106

This English version of *On With the Motley* is taken from the Imperial, Burke is in excellent voice; a fine spacious performance. *Questa O Quella* is recorded with a minimum of treble making the result somewhat dull. *La Donna* is much brighter as is the *Tosca* aria. *Because* and *Until* are both successfully transferred.

The Minstrel Boy was recorded by Burke three times, the one here being the middle Columbia Electrical 78, probably the best – and faithfully re-recorded. The brilliant *Invictus* is the acoustic Columbia which is very defiant but not quite so grand as the one he did for Dominion in 1929. *Killarney* is very welcome because this was never available in Europe, and it receives a fine vigorous performance here, with one or two lovely touches. *For You Alone* is the Electrical Columbia, and as usual the climax is really a strain, usual that is for all tenors apart from Caruso.

– – – – – – – – – – –

The three LP's reviewed are a good cross section of Tom Burke's recorded output. All three are well worth a place in anyone's collection, and they all contain several items which are vintage Burke i.e. singing, Italian style, at its very best.

FURTHER NOTES AND APPRECIATIONS OF THE "78" RECORDINGS

By Sydney Winstanley

Che Gelida Manina:

Another good, unmannered performance; there are two or three rather low notes in this aria and they tax him, but they are there and quite steady. The higher notes are free and true, and the high C is quite effortless.

Celeste Aida:

Frankly, he sounds a little young for the music; perhaps we have become used to heavier voices than the young Burke's. The phrasing is good, and the attack is clean. I'm sure Burke could have managed the last note 'p. e morendo', but he would not have been Burke if he had.

Lorraine:

This is a song almost without merit, yet his enthusiasm makes it quite enjoyable; there is a fair scattering of high notes and these are the only ones which really come out of the wax on this rather poorly recorded item.

For You Alone:

A great favourite with tenors of 40 years ago, and deservedly so. Burke's diction is clear, as always, and he makes good use of the words. The tone catches fire on the word 'flame', and the word 'glows' really does. He makes a fine thing of the climax; the highest note of the song is taken on the closed vowel in 'you' and is filled with tone.

Invictus:

This is a defiant song, usually sung by basses. Here in a higher key it rises out of the mists, and becomes an English 'Di quella pira', complete with flashing high C. Again Burke's excellent enunciation adds much to the enjoyment.

The Minstrel Boy:

The acoustic and electric versions are exactly alike in interpretation, but in the later version Burke's voice sounds more mature and there is more steel in it. This may be because he was a few years older, but it is certain that electric records do bring out the brilliance of the quality more than the acoustics. Note the contrast between the passage 'Ne're spoke again' and 'For he tore the chords asunder'. The first phrase is sung as though by an angel and the second like a Viking warrior.

Thank God for a Garden:

Burke uses his 'voce mista' technique almost all the way through this song, and the tone is most pleasing; there is a slightly exaggerated climax near the end but all is forgiven when you hear him float up for the last note.

Nessun Dorma:

His rocklike steadiness, and aggressive manner combine to make this the outstanding operatic record by Tom Burke. The declamation of the text is trenchant and the stream of thrilling tenor tone is in the authentic Italian manner.

O Vision Entrancing:

Again Burke sings softly and sweetly, raising his trumpet only on occasions, and always just at the right moment. His diction again is first rate, yet his legato is not halted by his scrupulous attention to consonants.

My Dreams:

This is to me an important record, perhaps more important than the song deserves. I think it is Burke's best record as it is a reflection of my idea of Burke. He sings the two verses with grace and sweetness of tone, and rather slower than one is used to, and then he hurls aside the niceties: he has lost his love and he is howling with rage. He works up to a climax which it seems quite impossible to maintain but he brings it off with a huge B flat, which only a flawless technique and giant diaphragm could produce.

"78" RECORDS MADE FOR OTHER COMPANIES

Queen of My Heart:

This is one of my favourites; I find the tune pleasing, and Burke's lightness of touch is very suited to the song. Occasional glimpses of his power are to be had, so we have a variety of tone – Burke was never boring.

Toselli's Serenade:

Burke's version of this delightful song is one of the best ever recorded, and it is possibly the best example to illustrate how the Italian idiom had been assumed by Burke.

Massenet's Elegie:

Again he is in fine voice, and none of the sadness is mising, even though he does use plenty of volume.

Excelsior: (with Foster Richardson)

Only Burke could save this ridiculous thing from being funny; in fact his contribution makes the record desirable.

O Primavera:

This, like the Toselli item, is full of spaghetti and sunshine.

Ombra Mai Fu:

Although shorn of the recit. in all other respects this reminds me of Caruso's version. Burke's breadth of tone is like a young baritone's and his Italian is a real pleasure to listen to. The swell on 'Soave piu' at the end is physical singing at its most exciting.

Invictus: (Dominion)

Even more striking than the Columbia. The voice is broader and used with even more force than before. The intensity of this late performance perhaps shows how Burke identified himself with this song.